BETWEEN PACIFISM

AND JIHAD

JUST WAR AND
CHRISTIAN TRADITION

J. DARYL CHARLES

InterVarsity Press
Downers Grove, Illinois

InterVarsity Press
P.O. Box 1400, Downers Grove, IL 60515-1426
World Wide Web: www.ivpress.com
E-mail: mail@ivpress.com

InterVarsity Press®️ is the book-publishing division of InterVarsity Christian Fellowship/USA®️, a student movement active on campus at hundreds of universities, colleges and schools of nursing in the United States of America, and a member movement of the International Fellowship of Evangelical Students. For information about local and regional activities, write Public Relations Dept., InterVarsity Christian Fellowship/USA, 6400 Schroeder Rd., P.O. Box 7895, Madison, WI 53707-7895, or visit the IVCF website at <www.intervarsity.org>.

Design: Cindy Kiple

Images: bullet: David Sacks/Getty Images
*   nail cross and peace symbol: Don Farrall/Getty Images*

ISBN 0-8308-2772-2

Printed in the United States of America ∞

Library of Congress Cataloging-in-Publication Data

Charles, J. Daryl, 1950-
  Between pacifism and Jihad: just war and Christian tradition /
J. Daryl Charles.
      p. cm.
  Includes bibliographical references and index.
  ISBN 0-8308-2772-2 (pbk.: alk paper)
  1. War—Religious aspects—Christianity—History of doctrines. 2.
Just war doctrine—History. 3. War—Religious aspects—Christianity.
4. Just war doctrine. I. Title.
BT736.2C43 2005
261.8'73—dc22

                                                                                    2005000231

P	18	17	16	15	14	13	12	11	10	9	8	7	6	5	4	3	2	1
Y	18	17	16	15	14	13	12	11	10	09	08	07	06	05				

"In this erudite, timely and helpful book, Daryl Charles surveys the landscape of just-war thinking past and present and helps us to understand why war should not be severed from ethical considerations and constraints. His book is a wonderful introduction to just war as well as a major contribution to the contemporary debate."

JEAN BETHKE ELSHTAIN, THE LAURA SPELMAN ROCKEFELLER PROFESSOR OF SOCIAL AND POLITICAL ETHICS, THE UNIVERSITY OF CHICAGO, AND AUTHOR OF *JUST WAR AGAINST TERROR: THE BURDEN OF AMERICAN POWER IN A VIOLENT WORLD* (BASIC BOOKS, 2003)

"Contemporary Christians tend to approach questions about the proper use of force in international relations naively, as though no one had reflected about them until our own time. In a fallen world, such ignorance is not only intellectually inexcusable but an invitation to moral disaster. *Between Pacifism and Jihad* is an excellent resource for evangelicals who desire to reacquaint themselves with the 'consensus' tradition on the ethics of justified war."

J. BUDZISZEWSKI, PROFESSOR OF GOVERNMENT AND PHILOSOPHY, UNIVERSITY OF TEXAS AT AUSTIN, AND AUTHOR OF *WRITTEN ON THE HEART: THE CASE FOR NATURAL LAW* AND *WHAT WE CAN'T NOT KNOW: A GUIDE*

"Daryl Charles has read widely and thought carefully about the role of government and the place of warfare in Christian thought. Arguing for a view that neither baptizes force whenever it is used for patriotic purposes nor rejects force when it is needed to serve just ends, Charles provides both helpful historical background and probing moral argument. Christians who want to reflect more carefully about these matters will find here a valuable resource."

GILBERT MEILAENDER, DUESENBERG PROFESSOR OF CHRISTIAN ETHICS, VALPARAISO UNIVERSITY

"Here is an intelligent, articulate presentation of just-war thinking by a leading evangelical scholar. The lure of pacifism and the call to holy war have both found their champions in the Christian tradition. Daryl Charles draws on the wisdom of Niebuhr, Ramsey, Elshtain and others to present a mediating position: the sanction of force by the state as a means of justice bearing peace. An important evangelical engagement with this debate."

TIMOTHY GEORGE, DEAN, BEESON DIVINITY SCHOOL, SAMFORD UNIVERSITY, AND EXECUTIVE EDITOR, *CHRISTIANITY TODAY*

"This is an important book. Daryl Charles helpfully surveys Christian perspectives, past and present, on the issues of war and peace. Then he offers some wise counsel about how we are to reappropriate just-war theory for the unprecedented challenges of our own day. And best of all he shows us why all of this requires careful theological reflection."

RICHARD J. MOUW, PRESIDENT AND PROFESSOR OF CHRISTIAN PHILOSOPHY, FULLER THEOLOGICAL SEMINARY

"Few people are reconsidering the just-war theory in light of the threat of radical Islam. Fewer still are doing it with the biblical insight, historical depth and careful moral analysis of J. Daryl Charles. An indispensable book in our age of terror."

JOSEPH LOCONTE, WILLIAM E. SIMON FELLOW IN RELIGION AND A FREE SOCIETY AT THE HERITAGE FOUNDATION

to James Turner Johnson
and Jean Bethke Elshtain,
voices of justice crying
in the academic wilderness

to David Corey
friend, teacher extraordinaire
and student of classic texts

to Jesse and Ian,
beloved sons and lovers of justice

Contents

1

INTRODUCTION

Is war ever—or *never*—justifiable? Should evil be confronted head-on in the present life? Is pacifism *the* Christian way? Doesn't Jesus require of the Christian an ethic of nonviolence? Is coercive force *always* immoral? Are government and political power inherently evil? Aren't we under obligation to "turn the other cheek" when evil occurs?

Such are questions that plague us. But we have further doubts. Is there a difference between self-defense and defending an innocent third party? Between insult and assault? Should we come to the defense of others when oppressive injustice or crimes against humanity occur? If so, on what grounds? If not, why not? If we invoke religious faith, shouldn't we trust that God in his sovereignty and without our "meddling" will protect others when evil occurs? Shouldn't we leave it to God to punish those who do evil?

And isn't there a basic theological issue at stake here? Don't we encounter a basic discontinuity between the Old and New Testaments? After all, it seems as if the God of the Old Testament is foremost a judge and warrior, visiting evil with the sword and judgment in human history, while the God of the New Testament is merciful, compassionate and forgiving, reserving judgment for the eschaton. Isn't war justified only for Israel as a theocracy under the old covenant and now forbidden under the new?

WRESTLING WITH A PERENNIAL ISSUE

This is a book about difficult issues. It is about the ethics of war and peace, the use of force and military conflict. But difficult as these issues are, they are perennial, ever with us. And for this reason we can be encouraged: we are not the first to wrestle with such matters. Early Christians—bishops and laypeople, monks and magistrates—agonized over them, and believers have continued to do so ever since.

Certainly the ancient question "How can the use of force serve just purposes?" loses none of its relevance today. And because Christians from the beginning have struggled with the ethics of war and peace, we are not without resources—enduring resources—to help us think about these matters. That is *not* to say that Christians have always agreed or that we will agree or that the issue is a test for religious or confessional fellowship; it is not. It is, however, to acknowledge that (1) clergy and laity alike have struggled throughout the centuries to formulate a Christian response, and (2) a consensual understanding of Christian thinking through the ages emerges.

To the surprise of some, Christian reflection on the ethics of war is rooted squarely within the mainstream of the Christian moral tradition; it is by no means a peripheral issue. As a result, a consensus among important Christian thinkers emerges, offering much-needed political-moral wisdom for our time. It offers wisdom for the church as it wrestles with its own convictions, and for individual Christian believers as they consider vocational callings and attempt to embody responsible citizenship.

Sadly, much of Christendom—whether evangelical, mainline Protestant or Roman Catholic—has been divorced from the wisdom of this consensual tradition. The results of this divorce are quite unfortunate. At the most basic level the average layperson, even when he or she intuits what justice demands in a particular situation, is often unable to offer a rationale as to why this is or is not so.

In *The Unformed Conscience of Evangelicalism* I lamented the absence of moral formation in the church's teaching and preaching and in congregational life.[1] My basic argument was this: there is no such thing as an evangelical social ethic or a broadly Protestant ethic, for that matter. To be sure, we have elevated church growth to a virtual science. We have written and sold millions upon millions of heart-warming and inspirational Christian "breakthrough" books. We have made endless forays into the contemporary music scene. And we are as "seeker-friendly" as any group on the face of the earth. But when it comes to giving a *reason* for the hope within or pre-

---

[1]J. Daryl Charles, *The Unformed Conscience of Evangelicalism* (Downers Grove, Ill.: InterVarsity Press, 2002).

senting a *rationale* for Christian social ethics or offering an *explanation* of
the church's traditional teaching on perennial ethical issues, we are all but
clueless. And yet this is not merely a problem of our congregations. Our colleges and seminaries have not offered much in the way of equipment either.[2]
Something is very wrong with this picture.

But let's leave aside the absence of moral education for the moment. Another regrettable consequence of the divorce of Christendom from its moral
tradition is the lack of responsible conversation between the Christian community (including Christian ethicists) and policy-makers. Conspicuously absent today is the incisive linkage of Christian ethics to a broad range of
public-policy concerns in a manner that characterized people like John Wes-
ley and William Wilberforce two centuries ago or Reinhold Niebuhr, John
Courtney Murray and Paul Ramsey closer to our time. And as evidence of this
divorce the average Christian layperson today would be unfamiliar with most
if not all of these names. So we must intentionally enter into conversation
with the Christian tradition and probe its relevance for contemporary ethics.

This book represents the fruit of my own thinking about ethics in recent
years. While not the sole factor, the events of September 11, 2001, unquestionably played an important role in framing particular questions. I was
greatly dismayed at the many depressingly irresponsible comments made by
religious leaders in reaction to the terrorist bombings and mass murder of
9/11. These reactions, of course, ran the gamut from "America got what it
deserves" to "Let us remember to forgive our enemies." Both excesses, in
the context of the events themselves, are theologically vacuous and fail to
take seriously the role of governing authorities in preserving the social order
and confronting moral evil. My guess is that these responses will contribute
precious little to civil society.

But the events of 9/11 only crystallized what had been perplexing me for
years. The inability of many Christians—clergy as well as laity—to articulate
a theologically, morally and politically responsible response to evil tends to
confirm my own experience of doing criminal justice research in Washington, D.C., in the early to mid 1990s. At that time there was a conspicuous
lack of thoughtful Protestants involved in policy analysis. I particularly won-
dered, *Where are the evangelicals? Why is it,* I continually asked myself, *that*

---

[2]In chapter ten of *Unformed Conscience* ("Thinking with the Church"), I have attempted to address this lack by offering some specific recommendations for instruction both in congregational life and in college and seminary curricula.

Roman Catholics are making the most significant contributions to policy analysis and debate? Was there a Protestant "public philosophy"?[3] Since then, I must confess, I keep returning to a nagging question: Is it likely that the evangelicals' relative absence in the public square is due, among other things, to an underdeveloped theology of creation, humanity and culture? Have all of these been overshadowed by a skewed eschatology? (I have in mind our fixation with end-times scenarios—often understood as "biblical prophecy"—that hamstrings the church's ability to wrestle with the *already-but-not-yet* tension of the kingdom of God.)

Another thought. What is it in the contemporary Protestant-evangelical mindset that causes us to think about ethics after the fact? That is, only when lightning-rod issues come down the pike or an important election rolls around? Can it be that as offspring of the Protestant Reformers we have been so consumed with elevating faith and grace that our aversion to anything that smacks of "works righteousness" prevents us from meaningfully engaging culture (which frankly is hard work)? Or when we finally *do* discover the social implications of the gospel, do we tend only to become social activists, pausing infrequently to reflect theologically on what is just, what is distinctly Christian, and what the church historically has believed and taught?

CONTEMPORARY GEOPOLITICS

With the collapse of the Soviet empire just over a decade ago, for many—from the average layperson to the policy-maker—the question of military force lacked urgency. Yet it is precisely the developments *since* the end of the Cold War that call forth the need for reexamining the merits and moral substructure of armed conflict. Consider, for example, Iraq's occupation of Kuwait and genocidal treatment of its own people, notably the Kurds; the starvation of civilians in Somalia; exile and enslavement of Christians in Sudan; the slaughter of between five hundred thousand and a million people in Rwanda;[4] genocide in Bosnia and Kosovo; the need for massive humanitarian efforts in Burundi, Rwanda, Liberia, Sudan and Afghanistan; the production of chemical and biological weapons in Libya and Iraq; drug-trafficking on several continents; the breathtaking rise of maturing international

---

[3] I am an orthodox Christian with a broadly evangelical background and ecumenical sympathies. In terms of my own academic training and work experience, I am indebted chiefly (though not solely) to Catholic social thought for the substructure of my ethical thinking.

[4] It is difficult to get a precise number, although the best estimates are in the 800,000–850,000 range.

terrorism worldwide; and the Talibanization of Afghanistan, Pakistan, portions of central and southeast Asia as well as northern and western Africa.[5]

These diverse crises force laypeople, educators, politicians and policymakers alike to reflect on the morality of war, the use of force and military intervention. Should we intervene? When? Why or why not? By what criteria and in what measure? What about the place of private conscience and conscientious objection? What role does the church assume in national debate over war? But at a more basic level, does the church have a "worldly" mission? What is the proper relationship between the church and the world? Between Christ and Caesar? Between Christians and social-political evil?

The attacks of September 2001 and their aftermath represent something of a watershed regarding U.S. foreign policy—events that could not have been foreseen by most people a mere decade earlier. What sort of reassessment will this mean for all Americans but especially for people of Christian faith? The cluster of related issues certainly transcends our personal lives and the life of our particular congregation. Perhaps we should confine our thinking to issues of piety, personal devotion or church growth and leave things like public policy to the experts. But what about basic issues of justice? What about terrorism? And what about governments and regimes that directly or indirectly abet terrorist activity?

Clearly, in raising such questions, we have waded well past the shallow waters of much contemporary teaching and preaching. And other difficult issues remain. Should we—Christians included—work to promote abroad such democratic features as the rule of law and respect for human rights? Is it legitimate for Christians to work for a just international order? Given the fact that terrorists emerge from those cultures where democracy and freedom—religious as well as political—have not made significant inroads, these cultures are "ill-equipped to wage necessary political, ideological, and

---

[5]See Paul Marshall, *Their Blood Cries Out: The Untold Story of Persecution Against Christians in the Modern World* (Dallas: Word, 1996). Organizations such as the Center for Religious Freedom and Freedom House deserve credit for their attempts to inform the Christian community of the plight of Christian persecution in Islamic cultures—particularly those where fanatical Islam is on the rise. See, for example, the important book by Philip Jenkins, *The Next Christendom* (New York: Oxford University Press, 2002) as well as his cover article "The New Iron Curtain," *American Outlook,* fall 2002, pp. 25-30, which explain why Americans should simultaneously be alarmed by anti-Christian oppression in Muslim nations and remember their Christian brethren in these cultures. See also Paul Marshall, "Radical Islam in Nigeria," *Weekly Standard,* April 15, 2002, pp. 15-16, as a specific case in point. As I was preparing this manuscript a new publication arrived in my mail: Timothy Shah, *The Rise of Hindu Extremism* (Washington, D.C.: Center for Religious Freedom/Freedom House, 2003).

military struggles against the revolutionary political extremism that masks it-self as a great faith."[6] Can Christians affirm the use of military force for the purposes of restraining growing extremism and the terrorist threat? Why or why not? And does it really matter?

I must confess, as a Christian who teaches theology and ethics, that I did not receive much help from prayers that were prayed and admonitions that were made following 9/11 and up to the present. Few religious leaders and commentators seem capable of linking theological belief to responsible cit-izenship and to the culture of which we are a part. Sadly, many Christian ethicists and not a few Christian writers lack a basic intuition for moral rea-soning that is historically informed and theologically faithful.[7]

At the most basic level, what might be said—and *should* be said—about the terrorist bombings and the murder of innocents, from a Christian stand-point? What is a proper response when catastrophe and violence come calling?

Regardless of our political differences, even within the Christian commu-nity, certain things not only *might* be said but *must* be said at a time when evil manifests itself so grotesquely as it did on September 11, 2001. For start-ers, such occasions remind us of the hard truths that we typically ignore dur-ing times of peace and prosperity. They remind us of what really counts in life, what is truly important and what is not. We discover—if we care to, that is—the comfort of a God who rules history and calls nations to account—ours included. And as an atomized, fragmented society, we discover that we need community; we need each other. If we learned nothing else from these difficult days, the New York Fire Department taught us that. Moreover, such

---

[6]Michael Goldfarb, "Freedom House Reacts to Terrorist Attacks," *Freedom House Monitor* 18, no. 3 (2001): 3.

[7]Take the column written by Philip Yancey in the February 2002 issue of *Christianity Today* ("I Was Just Wondering . . ."), which contains "twenty questions that nag me after September 11." Among his nagging questions: "How much would it have cost to reconstruct Afghanistan after their [sic] war with the Soviet Union?"; "Why is the United States so much better at destroying buildings and then rebuilding them—as in Germany, Japan, Korea, Kosovo—than in keeping them from being destroyed in the first place?"; "How do you demolish an ideology of fanati-cism when, by killing those who preach it, you attract even more converts to their fanaticism?"; "Why is it so much cheaper to prevent war than to conduct it?"; and "Why do we Americans, who consider ourselves friendly and compassionate, arouse such hatred in some parts of the world?" It seems that Yancey is struggling with guilt for being an American. But fully aside from his internal struggles, his questions fail at the most basic level to address concretely what is a just response to evil when it occurs. Fully absent is any attempt to engage in moral rea-soning. Unfortunately, Yancey's "nagging questions" do more to obscure than they do to high-light justice and Christian responsibility.

occasions also force us to enter into basic moral reasoning—what contemporary Americans typically have little time or motivation to do: suddenly we are forced to discriminate between basic evil acts—for example, mass murder—and acts that are humane.

But there is more. We are not merely quagmired in the events that beset New York City in 2001. While religious leaders and some within the academy piously remind us that we must seek to understand what motivates terrorists who engage in mass murder, we must also reconsider the meaning of justice. Empty calls to forgive are not the first order of business when evil rears its ugly head. In times of social upheaval and moral barbarism, our governing authorities—whether city, state or federal—do *not* conclude that *less* civil restraint and a *lesser* degree of retribution are needed because of the fear that apprehending and punishing criminals might motivate future criminals to retaliate. Rather, they make calculated efforts to restrain and prevent crime in the future. This is only the beginning of the criminal justice process, part of which entails apprehension, incarceration and punishment. Such a response issues out of prudential wisdom, not vengeance.

Of course, in making such a claim I can anticipate the objection. While reserving more extensive comment on retribution versus revenge for a later chapter, let me respond. It is true that a certain aspect of judgment *is* reserved for God beyond this life. Vengeance does belong to the Lord, and he will repay. But this is not to restrict divine vengeance only to the eschaton. Neither is it to remove divine recompense from the hand of the governing authorities, which is the clear, unambiguous argument of the New Testament. God has ordained "the sword" in the hand of governing authorities for the express purpose of limiting as well as punishing evildoers, thereby safeguarding society.

While taking justice into one's own hands—let us call it "vigilante justice"—is *proscribed* by Paul in Romans 12, justice is *prescribed* in another context, namely, in the hand of the magistrate, according to Romans 13. Not to respond to the attacks of September 11, or any other moral atrocity, would be an abdication of the most fundamental responsibility of government. That God has instituted government is not to say that government is godly; rather, it means that government is ultimately accountable to God to restrain evil. As one social critic observes, "None of the goods humans cherish, including the free exercise of religion, can flourish without a measure of civic peace and security. If evil is permitted to grow, good goes into hiding."[8]

Still more remains to be said. Firm as our resolve must be to address evil and gross injustice, we must at the same time reexamine our allegiance to our own nation and with humility recognize an ultimate allegiance—to the Creator, the Ruler of the nations. Otherwise, we can slip into the danger of national idolatry. From the Christian standpoint it is necessary to distinguish between our earthly and heavenly citizenship, even when both place responsibilities on us. But in struggling with this tension, we are not alone. We look to people such as Augustine, who takes both citizenships quite seriously. Living in a time of social decay, Augustine penned *The City of God* as a response to those who held Christianity responsible for Rome's demise.

In this important work Augustine's treatment of justified war, significantly, is found in the broader context of duties of citizenship.[9] Christian faith, Augustine contends, will not lead us to abdicate our duties in the present life, even when we must confront—and on occasion denounce—the powers of the present. In an unjust world we are still to work for justice, motivated by charity. We do not disassociate ourselves from the affairs of society as we await the eschaton.[10] Fundamentalists, radical separatists and certain evangelicals, take note.

At the same time we need not adopt, as do some religious critics of our foreign policy, the self-righteous attitude of "America as empire" (and here I write in the American context), attributing to our nation imperial or imperialistic designs that are reputedly causing the ills of the whole world. While recognizing our national problems we may indeed still acknowledge that there is much good in this nation. Nevertheless, we temper the requirements of justice with humility and the resolve to resist the nationalistic impulse. In the end it is not within our ability to make our lives, or our nation, "secure." Terror and evil abound, and there is no guarantee that we as a nation will be spared untold suffering.[11] After all, what we export to the world cuts both ways.

---

[8]Jean Bethke Elshtain, "Seeking Justice," *Christian Century,* November 14, 2001, p. 26.

[9]See chapter two for further development.

[10]A helpful guide for the church as it struggles with its relationship to pagan culture is Curtis Chang, *Engaging Unbelief: A Captivating Strategy from Augustine and Aquinas* (Downers Grove, Ill.: InterVarsity Press, 2000). Chang considers what it means to be Christian in a culture that is increasingly fragmented and religiously pluralistic.

[11]Lutheran ethicist Gilbert Meilaender has captured this attitude quite appropriately in "After September 11," *Christian Century,* November 14, 2001, pp. 7-8.

PRESUMPTION AGAINST WAR OR AGAINST INJUSTICE?

How Americans—and American Christians—think about war *cannot* be properly understood apart from reflecting on the American experience of the last half-century. And although the language of "just war" is frequently heard among politicians, journalistic pundits, policy analysts and even religious spokespersons, particular obstacles nevertheless impede our understanding of what the just-war tradition really is. These impediments are both cultural and theological in nature.

Consider, for example, how the last fifty years have molded the way in which we think about war and peace, especially in the church and in the academy. Our national experience as a result of the way World War II ended (at least in the Pacific theater) and our experience in Vietnam in particular have powerfully combined to shape our national ethos, whether we are Protestant or Catholic. When we add to this the proliferation of nuclear as well as chemical and biological weapons in the last forty years, many religious people believe that the proportions of modern warfare are so inherently evil that war or the use of military force is *intrinsically* immoral.[12] Thus we have today—perhaps less so among laypeople but overwhelmingly so in academic circles and in many religious quarters—a presumption against *war and force* in general rather than a presumption against *injustice*.[13] While the heart of the just-war tradition has been based on opposition to injustice, recent reinterpretations of just-war thinking are based instead on a presumption against *war itself*. This mutation has led to what James Turner Johnson calls "the broken tradition."[14]

We find this illustrated in statements by many Protestant denominations during the 1980s due to the escalation of Cold War tensions prior to the col-

---

[12]Thus already in 1960 Roman Catholic theologian John Courtney Murray wrote: "The use of force is not now a moral means for the redress of violated legal rights. The justness of the cause is irrelevant; there simply is no longer a right of self-redress; no individual state may presume to take even the cause of justice into its own hands. Whatever the grievance of the state may be, and however objectionable it may find the status quo, warfare undertaken on the sovereign decision of the national state is an immoral means of settling the grievance and for altering existent conditions" (*We Hold These Truths* [New York: Sheed & Ward, 1960], p. 256).

[13]Among ethicists, see, e.g., Richard B. Miller, *Interpretation of Conflict: Ethics, Pacifism, and the Just-War Tradition* (Chicago: University of Chicago Press, 1991), and James F. Childress, "Just-War Criteria," in *War or Peace?* ed. Thomas A. Shannon (Maryknoll, N.Y.: Orbis, 1980), pp. 40-58.

[14]James Turner Johnson, "The Broken Tradition," *National Interest,* fall 1996, pp. 27-36.

lapse of the Soviet empire.[15] War could not *possibly* be justified, we were scolded, regardless of the gulf between democratic self-government and totalitarianism. *Both* superpowers, it was argued, are immoral in "threatening" the world. We also see this presumption against war in the writings of influential Christian ethicists, who make calls for the elimination of war and strife in the present age.[16] And we see it with regularity in statements made by religious leaders in response to geopolitical events.

In 1983, at the height of Cold War tensions, a statement was published by the U.S. Catholic Bishops' Conference titled *The Challenge of Peace*.[17] In this document the bishops appear to want to synthesize just-war thinking and pacifism while deemphasizing the differences between the two.[18] They write:

> The church's teaching on war and peace establishes a strong presumption against war which is binding on all; it then examines when this presumption may be overridden, precisely in the name of preserving the kind of peace which protects human dignity and human rights. . . . The moral theory of the "just-war" or "limited war" doctrine begins with the presumption which binds all Christians: We should do no harm; . . . how we treat our enemy is the key test of whether we love our neighbor; and the possibility of taking even one human life is a prospect we should consider in fear and trembling. How is it possible to move from these presumptions to the idea of a justifiable use of lethal force?[19]

---

[15]E.g., see the 1986 statement by the United Church of Christ, "Affirming the United Church of Christ as a Just Peace Church"; the United Methodist bishops' statement, *In Defense of Creation* (Nashville: Graded Press, 1986); the 1987 report by the Episcopal Diocese of Washington, D.C., *The Nuclear Dilemma: A Christian Search for Understanding* (Cincinnati: Forward Movement Publications, 1987); and the statement in 1988 by the 200th General Assembly of the Presbyterian Church (USA), *Christian Obedience in a Nuclear Age* (Louisville: Office of the General Assembly, Presbyterian Church [U.S.A.], 1988).

[16]See, e.g., John Howard Yoder, *The Original Revolution: Essays on Christian Pacifism* (Scottdale: Herald Press, 1971); *Christian Attitudes to War, Peace, and Revolution: A Companion to Bainton* (Elkhart, Ind.: Co-op Bookstore, 1983); *He Came Preaching Peace* (Scottdale: Herald Press, 1985); *Nevertheless: The Varieties and Shortcomings of Religious Pacifism* (Scottdale: Herald Press, 1992); *When War Is Unjust*, 2nd ed. (Maryknoll, N.Y.: Orbis, 1996); Stanley Hauerwas, *The Peaceable Kingdom* (South Bend, Ind.: University of Notre Dame Press, 1983); *Should War Be Eliminated?* (Milwaukee: Marquette University Press, 1984); and Glen Stassen, *Just Peacemaking: Transforming Initiatives for Justice and Peace* (Louisville: Westminster John Knox, 1992).

[17]*The Challenge of Peace* (Washington, D.C.: United States Catholic Conference, 1983). In the bishops' sequel, *The Harvest of Justice Is Sown in Peace* (Washington, D.C.: United States Catholic Conference, 1993), which was published ten years later, a firmer attempt was made to distinguish between just war and pacifism.

[18]The bishops' position, which might be called "relative" or "nuclear" pacifism, is indebted, more accurately, to pacifist thinking than to a proper understanding of just-war assumptions. See the discussion below as well as that of chapter five.

[19]*Challenge of Peace*, ¶70, 80.

The bishops give the strong impression that they want to have it both ways. They wish fervently to affirm peace and stop just short of saying that war is *never* justifiable. In contrast to the bishops' emphasis, the historical moral basis of just-war teaching is the presumption not against war or lethal force per se but against evil that is directed toward my neighbor, against injustice and oppression. Just-war thinking, properly understood, begins with the presumption to restrain evil and protect the innocent, not to forbid coercive force.[20]

In their statement the bishops imply that peace is the starting point for thinking about justice. The just-war tradition, however, proceeds on the reverse assumption. Without justice, peace itself can be illegitimate. The animating spirit of just-war thinking is that "social charity comes to the aid of the oppressed."[21] Therefore, anyone who categorically rules out the possibility of war or coercive force violates the presumption against injustice, which is a requirement of love rightly construed. The just-war tradition, hence, strongly qualifies peace, acknowledging that if this peace is not justly ordered, it may well be illegitimate, even oppressive. Peace, therefore, is not merely the *absence of conflict.* The bishops, mistakenly, assume that the just-war tradition begins with a presumption *against war.* It does not. In its development, the Christian just-war tradition issues out of a presumption *against injustice.*

Properly understood, the just-war tradition understands itself as a mediating or moderating position between two poles that are absolutist in their attitude toward coercive force. On the one hand, the militarist—whether secular (sometimes called the "political realist") or religious (the jihadist or crusader)—views war and coercive force as justifiable under any circumstance. No moral restraints beyond political expediency or the "command of God" need be applied. On the other end stands the pacifist. Given the suffering and bloodshed caused by violence and war, the pure or principled pacifist believes that war and coercive force are *never* permissible; war is to be rejected under any and all circumstances.

The just-war position—an expression of consensual Christian thinking through the ages—seeks to mediate this tension. This mediating position is rooted in a certain Christian realism: we must never believe that nothing is

---

[20]Protestant ethicist Paul Ramsey was acutely critical of those who argued that pacifism and just war have in common the same presumption against violence (*Speak Up for Just War or Pacifism* [University Park: Pennsylvania State University Press, 1988], pp. 109-10).
[21]Ibid., p. 109.

permissible, nor that everything is. There *are* occasions in which, reluctantly, we may need to apply coercive force, even if this means going to war, for the protection and preservation of a third party. Resort to war is sometimes, though not always, unjust. The difficulty with the bishops' attempt to blend pacifism and just war is that pacifists in the end reject the validity of just-war criteria (which are discussed in chapter six). For the ideological pacifist, coercive force and war can *never* serve a just end.

The distinction between a presumption against war or coercive force and a presumption against injustice is not merely academic. It is critical as a starting point for thinking about war. And it is a distinction made again and again by Christian moral thinkers.[22]

Aquinas begins his discussion of war (*Summa Theologiae* 2-2.Q40) with this distinction in mind. He asks, "Is it always a sin to fight in war?" As he frequently does, Aquinas answers typical objections that cause someone to answer incorrectly. He identifies two common objections that he says are lodged in a misunderstanding of two biblical texts—Matthew 5:38-39 (not resisting evil and turning the cheek) and Romans 12:17-21 (not returning evil for evil). In response Aquinas is at pains to show that coercive force per se is not a category of injustice but rather that it is necessary to what Augustine called the *tranquillitas ordinis,* the civic peace.[23] Theologian John Courtney Murray's distinction between force and violence, I think, is useful here: "Force is the measure of power necessary and sufficient to uphold . . . law and politics. What exceeds this measure is violence, which destroys the order of both law and politics. . . . As an instrument, force is morally neutral in itself."[24]

When we speak of just war, we do not mean a war that, narrowly speaking, is just. Rather, we refer to warfare undertaken that is in conformity with the demands of charity, justice and human dignity, and that seeks to protect the innocent third party from gross injustice and social evil. These are the fundamental assumptions of just-war thinking.

I am fully aware of the strong disagreements that separate Christians regard-

---

[22]An attempt to address fundamental misconceptions about just-war theory lies behind Oliver O'Donovan's recently published work *The Just War Revisited* (Cambridge: Cambridge University Press, 2003). This deceptively brief volume (139 pages including the index) navigates deftly between politics and theology. While it omits any historical development of just-war thinking it focuses rather on contemporary dilemmas such as biological weapons, economic sanctions, international conventions and war crimes trials.

[23]*Summa Theologiae* 2-2.Q40a.1; see also Q7a.3-4 as well as Q18.

[24]Murray, *We Hold These Truths,* p. 274.

ing war and the use of force. As one who grew up in the Anabaptist (and specifically Mennonite) tradition, I am grateful for the influence of this tradition on my social ethic and spiritual formation. At the same time I reflect on my experience doing criminal justice work in Washington, D.C., and on the relatively unformed social conscience of so many Christians today—whether in the congregation or the classroom. The crying need of the hour has less to do with pacifism than an understanding of peace that is not divorced from the obligations of justice. *The challenge before us is neither to renounce war and coercive force in absolutist terms nor to affirm militarism with its disdain for moral reasoning.* What applies to domestic policy also applies to foreign policy; so a useful analogy holds: there is a choice—an alternative—between permitting crime on the one hand and police brutality on the other. That choice lies somewhere in the middle. It is this messy middle that requires that we roll up our sleeves and get our hands dirty, and such is the focus of the present volume.

But first things first.

MAKING MORAL JUDGMENTS

Society's and the church's deep-seated skepticism about force as a moral enterprise is exacerbated by the broader cultural climate. I speak here of the climate of postmodernism that fosters radical moral pessimism and stubbornly refuses to identify moral markers at all. It is difficult to overstate this point: not only does our culture fail to assist us in making moral judgments, it *discourages* us from doing so.

This should come as no surprise, however, since leading social scientists have been telling us for decades that moral beliefs and values are all products of particular cultures, evolving and adapting over time and circumstances. If all moral judgments are relative to the values of a given society, then everything can be justified, even aberrant forms of sexuality, torture, child molestation and slavery.[25] Intellectual honesty requires then that nothing binding prohibits such actions.

But on the practical side the empirical evidence around us overwhelm-

---

[25]While a list of those holding to moral relativism would be endless, representative of this thinking are William Graham Sumner, "Folkways," Ruth Benedict, "Anthropology and the Abnormal," and J. L. Mackie, "The Subjectivity of Values," all of whose essays have been gathered in *Moral Relativism: A Reader*, ed. Paul K. Moser and Thomas L. Carson (New York: Oxford University Press, 2001), pp. 69-79, 80-89, 259-76 respectively. A test case to demonstrate how moral relativism is self-refuting is found in Loretta Kopelman, "Female Circumcision/Genital Mutilation and Moral Relativism," which has been appended to the same volume, pp. 307-25.

ingly points to the existence of two diametrically opposed forces—"good" and "evil." And why is it, given the omnipresence of evil in the world, that society flatly and resolutely refuses to acknowledge it as an entity? To call it by its name, much less to confront it?

To avoid the tension between fact and fantasy, some people, for example, deny that evil exists. Period. This, of course, is the tactic of the materialist, the secularist, the atheist. To acknowledge the realm of evil is to acknowledge that there is a dimension of reality, after all, that exceeds the bare material world. But this is not the only strategy of evasion. Others seek to minimize evil in order to make it more manageable. Change the language of morality, redefine what is acceptable and unacceptable, and voilà! Then we need not be encumbered by the "oppressive" restraints of "traditional morality"! What used to be unthinkable now has become the norm for society. Such a strategy, of course, has enormous implications for public policy. And if we relegate evil to a few notorious cases in history—Mao, Stalin, Hitler, Pol Pot and the like—we can successfully dodge the bullet of universal depravity ourselves.

Yet another evasive tactic is to engage in moral equivalence, a sort of moral calculus that works through comparison and refuses to make moral discriminations of any sort. No action, in the end, is better or worse than another. Examples of this abound in daily life. Two superpowers, regardless of their ideological commitments, are an equal threat to the world's peace.[26] Two presidential candidates, we were told, are equally noxious as they vie for several thousand uncontested votes in the state of Florida, even though the lawyers of the one candidate engage in six weeks of legal (and illegal) street-fighting to overturn the election's outcome. And evangelical Christians are routinely lumped together with Muslim fanatics as "fundamentalist extremists" who, we are condescendingly reminded, threaten good folk everywhere with their narrow-minded way of thinking.

A further tactic—one that has become increasingly common in contemporary culture—is to accuse anyone who does make moral judgments of being judgmental. This very effective strategy in our day has the effect of

---

[26]One religious writer, suspicious of U.S. propaganda efforts in the 1980s, with a bit of self-righteous clairvoyance dismisses what was in fact common knowledge: "At other times, the propaganda weaves together disparate events to present an intricate (if not paranoid) vision of conspiracy; such was the Reagan-era claim that there was a 'global terror network' directed from Moscow" (Lee Griffith, *The War on Terrorism and the Terror of God* [Grand Rapids: Eerdmans, 2002], p. 18).

paralyzing most people (even good people) into nonaction. After all, given the exalted stature of tolerance as a contemporary virtue, what is the cardinal postmodern sin, if not judgmentalism? Anyone today who dares to make moral pronouncements is labeled an imperialist, a bigot and narrow-minded in the extreme. Most contemporary Americans would rather be branded as criminals than bear the mark of Cain that is judgmentalism.[27]

The present character of Western societies is often described as "pluralistic." But we are naive—or disingenuous—if we fail to distinguish between a pluralism of social and cultural differences and a pluralism that is ideological and moral. Thus we will need to qualify the term wherever it used. One social critic has depicted Western societies collectively (and North American society, in particular) as a "regime of toleration," in which personal lifestyles and choices have supplanted a common way of life and the acknowledgment of any higher moral authority. Western "democracies" are perhaps the most individualistic—and amoral—societies in history:

> Compared to the men and women of any earlier . . . [era], we are all radically liberated. We are free to plot our own course; to plan our own lives; to choose a career, a partner (or a succession of partners), a religion (or no religion), a politics (or an antipolitics), a lifestyle (any style)—we are free to "do our own thing."[28]

While social-cultural pluralism is to be celebrated and is part of the fabric of creation, ideological and moral pluralism—by which we deny that there is a binding moral authority over our lives—is not benign. Rather, this form of pluralism, among individuals and societies, inevitably descends into a pluralism—indeed, a plethora—of moralities, out of which only moral barbarism ensues. Barbarism, it should be observed, is not merely the huddling together of people under the brute force of violence and fear. Society becomes barbarian

> when economic interests assume the primacy over higher values; when material standards of mass and quantity crush out the values of quality and excellence; when technology assumes an autonomous existence . . . without purposeful guidance from the higher disciplines of politics and morals.[29]

---

[27]The social commentator Dennis Prager, in a most concise and lucid manner, has developed a similar "taxonomy of denial" in his essay "Why Aren't People Preoccupied with Good and Evil?" *Ultimate Issues* 7, no. 2 (1990): 6-9.

[28]Michael Walzer, *On Toleration* (New Haven, Conn.: Yale University Press, 1997), p. 100.

[29]John Courtney Murray, *We Hold These Truths* (New York: Sheed & Ward, 1960), pp. 13-14.

Barbarism also looms when people cease talking to one another or when they lack a common moral grammar and cannot talk at all with one another. Civility dies, then, as a result of "the death of dialogue."[30]

But common sense, not merely Christian faith, tells us that people are stronger when they contribute to a common cultural life, when there is a strong sense of civic engagement and where civility is found. "Love your neighbor as yourself" is not merely a religious platitude; it has enormous social ramifications. In fact community, civility and cultural engagement are inevitable byproducts of neighbor love.

No society can be founded on (let alone survive) the radical individualism, with its pluralism of morality, that presently holds sway in American culture. To refuse to choose for the good—and *good* is to be understood in terms of *what benefits the community or society, not myself*—is to allow room for evil to flourish. And if we live in a moral universe, a vacuum is created when goodness and justness fail to assert themselves. With a pluralism (or plurality) of moralities, society becomes ungovernable. Ordering itself and dealing with external threats become impossible under such conditions.

RELIGIOUS ATTITUDES TOWARD WAR

Religious people—and certainly Christians around the world—differ strongly in their views of war and peace and the use of coercive force. They approach the question with radically divergent assumptions. Writing on the brink of World War II, British evangelical Martin Lloyd-Jones observed among Christians of his own day three general prevalent attitudes. One was preoccupied with the causes of war, much like sociologists who attempt to identify the "roots causes of crime" and focus on political, economic and sociological factors. These persons, Lloyd-Jones observed, tend to discuss the question of war apart from purely theological considerations such as the nature of God and human nature. They also assume that, given its horrors, the avoidance of war and all conflict is of utmost importance. Participation in war itself is presumed to be sin.

A second type of person tended to evaluate war in relation to God's rule over the nations but wholly divorced from Christian living. This person more often than not was found to be a very pietistic sort of Christian, with a devotional approach to faith and life. He or she demonstrates little interest in

---

[30]Ibid., p. 14.

theology or systematic study of the Bible and little concern for the intellectual or rational component of Christian faith. The experiential and subjective aspect of faith is of paramount importance. As a result, war poses a severe dilemma for this sort of person simply due to the enormity of the issues raised that appear to be outside of one's "experience."

A third type of person seems to share elements of types one and two. His or her idea of God tends to be somewhat vague, usually conformed to that of surrounding culture. Not surprisingly, it is the love of God, among all divine attributes, that becomes the singular focus of this person. The notions of divine wrath, judgment or punishment are utterly foreign to this outlook, typically overshadowed by God's benevolence, compassion and condescension. Human happiness, not cruelty and suffering, are understood to be the promises of this loving God in this life.[31]

What Lloyd-Jones found several generations ago would be a near-accurate typology of Christians today. And despite their differences, what is notable about all three types is that they all share an aversion to theology. Consider our own congregations for a moment. Few Christians tend to think in terms of a broader Christian worldview, which rests on explicit theological foundations. Rather, they focus on the personal benefits that faith can add to their private lives. Consequently, wrestling with perplexing questions such as the ethics of war is to be left to the "professionals"—those who have studied such matters. Where God *does* enter the picture for many, he frequently does so in the form of the standard question, Why does God allow war? or How can God allow war? And that is about as far as it goes.

In response to this standard question several things need to be affirmed that affect our starting point. The confessing Christian must begin to think about war and suffering in general *based on what Scripture reveals about the divine nature and human nature.* What assumptions form the bedrock of historic Christian faith?

God's sovereign reign is established. He is the Lord "almighty," as the creeds confess. Therefore, nothing—not even war—is outside of his providential rule, knowledge, power and dominion.

➔ ✶War is properly understood as belonging to the consequences of sin that attend the present age. It is part of our fallenness, which means that it is part of the present world, a permanent fixture, and will be with us until the es-

---

[31]Martin Lloyd-Jones, *Why Does God Allow Suffering?* (London: Hodder & Stoughton, 1939), reprinted by Crossway in 1994.

chaton, when (and only when) the effects of the Fall are no more. Therefore, its elimination is utopian and optimistic at best and wrong-headed at
worst, even when we work to reduce both its intensity and infrequency.
World peace is impossible due to the human condition. Punishment and
judgment of sin are not fully postponed until the next world; they are temporal realities as well, for "whatever a man sows he will reap." Even most
postmoderns know this reality: "what goes around comes around."

Because peace is a prominent biblical theme and a highly prized human
commodity, it must be strongly qualified. Peace is not merely the absence
of conflict or war, which suggests that some versions of peace may be unjust.[32] The peace that is depicted through various Old Testament images—
for example, the lamb laying down with the lion (see Is 11:6-9; 65:25) and
humans beating their swords into ploughshares and spears into pruning
hooks (Is 2:4; Mic 4:3)—is intended to foreshadow a future, eschatological
peace. These metaphors represent ultimate, not penultimate, reality. The
ideal must not be mistaken for the real. God has not promised a world without war and strife, nor may it be argued that he intends to abolish them in
the present. Peace as most humans know it can be a false security that hides
a waning of religious commitment, a decline in general morality and an in-
crease in material decadence.[33] It can even be idolatry itself. An authentic,
properly motivated peace, by contrast, is based solely on the desire to live
a godly life (cf. 1 Tim 2:1-4). Moreover, peace among humans in the present
must be justly ordered, the *tranquillitas ordinis* described by Augustine;[34]
otherwise, it is no peace at all and may serve unjust ends. The presence—
or possibility—of war therefore need not shake our faith.

While murder is proscribed by the Creator (Ex 20:13; Deut 5:17), based
on our creation in the image of God (Gen 1:27; 9:6), there is no absolute
sanction against the taking of life. Manslaughter is not the equivalent of murder, as the Old Testament narratives describing the cities of refuge indicate
(Num 35:6-33; Josh 20:1-9). Moreover, capital punishment was prescribed by
Mosaic law for various crimes, and killing in self-defense was not considered
a criminal offense. While life is a gift and thus is sacred (hence the sixth

---

[32]The Latin *pax* and the English word *pact* (an agreement not to fight) derive from the same
root. Augustine writes in *The City of God* of the "cruel peace" that went under the guise of
the pax Romana.

[33]For this reason, World War I was frequently and mistakenly referred to as "the war to end all
wars."

[34]I discuss this aspect of Augustine's thinking further in chapter two.

commandment), it is not to be valued above the soul. Therefore, loss of life as punishment for crimes against humanity is not the moral equivalent of murdering the innocent (a fundamental distinction that is present in Gen 9:6 as part of God's covenant with Noah and forms the basis of our criminal justice system). Jesus' teaching regarding the body and soul seems to infer this distinction, even when it is not his aim to elaborate on the distinction: "Do not be afraid of those who kill the body but cannot kill the soul. Rather, be afraid of the One who can destroy both soul and body in hell" (Mt 10:28). "Thou shalt not kill" cannot be interpreted to rule out all killing, including war. The purpose of war, furthermore, is to stop the strong man, not to kill as such. Therefore, killing in war is not the equivalent of murder.

The use of force in resisting or punishing evil is not entrusted to individual people. It rests with governing authorities, whose responsibility it is to protect the moral-social order. In this way, justice and retribution show themselves to be moral entities and are to be distinguished from vengeance (Rom 12:17—13:10; 1 Pet 2:13-14; cf. 1 Tim 2:1-4).

War can—and usually will—cause people to reflect on the important issues of life—God, justice, sin, human community, civility and so forth. Therein we are reminded of our humanity, our fallenness, our utter dependence on God and the extent to which human relationships should mirror— ever so dimply—divine justice. In such times we are brought to the deepest place of soul-searching, spiritual awareness and heart-felt repentance.

War raises a host of complex questions, not the least of which is: What about the innocent who suffer? This question, over which philosophers have agonized for millennia, requires our thinking at two levels—the theological and the prudential. As to the latter, just-war principles as found in the Christian moral tradition deliberately *seek to protect* the innocent. Safeguarding the innocent third party serves as moral justification for going to war, and once in conflict it seeks to safeguard the innocent by granting them noncombatant immunity.[35] The theological grounds for why the innocent suffer are less clear-cut. The "wisdom" perspective of Jesus and Job, while a necessary corrective to an overdone "retribution" theology (such as advanced by Job's friends), leaves much unexplained: it rains on the just and unjust, and bad things *do* happen to good as well as bad people. What we may say with certainty is that we all share in Adam's sin; Adam's sin therefore affects

---

[35]The particular moral criteria that comprise the just-war tradition are discussed in chapter six.

us all. We share in the plight of the human race. All have sinned and fall short of divine standards. Thus no one is innocent—no one, that is, apart from the Son of God, who suffered innocently and vicariously on our behalf.

Difficult as it is, the question Why does God allow war? in the end is overshadowed by other theologically informed questions. We begin to sense this adjustment of perspective, and alter our own perspectives, once we enter into centuries-long conversation with prior generations of Christians and place these considerations alongside our own study of Scripture. What did the church in prior generations believe and teach? What insights might historic Christian reflection on war, suffering and evil afford us today as we wrestle with perennial issues? At the very least, we might begin to ask slightly different questions—for example: Why doesn't God allow humankind to self-annihilate? Why does his grace restrain evil? Why does God redeem what is evil? Why does God transform evil into good? What is God's greater purpose (the "deeper wisdom" alluded to in passages such as 1 Cor 2:6-10)? While the mystery and tragedy of being human do not go away, the human perspective is altered—indeed, transformed—as we begin to think biblically and theologically.

JUST-WAR THINKING AND THE TERRORIST THREAT

In the 1980s many books on the ethics of war appeared as a response to heightened tension in U.S.-Soviet relations. Most of these volumes pressed the same argument. They decried the arms race as immoral and argued that modern technology, especially nuclear weaponry, altered the ethical landscape so that just-war theory was hopelessly irrelevant.[36] Contrary to this standard argument, I contend that just-war thinking loses none of its relevance today as we sit on the cusp of the third millennium. In fact, two developments since 1990 invalidate and render obsolete much of what was written before 1990. I speak of the end of the Cold War and the breathtaking rise of international terrorism. These two factors altogether alter the geopolitical landscape. And it is the maturing of the terrorist threat that underscores the abiding relevance of the just-war tradition.

If war poses moral dilemmas, terrorism in its contemporary form thrusts moral dilemmas in our faces with a vengeance. This book is not written merely to engage in sterile discussions of ethical theory. Enough of aca-

---

[36]Representative is Bernard T. Adeney, *Just War, Political Realism, and Faith* (Metuchen: American Theological Library Association, 1988).

demic ethics is so oriented. Rather, the problem of terrorism forces us to (1) make moral judgments, (2) give account of those judgments and (3) act on those judgments. The fact that many of our contemporaries lack the fortitude to embark on this project does not let us off the hook. When catastrophe comes calling, we will need to act on the convictions generated by our worldview.

In the face of moral evil Christians will need to know how to respond and justify that response. Assuming the Christian fundamental inclination to prevent conflict and avoid bloodshed wherever possible, are there ever situations in which it is better to use lethal force or go to war than permit terror and heinous evil to go unimpeded and unaccountable? What is a moral response to social-political evil when it strikes?

Terrorism is a particularly heinous form of evil, due to its intent. It seeks to undermine the social order and thus poses a political as well as a moral challenge. How a society responds to its challenge will be determined by how that society defines and understands justice. The very principles of just cause, right intent, legitimate authority, proportionality and discrimination, which form the backbone of the just-war tradition, address head-on the evils of terrorism and therefore commend just-war thinking to us as a response to current geopolitical challenges.

Questions raised in this book remind us that these are difficult days. But they are made more difficult by our inability (or refusal) to make moral judgments and then to act on those judgments. The terrorist threat is by no means the only political, moral and social challenge that faces us. Nor is it the primary focus of this book. But it does test our will—and our ability to do justly—perhaps as nothing else can.

This book represents an attempt to wrestle with the moral obligations of justice. It seeks to locate itself within the mainstream of historic Christian thinking, whereby it is understood that there is such a thing as a just use of force. It wishes to draw upon the collective wisdom of the just-war tradition—a part of the Christian moral tradition that is rich, complex and longstanding. In the following chapters we will become reacquainted with this tradition, or perhaps for many readers, to become acquainted for the very first time. Political ethicist Jean Bethke Elshtain correctly points out the risks we run if we fail to interact with this tradition:

> If we try to avoid the complexity of what is at issue when we debate the use
> of force, simplistic solutions are likely to win the day, whether of a pacifist or

militarist bent. The just war tradition requires that the philosopher, the moralist, the politician, and the ordinary citizen consider a number of complex [moral] criteria when thinking about war. These criteria shape a continuous scrutiny of war that judges whether the resort to force is justified, and whether, once force is resorted to, its use has been kept within necessary limits. Although never regarding war as desirable, . . . the just war tradition acknowledges that it may be better than the alternative.[37]

Because this tradition has a long and varied history, our first order of business is to consider some of the seminal thinkers who have contributed to its development.

---

[37]Jean Bethke Elshtain, *Just War Against Terror* (New York: Basic Books, 2003), pp. 56-57.

2

JUST-WAR THINKING
IN ANCIENT AND
MEDIEVAL THOUGHT

Although Christian thinkers wrestle with justice in war as a potential obligation of Christian charity to one's neighbor, just conduct of war is also found in other cultures that predate Christianity. What is ethically refined by Christian faith finds precursors in pagan societies.

PRE-CHRISTIAN JUST-WAR THINKING

Lao Tzu, a sixth-century B.C. Chinese philosopher (and founder of Taoism), warns that wisdom will "oppose" all attempts at overreliance on force of arms, for "such things are likely to rebound." "Where armies are, thorns and brambles grow. . . . Therefore a good general effects his purpose and stops" to consider wisdom. This wisdom will not rely wholly on strength of arms, nor will it glory or boast therein.[1]

Wisdom, rather, will view armed conflict as "a regrettable necessity" and "not love violence," since "violence would be against the Tao, and he who is against the Tao perishes young." And because "soldiers are weapons of evil," they are "not the weapons of the gentleman." However, when "the use of soldiers cannot be avoided, [t]he best policy is calm restraint. . . . He who delights in slaughter will not succeed in his ambition to rule." In addition to counseling restraint, Lao Tzu distinguishes between combatants and the innocent masses: "The slaying of multitudes should be mourned with sorrow. A victory should be celebrated with the Funeral Rite."[2]

---

[1]Lao Tzu *The Wisdom of Lao Tzu* 30-31, in *War and Peace,* Classical Selections on Great Issues 1 (Washington, D.C.: University Press of American, 1982), 5:562.
[2]Ibid., pp. 562-63.

The fifth-century B.C. philosopher-soldier Sun Tzu states that because war is a matter of vital importance to the state, "it is mandatory that it be thoroughly studied." At the same time he states: "Weapons are tools of ill omen." The first of the essentials requiring examination, according to Sun Tzu, is the "moral influence." War, he writes, is "a grave matter; one is apprehensive lest men embark upon it without due reflection."[3] For Sun Tzu too, war is a regrettable necessity, and like Lao Tzu he contends for restraint. Chinese of the fifth century B.C. also recognized rules of engagement that required just cause to begin a war, notification of pending attacks, humane treatment of prisoners and the injured, noncombatant immunity for innocents, and not prolonging war. Generally, in war, the best policy is to take a state intact; to ruin it is inferior to this—to capture the enemy's army is better than to destroy it—the worst policy is to attack cities.[4]

Similarly, the Hindu civilization of India during the fourth century B.C. codified in the *Book of Manu* humanitarian rules that were to regulate warfare conducted by "honorable warriors." These rules granted various kinds of immunity to noncombatants, civilians, soldiers without weapons and armor, as well as those who were in flight.[5]

Both Plato and Aristotle, who view war as a necessary evil, nevertheless question what is sufficient warrant for going to war. In Plato's *Republic* the ravaging of enemy territory and property is outlawed, while immunity is granted to women, children and those men who are deemed innocent.[6] In *Laws* Plato acknowledges that only the commonwealth, that is, a properly constituted authority, can declare war or peace.[7] The goal of going to war, according to Aristotle, is that we may live at peace, not for the sake of war itself. War must be conducted with the virtue of nobility and grandeur, he writes, and is justified under the following conditions: as a result of aggression, to address a prior wrong, and when injustice is presently underway. Going to war is justified in the case of self-defense, defending our own as well as aiding our allies.[8]

Writing in the first century B.C., the Roman Stoic philosopher Cicero de-

---

[3]Sun Tzu *The Art of War* 1.1, in *War and Peace,* Classical Selections on Great Issues 1 (Washington, D.C.: University Press of America, 1982), 5:301.
[4]*The Wisdom of Lao Tzu* 30-31, pp. 562-67, and *The Art of War,* pp. 301-4.
[5]*The Law of War* (New York: Random House, 1972), 1:3.
[6]Plato *Republic* 4 (471a-b).
[7]Plato *Laws* 12 (955b-c).
[8]Aristotle *Nicomachean Ethics* 10 (1177b), and *Politics* (1425a-b).

velops criteria that justify going to war.[9] These include last resort where diplomatic and peaceful efforts to avoid war have failed, formal declaration by delegated authority, and just cause in the sense that war must be provoked. Cicero advocates restraint in war even with those who have committed wrongs against Rome, arguing that "there is a limit to retribution and punishment."[10] One part of Cicero's definition of just cause is a defense against dishonor. And although Augustine, writing at the time of Rome's demise, extends the rules of war delineated by Cicero, he and Christian thinkers to follow restrict just cause to defense against aggression, the righting of wrongs and the restoration of peace. But most notably they root justice in the concept of Christian charity and neighbor love.

Whether or not Rome embodied the principles as explained by Cicero, to be sure, is another question. But this is not our present concern. The point to be emphasized is that Christian moral thinkers root proper motivation for just war in charity, which *may* express itself in some situations by actively and directly defending an innocent third party.

Regardless of Rome's track record, a very elaborate procedure by Rome ensued when a grievance against another city or nation arose. Historian Paul Christopher describes certain aspects of this procedure:

> Ambassadors under the direction of a distinguished statesman would go to the offending city and demand reparations. The ambassadors then returned to Rome and waited thirty-three days for a response. If they received none, the same representative and his party would again travel to the other nation and threaten war. If the offending nation still refused, the designated statesman would inform the Roman Senate of the failure to achieve reparations, and the Senate could decide to resort to force to carry out its claims. Once the Senate voted for war, the ambassadors were again sent to the hostile nation to announce the declaration of war and symbolically throw a javelin on enemy soil.[11]

The only time these elaborate procedures were not followed was when the enemy was not organized as a state, when Rome was already under attack or in the case of civil war.

Whether or not Rome embodied these principles remains outside our dis-

---

[9]Cicero *De Republica* 3.23, and *De Officiis* 1.11.

[10]Cicero *De Officiis* 1.11.

[11]Paul Christopher, *The Ethics of War and Peace*, rev. ed. (Upper Saddle River, N.J.: Prentice Hall, 1999), p. 13.

cussion. The point to be made is this: conditions existed according to Roman law to measure the justness of its cause among the nations and people groups. Military campaigns undertaken in accordance with these criteria were declared *formally* just.

EARLY CHRISTIAN ATTITUDES TOWARD WAR AND SOLDIERING

Although just-war thinking is found in Ambrose (A.D. 340-396) and his convert Augustine (A.D. 354-430), well before their time Christians who wrestled with their duties to organized society had begun serving in the Roman legions—a portrait that already is suggested in the pages of the New Testament. We learn of this directly and indirectly from several of the pacifist early church fathers.

In Tertullian's treatise *On the Soldier's Crown* we learn that Christians had been serving in the Roman army in North Africa. In his late-second-century work *On Idolatry,* Tertullian writes for the purpose of describing specific vocations that are thought to imperil one's faith. Included in this list were Roman civil service and military service. Both, he believed, were forms of pagan sacrifice. As to the latter we know from military history that higher ranks in the Roman legions sacrificed to the emperor. And while lower ranks traditionally did not participate directly in this practice, they were present at such ceremonies, swore allegiance to the emperor and wore badges that bore the emperor's effigy.[12] Tertullian adopts a very literal rendering of Jesus' words: "One soul cannot be owing to two masters—God and Caesar."[13]

But the danger of idolatry, according to Tertullian, is widespread.[14] One cannot be too careful. His list of forbidden occupations is not limited to the state. The danger of idolatry should also prevent Christians from becoming teachers and students because both require studying the classics of Greek and Roman literature. In addition, trades such as gold- and silversmithing as

---

[12]Ibid., pp. 17-18. See also John Helgeland, "Christians and the Roman Army, A.D. 173-337," *Church History* 43, no. 2 (1974): 149-63.

[13]*On Idolatry* 19. Tertullian was opposed to a Christian wearing garlands *anywhere* simply because of the close connection between military garlands and pagan deities, and thus, the fear of idolatry (*De Corona Militis* 11.6; 12.1). He was also keenly aware of the *sacramentum,* the military oath taken upon enlistment and then twice a year by every soldier.

[14]Tertullian's argument in *On Idolatry* is not always correctly understood. His main preoccupation in this treatise is not whether a Christian could serve in the army. Rather, he writes for what apparently are fairly recent converts; thus, his fear of situations that could lead to compromise, and as a result, idolatry, is understandable.

well as woodcarving are to be avoided by Christians, since these vocations so frequently entail making pagan idols for clients.[15] And not only vocations, but our lifestyles are potentially idolatrous. So, for example, fancy hairstyles and outer adornments are to be eschewed.[16]

What is remarkable well before Tertullian's time is that the early-second-century letter of Pliny to the emperor Trajan (A.D. 112) concerning the problem of Christians fails to mention anything about their unwillingness to serve in the military.[17] Given the tenor of the letter, nonservice would have been conspicuous—and scandalous—to Pliny since, as Origen writes, the emperor required service.[18] It should be noted that the two chief pacifist church fathers, Tertullian and Origen, both of whom prohibit Christians from bearing the sword, neither denied to government the moral duty of self-defense nor denied that Christians actually served in the military. In fact, Tertullian indicates that considerable numbers of Christians were already serving in the Roman legions, and he concedes certain conditions under which he believes a Christian could serve as a magistrate, provided that he avoid certain idolatrous contexts.[19] (And we know from Eusebius that before the fourth century there were Christian governors in the provinces.) What is more, Tertullian prays for "security to the empire; for protection to the imperial house; for brave armies."[20]

An allusion by Eusebius to an event roughly contemporary with the early part of Tertullian's life is intriguing. Eusebius informs us of a military band called Legio Fulminata ("the Thundering Legion"), which was credited with miraculously helping Marcus Aurelius in the year 173 against Germanic horses on the Danube frontier.[21] With troops dehydrated due to a lack of water in the region, soldiers prayed. As a result, lightning struck and rain poured down, putting to flight the enemy. Following this remarkable incident, the emperor wrote to the Senate, crediting Christians in the army with the victory. In his account Eusebius notes in passing that Tertullian knew of

---

[15]It is significant that Tertullian looks past the soldiers who come to John the Baptist and the centurion who came to Jesus and exhibited faith. Rather than questioning why neither the Baptist nor Jesus called soldiers away from a "violent" vocation, Tertullian grounds his view of the sword as idolatry in Jesus' rebuke of Peter in the Garden as recorded in Mt 26:52 (*On Idolatry* 19).

[16]*De Cultu Feminarum* 2.9; 3.1.

[17]*Epistle* 10.96, 97.

[18]Origen *Contra Celsum* 8.73, 75.

[19]Tertullian *On Idolatry* 17.

[20]*Apology* 30.

[21]*Church History* 5.43–5.7.

this event (cf. *Apology* 5). It is reasonable to assume that these soldiers were not the first Christians to serve in the Roman army.

In the third century Origen sought to defend Christianity in the light of attacks made by the pagan philosopher Celsus. Celsus had pressed the argument that Christian who did not serve in the Roman legions would contribute to Rome's collapse at the hands of barbarian hordes. Origen's response is noteworthy. He concedes that some believers are in fact soldiers, although most are not, since killing is not the way of Christ.[22] More importantly, he maintained, Christians supported the empire in equally valid ways through their prayers for its leaders. In this way the forces of evil are also combatted.[23] Significantly, Origen, unlike Tertullian, acknowledges the possibility of the military "fighting in a righteous cause."[24] What's more, Origen wishes to affirm that, as Christians, "we do take our part in public affairs." Indeed, "none fight better for the king than we do. . . . We do not indeed fight under him . . . ; but we fight on his behalf, forming a special army—an army of piety— by offering our prayer to God."[25] Unfortunately, in all of his writings this is the only work—*Against Celsus*—in which Origen addresses the issue of war. And even here the concern is not the ethics of war per se.

Cyprian, also writing in the mid-third century, laments the degeneracy and savagery of his own day, and specifically that both the numbers and the efficiency of soldiers were in decline. Yet at the same time he acknowledges Christian acquaintances who are serving in the military.[26]

The conventional portrait of the early church that comes to us is that the early Christians were uniformly pacifistic, followed by the church's fourth-century compromise with the Roman Empire. Beginning with Constantine's rule, it is typically argued, Christians prostituted themselves to secular authority. This portrait, however, does not bear up under close scrutiny. It errs both in its oversimplifying early Christians' relation to the state and in its attributing to fourth-century Christians an overly uncritical attitude toward governing authorities. As Augustine painstakingly argues in his magisterial *City of God,* there are civic duties that are required of the Christian believer, even in a culture that is (quite literally) crumbling.

The limited evidence we have of the early Christian attitudes toward war

[22]Origen *Contra Celsum* 3.7.
[23]Ibid., 8.73.
[24]Ibid.
[25]Ibid.
[26]Cyprian *Epistle* 39.

is inconclusive. Both strands—pacifist and nonpacifist—can be detected. Clearly, many Christians did oppose military service, but this was not universal. Nor was opposition due to explicit prohibitions in the New Testament, evidenced by the fact that soldiers in the New Testament are never called to abandon their profession. Even Christian historian Roland Bainton, who as a Quaker has contributed substantially to a pacifist reading of the early church, concedes from the existing evidence that while "ecclesiastical authors before Constantine condemned participation in warfare," this was not the case regarding military service "in time of peace" and soldiering in general.[27] James Turner Johnson has also closely examined the writings of the early church fathers that mirror attitudes toward war and soldiering. His conclusion, following a careful and even more judicious reading of these sources than Bainton's, is that evidence is mixed.[28] Thus it is fair to contend that the early church was not absolutist on either pacifism or military service.[29]

EARLY CHRISTIAN DEVELOPMENT OF JUST-WAR THINKING: AMBROSE AND AUGUSTINE

We will begin to explore the emergence of early Christian just-war thinking in Augustine and his spiritual father Ambrose, bishop of Milan. In the writings of both two elements are striking: (1) the concern that Christians not remain aloof from affairs of the state as they wait for the eschaton, and (2) that both renounced the right to self-defense.

What is significant about Ambrose is his location and his position. Before he became a bishop, he was a Roman governor in the northern military outpost of Milan. While it is tempting to portray Ambrose as something of a crusader because of his background, this is simply not the case. Very much the opposite might be argued. In his preaching and teaching he acknowledges that the continuous assaults on the Roman Empire by barbarian hordes were

---

[27] Roland Bainton, *Christian Attitudes Toward War and Peace* (New York: Abingdon, 1960), pp. 66, 81.

[28] See James Turner Johnson's detailed discussion of Christian attitudes in the first four centuries in chapter one of *The Quest for Peace* (Princeton, N.J.: Princeton University Press, 1987), pp. 3-66. Johnson offers a more nuanced assessment of early Christian attitudes than the standard portrait offered by Bainton.

[29] In their important volume *Christians and the Military: The Early Experience* (Philadelphia: Fortress, 1985), John Helgeland, Robert J. Daly and J. Patout Burns concur. They maintain that the New Testament's primary call is not to nonviolence but to love, which is why the experience in the early church regarding military service is mixed (pp. 15-16). See further David G. Hunter, "A Decade of Research on Early Christians and Military Service," *Religious Studies Review* 18, no. 2 (1992): 87-94.

part of a larger pattern of divine judgment on Rome's paganism. Nevertheless, he admonishes those under his watch *not* to extract themselves from civic affairs as they await the coming age.

What particular advice does he give those who are part of his spiritual oversight? His advice comes in the form of outlining duties of the clergy, who have been entrusted with shepherding the flock. The language of these duties, curiously, is the language of *virtue*—justice, temperance and wisdom. The nature of the virtuous life, as Ambrose understands it, has both vertical and horizontal dimensions; it applies to our service to society as well as to our serving God, to bodily usefulness as well as godliness.[30]

But why the emphasis on temporal duties? Doubtless, Ambrose was responding to a version of Tertullian's perennial question, "What does Athens have to do with Jerusalem?" Tertullian's answer, of course, represented the sentiment of many in the early church: "Absolutely nothing. The world is an ash heap, destined to go up in smoke. Why rearrange chairs on a ship that anyway is sinking?" Ambrose, like Augustine after him, seems to have had two aims in mind: to rebut those pagan contemporaries who had laid Rome's demise at the feet of otherworldly Christians, and to exhort the Christian community *not* to retreat from the affairs of the present life while awaiting the next.

Historian Paul Christopher has astutely called attention to the fact that right conduct in war is one of several practical illustrations utilized by Ambrose to underscore duties that are part of our temporal lives.[31] Cardinal virtues such as justice, temperance, courage and wisdom, for Ambrose, are integrated in the Christian's life; indeed, faith maximizes the expression of these virtues. Ambrose's discussion of these virtues contains moral criteria that are applicable to the question of whether or not to go to war—what is known in the just-war tradition as *ius ad bellum* (Latin for "justice toward war"):

> It is clear, then, these [cardinal] and the remaining virtues are related to one another. For courage, which in war preserves one's country from the barbarians, or at home defends the weak or comrades from robbers, is full of justice; and to know on what plan to defend and to give help, how to make use of opportunities of time and place, is the part of prudence and moderation, and temperance itself cannot observe due measure without prudence. To know a fit opportunity, and to make return according to what is right, belongs to justice.[32]

---

[30]Ambrose *On the Duties of the Clergy* 2.6-7.
[31]Christopher, *Ethics of War and Peace,* pp. 23-27.
[32]Ambrose *On the Duties of the Clergy* 1.27.129.

Ambrose also believes that justice is applicable in the midst of military conflict itself, what the just-war tradition refers to as *ius in bello* (Latin for "justice in war"). He maintains the need for justice in dealing with those who have been defeated and in granting noncombatant immunity to those deemed innocent. As a model of how to proceed in conflict he looks to David in the Old Testament, whose actions were measured and restrained. David required that fairness be meted out even toward those who had opposed him. He honored Abner, who led the opposition against him, even to the point of mourning Abner's death. Most importantly, he was constantly vigilant to distinguish between retribution and vengeance, eschewing the latter. David was quick to exonerate the innocent.[33]

Ambrose firmly believes that it is not virtuous to gain victory by unjust means such as excessive cruelty. For this reason he condemns in the strongest terms the lack of restraint exercised by the Emperor Theodosius who lay siege to the city of Thessalonica (late fourth century) to quell an insurrection. As evidenced by his letter to Theodosius, Ambrose is doubly pained. He mourns the injustice of the slaughter, and his prior friendship with the emperor makes this travesty all the more difficult:

> There was that done in the city of the Thessalonians of which no similar record exists, which I was not able to prevent happening; which, indeed, I had before said would be most atrocious when I so often petitioned against it. . . . When it [the siege] was first heard of, a synod had met because of the arrival of the Gallican Bishops. There was not one who did not lament it, not one who thought lightly of it; your being in fellowship with Ambrose was no excuse for your deed. . . . Are you ashamed, O Emperor, to do that, which the royal prophet David, . . . according to the flesh, did? . . . For if you listen obediently to this, and say: "I have sinned against the Lord," . . . it shall be said to you also: "Since thou repentest, the Lord putteth away thy sin, and thou shalt not die." . . . I urge, I beg, I exhort, I warn, for it is a grief to me, but that you who were an example of unusual piety, who were conspicuous for clemency, who would not suffer single offenders to be put in peril, should not mourn that so many have perished. . . . Do not add another sin to your sin by a course of action which has injured many.[34]

---

[33]Ibid., 2.7.32-39. Christopher's discussion of *ius ad bellum* and *ius in bello* criteria as found in Ambrose is quite helpful and aims to make contemporary application (*Ethics of War and Peace,* pp. 23-27).

[34]*Epistle* 51.6-12 ("To Theodosius"), in *Nicene and Post-Nicene Fathers* (Grand Rapids: Eerdmans, 1955), 10:450-53.

Through Christian reflection on justice, Ambrose begins laying the groundwork for the development of just-war war thinking. And as Christopher notes, by making justice the highest virtue, Ambrose lays the ground rules for how conflicts between competing duties are to be arbitrated as well as how conflict between parties, even nations, is to be handled.[35]

Born in A.D. 354 and converted to Christ at the age of thirty-two, Augustine lived in a period akin to our own—a period of disintegration and upheaval.[36] In fact, two decades after the formal sack of Rome (411) by the Visigoths, Augustine's own town of Hippo in northern Africa would belong to the Vandals. Augustine's inquiring mind and hunger to know truth made him well-suited to the challenges of his era. Before his conversion he was a student of philosophy and thus was able to interact with the moral philosophy of Plato, Aristotle and Cicero. He was also a champion of Christian orthodoxy, living in a time of great theological controversy and upheaval.[37]

Augustine's views on war and Christian faith do not come to us neatly packaged. We must glean his views from multiple sources—for example, from letters written in reply to inquiries about the viability of Christian faith as well as from his reflections written as a response to pagan challenges to the faith (for example, *The City of God*). Augustine evades any attempt on our part to find a neat, systematic and single coherent treatment of war in his writings. But what he does say is very significant.

Like his spiritual mentor Ambrose, Augustine rejects self-defense, with one exception: the soldier who acts in self-defense and in defense of others.[38] At the same time he argues for the morality of defending others. In a letter to Marcellinus, who needed help defending the Christian faith before influential pagans, Augustine writes that a righteous man privately should be willing to endure evil rather than respond with malice.[39] Matthew 5:38-39 (on turning the cheek and not resisting evil), he notes, refers to a *dispo-*

---

[35]Christopher, *Ethics of War and Peace,* pp. 24-25.
[36]Christianity became the official religion of the empire (formally in A.D. 383), even though several emperors had professed Christian faith since Constantine, whose Edict of Milan in 312 ended the persecution of Christians.
[37]As a champion of orthodoxy, Augustine would defend the faith against Manichaean, Pelagian and Donatist heresies.
[38]Augustine *Epistle* 47.5, "To Publicola." Augustine's thinking in the matter of self-defense seems to have evolved somewhat. Earlier, in *On Freedom of the Will,* he had expressed strong reservations.
[39]Augustine *Epistle* 138.9, "To Marcellinus." The same argument is presented by Augustine elsewhere to his friend Evodius on the matter of free choice (*On Freedom of the Will* 1.5.11-6.15).

sition of the heart and not the external act. In another letter, to Publicola, he writes: "In regard to killing men so as not to be killed by them, this view does not satisfy me."[40] (Luther, it should be pointed out, took Augustine to task on the matter of self-defense,[41] and Aquinas considers self-defense by force not only legitimate but virtuous to the extent that it is proportionate.)[42]

Nevertheless, despite their rejection of self-defense, both Ambrose and Augustine believe it to be *the obligation of Christian love* to defend and protect the *innocent third party*. Not to apply what Augustine calls "benevolent harshness" to the evildoer is as much an evil as to cause it.[43] If there is one strain of thinking throughout his writings that serves as justification for coercive force, it is this notion of "benevolent harshness." By this he means *just retribution that is rooted in charity with the aim of securing peace.*

For Augustine, justice and charity are not at odds. Justice is concerned with a right ordering of society for the sake of social peace, what Augustine calls the *tranquillitas ordinis.* He acknowledges the existence of both a just peace—*iusta pax*—and an unjust peace—*iniqua pax;* the distinction is critical. For this reason peace requires the ordering of justice. Even robbers, he observes, have order and maintain a certain peace within their own orbit in order to plunder the innocent.[44] Peace as a good, even in its relative state this side of the eschaton, must be guarded since it furnishes for people the environment in which to contemplate life's mysteries. While ultimate peace that is consummated in the kingdom of God requires no restraints, penultimate peace does.[45]

Charity, as Augustine conceives of it, must motivate all that we do. It is at the center of human experience, motivates human virtue, is self-sacrificing

---

[40]Augustine *Epistle* 47.5.

[41]*Luther's Works* (Muhlenberg ed.) 3.249-50. Paul Ramsey makes the interesting observation that modern pacifists have reversed this: that is, they reflect a debt to secular, non-Christian thinking by insisting that individuals should resist injustice by going to court and legal means while at the same time refusing to acknowledge the morality of resisting injustice in the context of the military (*Basic Christian Ethics* [New York: Charles Scribner's, 1950], p. 182).

[42]Aquinas *Summa Theologiae* 2-2.Q64a.7, Q108a.1.

[43]Augustine *Epistle* 47.147.5. In *Duties of the Clergy* 1.24.115; 3.4.27, Ambrose poses questions such as: "In the case of a shipwreck, should a wise person take away a plank of wood [on which to float] from an ignorant sailor [who cannot swim]?" Augustine uses the examples of highway robbery, assassination and soldiering to develop his argument in *On Freedom of the Will* 1.5, and *Contra Faustum* 22.70.

[44]Augustine *City of God* 19.12.

[45]Ibid., 15.4; 19.112, 27; 22.24; *Epistle* 189.6.

and expresses itself toward one's neighbor. Charity orders all human actions, even the use of coercive force and going to war. Furthermore, it is willing to order itself toward justice in society. As a social force, this "rightly ordered love"[46] is foremost concerned with what is good—for the perpetrator of criminal acts as well as for society, which has been victimized by criminal acts. When "men are prevented, by being alarmed, from doing wrong, it may be said that a real service is done to them."[47]

In Augustinian thought, justice working through charity is further buttressed—and clarified—by a thoroughly biblical concept: not the external action per se but one's intent determines the morality of one's actions. Thus, for example, in his "Letter to Publicola," Augustine renders legitimate, based on the wedding of justice and charity, an exception to the prohibition of killing. It is legitimate precisely when it involves the public good—for example, in the case of the soldier or public official who is carrying out his public trust by establishing a justly ordered peace.[48] For this reason Augustine writes elsewhere to Boniface, a governor of a northern African province, "Do not think that it is impossible for anyone serving in the military to please God."[49] In the event that military commands do contravene the divine will, Augustine is clear, using idol worship as his illustration, that Christians soldiers can soldier but do not sacrifice to pagan deities.[50] Actions are subordinated to intentions.

In our reading of *The City of God* it is important to understand Augustine's treatment of war as a subset of his discussion of citizenship. A major theme in this part of *City of God* is that one can simultaneously be a devout Christian *and* a good citizen. This emphasis, of course, is necessary if pagans are accusing disinterested or apathetic Christians for Rome's demise and challenging the basis for Christian belief. But it is also extremely important if many Christian believers are viewing Rome's collapse—and with it, the disappearance of the vaunted pax Romana—as a sign that the end is near, that the eschaton is imminent. Certainly, if Christians are by nature reticent to involve themselves in culture, they are severely tempted to withdraw at a time of cultural upheaval. But our temporal responsibilities are not to be abdicated.

---

[46]Augustine *City of God* 15.22 and *Contra Faustum* 22.78.
[47]Augustine *Epistle* 47.5.
[48]Ibid. Augustine argues similarly in *City of God* 1.21.
[49]Augustine *Epistle* 189.4 ("To Boniface").
[50]Augustine *Sermon* 62.13.

The overarching framework of Augustine's *City of God* is a complex and rather dense philosophical explanation of history, anthropology and theology that is a response to pagan critics. This understanding of human history, human nature and human participation in the divine plan serves as the foundation for Augustine's convictions about war, citizenship and occupying this world. War is one instrument (though by no means the sole one) through which retribution and purification for our fallenness is exacted. Good and evil coexist in the earthly city, just as the earthly city and heavenly city comingle. The tension between good and evil cannot be fully resolved in the present life; evil is thus a social reality that must be confronted in the present life, not merely by God in the next. Augustine does not argue that people are (or can be) without sin; rather, through rational choice they can purpose—however imperfectly—to do what is just and good for others. The necessity of social order—a justly ordered peace—supersedes in Augustinian thought any need for individual rights or privileges.[51]

In his view of the magistrate Augustine stands squarely within the Pauline tradition: God uses as an instrument the temporal powers to restrict and restrain evil. It is out of necessity, writes Augustine, that the magistrate must act with "benevolent harshness"; that is, he must "cherish toward evil men a perfect hatred . . . [in order that] he hates the vice and loves the man."[52] In this light, war, which for Augustine is both a plague and at times a necessity, is not merely a legal remedy to punish or restrain injustice, though it entails that. It can also be morally justified, so long as the criterion of justice informs our considerations in both going to war and proceeding in war.[53]

The implication of this social reality, as Augustine understands it, is that the moral principles governing whether or not to go to war *(ius ad bellum)* and how to proceed amidst war *(ius in bello)* apply not merely to Christians (or even Romans); they are applicable to humans universally. Even when the ideals of justice and peace are only fully reserved in the *civitas Dei*, the heavenly city, they are still important goods that need protecting in the *civitas terrena* since the two cities comingle.

Several just-war principles can be gleaned from Augustine's collective

---

[51]While Augustine accepts the generic and traditional definition of justice ("to each his due"), first and foremost there must be a rendering to God what is due (*City of God* 2.21).
[52]Augustine *City of God* 14.6.
[53]Ibid. 18.13; cf. 19.12-13.

writings. These include just cause,[54] proper authority, formal declaration, the aim of securing a just peace, retribution as distinct from revenge and discrimination between innocence and guilt. Due to the present reality of evil, humans may justify going to war; however, they do so only reluctantly. Augustine serves to remind us that political judgments are at bottom moral judgments. Christian justification for coercive force is neighbor love that must be willing on occasion to protect the innocent third party. The law of love obliges us to use force in the aid of others.[55] Love for Augustine is dynamic, active and able to distinguish between the person and the sin. Therefore love on occasion may be required to be physical and coercive. Properly motivated, we are to rebuke, restrain, intercede and even reluctantly use coercive force. More will be said about neighbor love later in the book.

In its essence the just-war tradition, from Augustine onward, emanates from two fundamental concerns in Christian thought: when resorting to force is justified *(jus ad bellum),* and how to apply force in the midst of conflict *(jus in bello),* or, in two words, *permission* and *limitation.*[56] Augustine is no crusader, nor is he an uncritical, passive slave of the state. When political power forces one to do what is wrong, then "by all means disregard the power through the fear [of God]"; the ruler might threaten "with prison, but God [threatens] with hell."[57] War is not to be taken lightly and is a last resort because it is "a higher glory still to stay war itself with a word than to slay men with the sword."[58] Augustine is under no illusions regarding Rome's own record of aggression, for "peace and war had a competition in cruelty."[59]

---

[54]According to Augustine, war is justified only under certain conditions—for example, defending against an unjust oppressor, protecting or rescuing innocent victims in hostile territory, defending an ally, and repelling an assault while traveling (*City of God* 19.15). Both offensive and defensive action can be wrongly motivated (ibid. 22.6); nevertheless, both can be justifiable (*Quaestionum in Heptateuchum* 4.44 and *Contra Faustum* 22.71-72).

[55]An extensive bibliography on political thought in Augustine can be found in William R. Stevenson Jr., *Christian Love and Just War* (Macon, Ga.: Mercer University Press, 1987), pp. 153-58.

[56]Paul Ramsey's introduction to *War and the Christian Conscience* (Durham, N.C.: Duke University Press, 1961).

[57]Augustine *Sermon* 62.13

[58]Augustine *Epistle* 229.2.

[59]"External aggression," he writes sarcastically, should be added to Rome's pantheon, since "she contributed [as a goddess] greatly to the growth of the empire" (*City of God* 4.15). For this reason we reject the viewpoint of Frederick H. Russell (*The Just War in the Middle Ages* [Cambridge: Cambridge University Press, 1975], pp. 19-25), who argues that Augustine prepared the way for a "holy war" or crusader mindset that took root in the Middle Ages.

There is no such thing as a Christian polity; Christian wisdom and political power are distinct. In the end Augustine is a distinctly "chastened" patriot.[60]

THE MEDIEVAL DEVELOPMENT OF JUST-WAR THINKING IN THOMAS AQUINAS

Medieval thinkers use Augustine as their starting point, given his concern to defend theological orthodoxy, his dexterity in understanding history, philosophy and human nature, and his ability to synthesize elements of truth that are found in pagan thought with Christian revealed truth. In this sense Aquinas and Augustine share much in common. Both tended to be innovative thinkers, both were ardent defenders of historic Christian faith and both were conversant with intellectual currents of their day.

For Aquinas the matter of justified war hinges first and foremost on legitimate authority. Why? Given the frequency with which princes, nobles and criminals all engaged regularly and aggressively in combat, and this for private ends, it is not difficult to understand why this emphasis presses to the fore. For medieval thinkers the fear is chaos and the longing is for order. Hence, we find in Aquinas the strong distinction between *duellum* (the private quarrel or duel) and *bellum* (war). Insofar as war is a *public* matter, *bellum* must be adjudicated by political-legal means and not private citizens. At the center of this thinking, Thomas explains, lie three fundamental moral guidelines: sovereign authority, just cause, and right intention.[61]

Specific occasions permitting war for Aquinas include recovery of what has been stolen, punishment or restraint of evil, and protecting the innocent from harm. Thus, for Aquinas, moral legitimacy in going to war may be defensive or offensive in nature. Like Augustine before him he responds to the common objection that war is contrary to Jesus' teaching in the Sermon on the Mount not to resist evil (Mt 5:38-39). He notes that "a man avenges the wrong done to God and neighbor" because of *charity*. And he quotes Augustine: "Those whom we have to punish with a kindly severity, it is necessary to handle in many ways against their will. For when we are stripping a man of the lawlessness of sin, it is good for him to be vanquished."[62] For

---

[60]Jean Bethke Elshtain uses the notion of a "chastened patriot" to describe mediation between warring and pacifist positions (*Women and War*, rev. ed. [Chicago: University of Chicago Press, 1995], p. 252).

[61]Aquinas's argument regarding war is developed most fully in "On War" in *Summa Theologiae* 2-2.Q40.

[62]Augustine *Epistle* 138.11.

Aquinas, there is just cause for war when those being attacked "deserve attack on account of some fault."[63] That is, just cause consists in an appropriate response to prior wrongdoing.[64]

Given the priority of order over chaos, how did medieval thought address the matter of tyranny? James Turner Johnson offers this assessment:

> Even in the case of tyranny, the division between *bellum* and *duellum* was hard for medieval and early modern theorists to overcome; thus removal of a tyrant—"regime change" in contemporary parlance—was first the responsibility of proper sovereigns, who (by contrast with private persons of whatever social rank) had the right of using the sword for the public good.[65]

While sedition and strife for Aquinas are inherently evil, based on motivation and intent, *bellare* ("to wage war") may or may not be.

Thomas, it should emphasized, was no crusader himself, even when we are justified in calling him an interventionist. By the time he codified a Christian understanding of war, the crusading spirit was past. As to his rationale for military campaigns against "pagans and Jews," he offers this explanation: "The faithful of Christ . . . wage war against unbelievers not in order to compel them to believe . . . but rather to compel them not to hinder the faith of Christ."[66]

But what about the existence of military religious orders in his day? This would seem to make Aquinas appear to be a "holy warrior." But he takes up the matter of religious orders, significantly, in a different context than his discussion of the generic question, Is it permissible to go to war? And in Thomas' own words, "it was necessary for religious orders to be established for military service because of the failure of secular princes to resist unbelievers in certain lands."[67] These orders, moreover, did not operate autonomously; rather, they were accountable to a higher authority.[68] Even in religious wars, in which the same three moral criteria—legitimate authority, just cause, right intention—are applied, the goal must be the public

---

[63] *Summa Theologiae* 2-2.Q40a.1.

[64] See the lucid discussion of qualified justice in Thomas Aquinas' thought in Gregory M. Reichberg, "Is There a 'Presumption Against War' in Aquinas's Ethics?" *The Monist* 66 (2002): 337-67.

[65] James Turner Johnson, "Aquinas and Luther on War and Peace," *Journal of Religious Ethics* 31 (2003): 18 n. 1.

[66] Aquinas *Summa Theologiae* 2-2.Q10a.8.

[67] Ibid., Q188a.4.

[68] Ibid., Q188a.3.

good and the advancement of justice and *not* proselytizing.[69]

Recall that Thomas's father and several of his brothers were knights. Recall too that his family had locked him in prison for fifteen months at age eighteen to prevent him from joining the Dominican friars. Thomas was certainly under no illusions regarding military life. "Knights are rapacious," he lamented in at least one sermon.[70] Thomas Aquinas was many things; one thing he was *not* was a crusader.[71]

---

[69]Aquinas *Quodllibet Questionae* 2.16; *Summa Theologiae* 2-2.Q64 and Q66. For a contrast of religious and political war in Thomist thinking, see LeRoy Walters, "The Just War and the Crusade: Antitheses or Analogies?" *The Monist* 57 (1973): 584-94.

[70]Aquinas *Sermon* 41, cited in Edward A. Synan, "St. Thomas Aquinas and the Profession of Arms," *Medieval Studies* 50 [1988]: 424). Moreover, Thomas emphasizes that warring and the shedding of blood are incompatible with the ministry of the priesthood, thus remaining consistent with the Christian tradition that forbids clerics and bishops from taking up arms (*Summa Theologiae* 2-2.Q40a.2, ad 3).

[71]I examine the role of Ambrose, Augustine and Aquinas in the development of just-war thinking in "Justice and Just War in the Christian Moral Tradition," *Journal of Church and State* (forthcoming).

3

Just-War Thinking in the Late Medieval and Early Modern Period

The Protestant Reformers, with their attempt to abolish the medieval distinction between clergy and laity, teach that all vocations rank the same before God in terms of dignity; there is no difference between monk or magistrate. Luther, Calvin and Zwingli were one in this regard, sharing the Pauline conviction that the magistrate, not the church, wields the sword for the purpose of resisting evil. Moreover, due to the integrity of all vocations, Christians can carry out obedience to God as magistrates or soldiers.

THE PROTESTANT REFORMERS ON CHURCH AND STATE AND WAR

Calvin expresses the Reformation perspective, careful to dignify all types of work as worthy in and of themselves:

> The Lord . . . has appointed to all their particular duties in different spheres of life. . . . Every individual's line of work . . . is, as it were, a post assigned him by the Lord. . . . It will also be no small alleviation of his cares, labours, troubles, and other burdens, when a man knows that in all these things he has God for his guide. The magistrate will execute his office with greater pleasure, the father of a family will confine himself to his duty with more satisfaction, and all, in their respective spheres of life, will bear and surmount the inconveniences, cares, disappointments, and anxieties which befall them, when they shall be persuaded that every individual has his burden laid upon him by God. Hence . . . there will be no employment so mean and sordid (provided

we follow our vocation) as not to appear truly respectable, and be deemed highly important in the sight of God.[1]

The matter of dignity in vocation is addressed quite pointedly in Martin Luther's 1525 tract "Whether Soldiers, Too, Can Be Saved." Writing to a knight and friend, Luther makes the observation that many soldiers struggle to reconcile their profession with Christian faith. Emphasizing the need for a good conscience, Luther underscores the distinction between the occupation and the person filling it. The question reduces in Luther's mind to this: Is Christian faith compatible with soldiering, which may involve going to war and killing "as military law requires us to do to our enemies in wartime"?[2]

Luther begins by stating a founding assumption:

> For the very fact that the sword has been instituted by God to punish the evil, protect the good, and preserve the peace [Rom 13:1-4; 1 Pet 2:13-14] is powerful and sufficient proof that war and killing along with all the things that accompany wartime and martial law have been instituted by God. What else is war but the punishment of wrong and evil?[3]

This view is a product of his understanding of two realms, the sacred and the secular, that have their own authorities. The church, therefore, exercises no sway over government; neither does government over the church. Every Christian, contends Luther, is a citizen of both domains, with responsibilities in each.[4] This is a departure from medieval thinking, which had tended to conflate the two.

Like Augustine and Aquinas, Luther also believed that military service could be a work of charity. In "Temporal Authority: To What Extent It Should Be Obeyed" and his treatise "On War Against the Turk," a work filled with argument and counterargument that reflects the religious agitation of his own day, he argues similarly that it is a work of Christian love to protect and defend a whole community with the sword and not let the people be abused.[5] Luther acknowledges that slaying does not seem like it could possibly be a work of love. The "simple man," he notes, would conclude that

---

[1]John Calvin *Institutes of the Christian Religion* 3.10.6, trans. John Allen (Philadelphia: Presbyterian Board of Christian Education, 1936), 1:791.
[2]Martin Luther, "Whether Soldiers, Too, Can Be Saved," in *Luther's Works*, ed. Jaroslav Pelikan and Helmut Lehmann (Philadelphia: Fortress, 1967), 46:95.
[3]Ibid.
[4]Martin Luther, "Temporal Authority: To What Extent It Should Be Obeyed," in *Luther's Works*, ed. Jaroslav Pelikan and Helmut Lehmann (Philadelphia: Muhlenberg Press, 1962), 45:81-129.
[5]Ibid., and 46:161-205.

such is not possible. In truth, however, it can be an expression of charity properly understood. An analogy, for Luther, is necessary.

A good doctor in extreme circumstances may be required to amputate or destroy a hand, foot, arm or leg due to disease. Viewed externally, this person would appear to be cruel and merciless. Viewed medically, the doctor wishes to cut off what is defective in order to save the body and work for the greater good. In the same way, argues Luther, the soldier fulfills his office by punishing the wicked, even when this means using lethal force. This serves the greater good of families and communities. If the sword were not employed to preserve the peace, everything in the surrounding world would be spoiled. Therefore, "war is only . . . a small misfortune that prevents a great misfortune."[6] In order to "prevent some from becoming widows and orphans as a consequence [of war or plunder]," it is for Luther "both Christian and an act of love to kill the enemy without hesitation . . . until he is conquered. . . . And when victory has been achieved, one should offer mercy and peace to those who surrender and humble themselves."[7]

Luther acknowledges that war is a great plague; this he cannot deny. He does, however, remind his readers that they should consider how great the plague is that is actually prevented by war. In the end, he argues, one must look at the office of the soldier and see it as "useful to the world as eating and drinking or any other work"[8]

But what about abuse? What about those who kill needlessly and defile the office of soldier? Luther recognizes this possibility and states that this is the fault of the person, not the office. Just wars may be necessary in a world of injustice and unjust peace. As proof of his conviction that the profession of soldiering is honorable and necessary, Luther cites John the Baptist. When soldiers came to him with questions, the Baptist did not condemn their vocation or call them out of military service. Rather, he exhorted them toward justice and contentment.[9] That is, he denounced *abuse* of the office, but not the office itself.

Luther, despite his relatively high view of the political authorities, cannot be accused of being a crusader type, even when in his day the Ottoman Empire had extended as far as Hungary. He condemned Christian attempts, usu-

---

[6]Ibid., 46:96.
[7]Ibid., 45:125.
[8]Ibid., 46:97.
[9]Ibid., 45:98 and 46:97.

ally by popes, to incite war in the name of Christ. We should recall too his response to the Peasant Revolt. The peasants, it should be remembered, were sympathetic to his teachings. Yet despite the excesses of both the Church and the authorities, Luther advocated suppressing the peasants when they decided to turn violent. In "Against the Robbing and Murdering Hordes of Peasants," he writes: "If [the ruler] does not fulfill the duties of his office by punishing some and protecting others, he commits as a great a sin before God as when someone who has not been given the sword commits murder."[10]

And Luther further believed that not only should the Christian *not* shun military service, he should consider it a *duty* and means by which to order peace and justice. He writes:

> It looks like a great thing when a monk renounces everything and goes into a cloister, carries on a life of asceticism, fasts, prays, etc. . . . On the other hand, it looks like a small thing when a maid cooks and cleans and does other housework. But because God's command is there, even such a small work must be praised as a service to God. . . . For here [i.e., concerning secular and mundane vocations] there is no command."[11]

Luther takes up the question of a Christian serving as a soldier most pointedly in "Whether Soldiers, Too, Can Be Saved" and "Temporal Authority." Such service, for him, is a "work of love" done "for the sake of others." If the Christian did not serve as a soldier and bear the sword, he would indeed be acting "contrary to love," thereby "setting a bad example to others." While the Christian is free to endure abuse personally, the presence of one's neighbor alters the moral equation: "Although you do not need to have your enemy punished, your afflicted neighbor does."[12] Consistent with Ambrose, Augustine and Aquinas before him, Luther believed that bearing the sword was not inconsistent with Christian discipleship. It is not for the purpose of "avenging yourself or returning evil for evil, but for the good of your neighbor and for the maintenance of the safety and peace of others."[13]

---

[10]Ibid., 46:53.

[11]Ibid., 4.341; 5.102.

[12]*Luther's Works,* 45:94-95.

[13]Ibid., 45:96. Lest he be misunderstood, Luther reiterates: "In what concerns you and yours, you govern yourself according to love and tolerate no injustice toward your neighbor. The gospel does not forbid this, in fact, in other places [i.e., other than Mt 5:39] it actually commands it . . . on behalf of others." Luther stresses, a Christian "may and should seek vengeance, justice, protection, and help, and do as much as he can to achieve it" (ibid., 45:96, 101).

Trained in law and theology, John Calvin develops more explicitly than Luther the link between Scripture and natural moral law. The enactment of justice through civil law is predicated on the moral law, which God has woven into the fabric of creation. This linkage is developed at length in his *Institutes of the Christian Religion*. If the moral law of God forbids all Christians to participate in killing, then how can it possibly be, asks Calvin, that a magistrate, who is responsible to wield the sword, might be a pious individual?

If, however, we understand that in the infliction of punishment the magistrate is not acting of his own accord but merely executes justice as God requires of him, then the issue is not an embarrassment to us. Not all homicide, Calvin maintains, is punishable. It is not murder to utilize the sword in obedience to heaven. There is "no valid objection to the infliction of public vengeance, unless the justice of God be restrained from the punishment of crimes."[14] Citing Romans 13:4, Calvin speaks approvingly of Moses and David, who with integrity obeyed the Lord.

But someone will readily raise the charge of unnecessary cruelty and lay it at Calvin's feet. "I am not an advocate of unnecessary cruelty," Calvin wishes his readers to know,

> nor can I conceive the possibility of an equitable sentence being pronounced without mercy of which Solomon affirms, [namely] that "mercy and truth preserve the king, and his throne is upholden by mercy." Yet it behooves the magistrate to be on his guard against both these errors; that he not, by excessive severity, wound rather than heal; or, through a superstitious affectation of clemency, fall into a mistaken humanity, which is the worst kind of cruelty, by indulging a weak and ill-judged lenity, to the detriment of multitudes.[15]

Because it is sometimes necessary for those in authority publicly to take up the sword against those who perpetrate evil, Calvin reasons, "the same reason will lead us to infer the lawfulness of wars which are undertaken for this end." Kings and nations too "have been entrusted with power to preserve the tranquility of their own territories, to suppress the seditious tumults of disturbers, to succour the victims of oppression, and to punish crimes." If they are to be "the guardians and defenders of the laws," argues Calvin, it is incumbent upon them "to defeat the efforts of all by whose in-

---

[14]Calvin *Institutes of the Christian Religion* 4.20.10.
[15]Ibid.

justice the discipline of the laws is corrupted."[16] There is no difference between robbers who plunder private citizens and robber nations who do the same on a larger scale.

Civil law, for Calvin, is predicated on the natural moral law and the revealed truth of Scripture. It is

> the dictate both of natural equity, and of the nature of the office, therefore, that princes are armed, not only to restrain the crimes of private individuals by judicial punishments, but also to defend the territories committed to their charge by going to war against any hostile aggression.[17]

As an adequately trained lawyer worth his salt, Calvin anticipates objections. One comes readily to mind, with three possible answers. If we object that the New Testament contains no precept or regulations permitting Christian participation in war, three considerations suffice as a response. First, the same causes of war in the ancient world exist in the present time; therefore, governing authorities retain their primary function. Second, that no explicit teaching on the subject of war is found in the teaching of the apostles is to be expected; their chief aim is to proclaim the kingdom of Christ, not to organize and justify civil government. Third, Calvin cites Augustine's observation regarding John the Baptist: if Christian participation in all warring is illegitimate, then the soldiers who sought out the Baptist would have been directed to throw away their arms and leave their profession. To the contrary, they were admonished to act justly and be content with their pay. Military life was not at all prohibited.[18]

Can the sword be abused or unjust? By all means, says Calvin. Here the authorities "ought to be very cautious." If retribution is to be inflicted, it is "not to be precipitated with anger, exasperated with hatred, or inflamed with implacable severity." Rather, those bearing the sword should "commiserate our common nature even in him whom they punish for his crime."

In addition to just cause, Calvin cites right intent and last resort as moral criteria for going to war: "the evident object of war ought to be the restoration of peace, and "certainly we ought to make every other attempt before we have recourse to the decision of arms." Otherwise, he notes, the authorities "grossly abuse their power."[19]

---

[16]Ibid.
[17]Ibid.
[18]Ibid.
[19]Ibid.

For Calvin, equity is rooted in general as well as special revelation—in both the natural law and Scripture.

Significantly, historic religious pacifism, in its sixteenth-century Anabaptist expression, rejected the views of Luther and Calvin (and the Swiss reformer Zwingli, who stood in basic agreement with them) regarding Christian participation in the affairs of the state. The historic "peace churches"—so named not because other confessions are not concerned with peace but because these churches refuse participation in war, to the present day—prohibited Christians from bearing the sword or governing.[20] Where historic Anabaptists differ from many contemporary Anabaptist pacifists is in their understanding of the powers. Anabaptist writers today tend to have a much more negative (i.e., apocalyptic) view of governing authorities.[21] As evidenced by the sixth of seven articles of the Schleitheim Confession, penned in 1527 as a brief summary of Anabaptist beliefs,[22] historic Anabaptism affirms that the sword in the hand of the authorities is ordained by God for the twin purposes of punishment and protection:

> We are agreed as follows concerning the sword: The sword is ordained of God outside the perfection of Christ. It punishes and puts to death, and guards and protects the good. In the Law, the sword was ordained for the punishment of the wicked and for their death, and the same [sword] is [now] ordained to be used by the worldly magistrates.[23]

It should be emphasized that the separatism and pacifism of the Anabaptists did not occur in a social or political vacuum. Rather, there were very good reasons for it. It is against the background of rejection and persecution by both Catholics and Protestants that the position of the Swiss Brethren (as the earliest Anabaptists came to be known) on civil society and its use of the sword is best understood. Writes one historian:

> They became separatists in part because of the persecution suffered at the

---

[20]The "peace churches" are primarily three confessions: Quaker, Mennonite and Brethren. Not all groups or individuals associated with the "radical Reformation" were pacifist, though most were. An exception was the Anabaptist preacher Balthasar Hubmaier.

[21]This is especially the case among Anabaptist academics.

[22]At the time that the Schleitheim Synod was convened in 1527, the Swiss Brethren—who drafted the Schleitheim Confession—were persecuted by Catholics and Protestants alike. For this reason they became separatist, to distance themselves from religious persecution, not to deny the role of the sword or the governing authorities.

[23]I am dependent on the translation of "The Schleitheim Confession of Faith," by J. C. Wenger in *Glimpses of Mennonite History* (Scottdale: Mennonite Publishing House, 1940), pp. 206-13.

hands of civil authorities backed by . . . Reformers and Catholics; separation
from the affairs of these regimes was thus an attempt to distance themselves
from the evil use of power that was, in part, directed toward them.[24]

Notwithstanding the early Anabaptists' absolute separation, while the
Schleitheim Confession expressly forbids the Christian believer to use violent force, it does *not* reject violence per se in the hand of the magistrate.

In the main the Protestant reformers show continuity with previous just-
war thinkers. They assume a basis for war in Scripture and natural law, even
when the latter is not a strong emphasis of their writings. And like their pre-
decessors they believe that coercive force *may* on occasion be an expression of love, properly understood. Both Luther and Calvin inherit a high
view of the governing authorities. They understand the magistrate as divinely appointed for the purpose of maintaining justice. While Christian faith
may lead the believer to disobey the civil authorities, this resistance based
on conscience is vastly different from insurrection; for this reason, Luther
would not countenance the Peasant Revolt.

EARLY MODERN THINKING ABOUT INTERNATIONAL
LAW: VITORIA, SUÁREZ AND GROTIUS

An important adaptation of just-war principles for the early modern period
by theorists such as Francisco de Vitoria (1480-1546), Francisco Suárez
(1548-1617) and Hugo Grotius (1583-1645) is their appeal to natural law. It
cannot be thought coincidental that the chief architects of international law,
with its understanding of justice grounded in natural law, lived at a time of
cultural ferment and crisis. Justice has a deeper basis than mere religious
confession. It is known through nature and intuited universally as binding
on all people everywhere. Thus the law of nature becomes a law to the nations *(ius gentium),* holding them accountable to the unchanging demands
of justice. Just-war principles then find confirmation in natural law and are
not a mere appeal to religion.

The ages of Ambrose and Augustine and Aquinas differ greatly in the sort
of dilemmas that needed addressing. Given the cultural synthesis of the Middle Ages, medieval theorists developed their understanding of just war explicitly from Christian religion and secondarily from natural law. This relationship is reversed in the Age of Discovery and early modern period, which

---

[24]James Turner Johnson, *The Quest for Peace: Three Moral Traditions in Western Cultural History* (Princeton, N.J.: Princeton University Press, 1987), p. 164.

present new challenges to just-war thinkers. These challenges concern people outside of Christendom as well as a divided Christendom. Regarding the first: Does just-war thinking apply to non-Christian peoples? What about cultures and nations that find themselves outside of Christendom? Do the very same just-war criteria apply? Why or why not?

Vitoria. Francisco de Vitoria, a professor of theology at Spain's leading university, the University of Salamanca, lived during the period of Spanish conquest of the new world.[25] The struggle between expansionists and missionaries was protracted and bitter. Spain in the sixteenth century was the intellectual center of Europe as well as its most dominant military and colonial power. Spanish treatment of indigenous people, in war and peace, instigated necessary discussions about justice.

By the year 1510 reports had reached Spain that were disquieting—reports that native Americans were being denied basic liberty and property. The immediate challenge confronting Vitoria was the Spanish vision to colonize the new peoples of the Americas. Spain was prepared to justify war with native Americans to possess their land and seek their conversion to the Christian faith.

Vitoria's task was to challenge the Spanish king on the basis of the unjust treatment of the American Indians: the king has no right, even if he were lord over the whole earth—which he is not—to claim ownership of the land of the native Americans. Looking back five centuries we fail to appreciate how revolutionary Vitoria's work was at the time. The words of one fourteenth-century Spanish lawyer tell us much about the religious and political environment of the time:

> If anyone asserted that the Emperor is not the monarch of the entire world, he would be a heretic; for he would make a pronouncement contrary to the decision of the Church and contrary to the text of the Gospel which says: "A decree went forth from Caesar Augustus that a census should be taken of all the world," as St. Luke has it, and so Christ, too, recognized him as emperor and master.[26]

Against conventional thinking, Vitoria argued that the emperor was *not* the ruler of the world: *Imperator non est dominus orbis.* In fact, he main-

---

[25]Not insignificantly, Vitoria had done his theological studies in Paris and thus was a beneficiary of renewed interest in Thomist thought.

[26]Cited in the introduction to Francisco de Vitoria, *De Indis et de Iure Belli Reflectiones,* ed. Ernest Nys, trans. J. P. Bate (New York: Oceana, 1964), p. 76.

tained, the church is not subject to him, nor are other nations. In fact, neither the king nor the pope, for that matter, could authorize war against the Indians. Neither religious nor economic or political reasons alone make coercion and warfare just. Therefore, war with the Indians to acquire their land is unjust, he argues in *Reflections on the Indians and the Law of War;* Indians and Spaniards have equal rights. The only cause for war that is just is a wrong that is intuited through natural moral law, a wrong that is discernable to all people everywhere through reason. Going to war based on religious differences or "the spirit of discovery" is not justifiable.[27] No war is just that inflicts on a population unprovoked injustice. And even were the Indians to attack the Spanish, a just response would be only a defensive response that sought to minimize loss.

Vitoria's criticisms of Spain's unjust treatment of American Indians strikes us as all the more radical, given the existence of slavery as practiced in Spain and Portugal.[28] What the professor from Salamanca was willing to acknowledge was unpopular because Spain had been "guilty of numerous scandals, crimes, and impieties" against the Indians.[29]

What specific causes might warrant going to war? Here Vitoria is in line with just-war thinkers of the past: defense against aggression, recovery of that which has been stolen and punishment for wrongdoing. He is adamant in rejecting the prevailing view of his day. Force is *not* justified in the case of difference of religion, in promoting conversion to the faith or as a response to rejection of the faith, or to defend the magistrate's sense of vainglory. Right of passage denied by the Indians, however, could be forcefully required by the Spaniards, but only with "moderation and proportion," so as to "go no further than necessity demands, preferring to abstain from what they lawfully might do rather than transgress due limits."[30]

Consistent with traditional just-war thinking, Vitoria also affirms *in bello* requirements of proportionality and discrimination between guilty and innocent. Regarding the former, retribution is to be "proportionate to the offense, and vengeance ought to go no further." As to the latter, "The deliberate slaughter of the innocent is never lawful in itself" and is forbidden by natural law. "It is never right to slay the guiltless, even as an indirect and

---

[27]Vitoria *De Indis* 2.5.
[28]In Vitoria's day, Spanish slaves consisted of blacks, whites, Moors and Jews. See especially the overview of Spanish attitudes toward slavery in the introduction (ibid., pp. 84-95) by the editor.
[29]Ibid., p. 87.
[30]Ibid., 3.2.

unintended result." "The basis of a war," Vitoria observes, "is a wrong done. But a wrong is not done by an innocent person. Therefore war may not be employed against him."[31]

Vitoria is not unmindful of collateral damage and acknowledges that preventing harm to all innocents in war is impossible. Such a situation might include the storming of a fortress in a just war with the knowledge that innocent people are inside. Prudence in such a case is therefore necessary, always with the aim of avoiding potential abuses.[32]

What is striking about Vitoria's work is that it constantly challenges the authorities to consider moral alternatives. Rendering evil for unwarranted provocation is unacceptable in Vitoria's view, for it causes justice to go into hiding.

But a more delicate question presents itself: Can the fact of Indians' vices, morals and questionable practices be just cause for war? No, says Vitoria, even though their idolatrous practices (e.g., cannibalistic rites in parts of Mexico and South America) were considered abominable and savage. The Spanish should be allowed to carry on trade in the New World, and the barbarians may not impede such commercial activity. If the Indians do attempt to impede them, the Spanish should seek to reason with them without violence. If the Indians use violence, then the Spanish may repel them forcibly. If the Indians seek to destroy them, the Spanish may resort to all rights to war.[33]

In what specific cases might coercive intervention be justified? Vitoria identifies several. The Indians may not persecute those who convert to Christian faith. Indian chiefs, moreover, may not exercise tyranny. Other just causes include self-defense, defending allies, sedition, defending public safety and preserving general peace against tyrants and aggressors.[34]

The history of Spain's adherence to these principles, of course, is not a happy one. As the record bears out, more often than not peace was subverted by conquistadors who had no intention of acting justly.

Other relevant theoretical questions on war are addressed by Vitoria. May Christians go to war? He agrees with Augustine. Yes, Christians may soldier and participate in war. The gospel, he responds, does not forbid such. And

---

[31] *De Iure Belli,* art. 10.

[32] *De Indis,* art. 34-39. On the matter of taking women and children captive, Vitoria is less assertive. He notes that it is "received rule" that Christians do not becomes slaves as a result of war. Women and children may be held as ransom, though not as slaves in the formal sense. Children may not be killed and must, along with women, be presumed innocent (art. 36).

[33] These matters constitute virtually the whole of section 3 of *De Indis.*

[34] Vitoria *De Iure Belli,* art. 10-19.

not only the gospel but saints of the church, holy men from the past as well as the law of nature permit war that is justified. By what authority may coercive force be used? Individuals may defend themselves and their property. The prince, magistrate or king may defend—and declare war on behalf of— the community, republic or state. Like Aquinas, Vitoria stresses that authority to declare and go to war reside only in the hands of the governing authorities. The state cannot "adequately protect the public weal . . . if it cannot avenge a wrong and take measures against its enemies." Otherwise, "wrongdoers would become readier and bolder for wrongdoing."[35]

What constitutes just cause for conflict? In short, for Vitoria, all that is necessary for the defense of the public good. What is *not* just cause for war? Differences in religion, attempts by the prince or king to bring glory or honor to himself, and injuries that are slight and not grievous. And what is right intention in going to war? The establishment of peace and security, since these are basic inviolable human needs. Is there noncombatant immunity in the midst of war? Innocent people and children are to be spared. May these be taken captive? Yes. May they be enslaved? No.[36]

What we find in Vitoria is the beginnings of "international law," that is, principles governing all nations that are anchored in natural moral law. Vitoria's argument is significant because it acknowledges an international community of independent states or people groups that have rights, territorial sovereignty and reciprocal duties as to conduct. Unlike just-war thinkers before him, Vitoria grounds the notion of just war not in Romans 13 and Christian theology per se but in moral obligation that is known through natural-law reasoning. Natural reason has established among the nations that certain rights and privileges rooted in justice are inviolable. Nature establishes a bond between all humans; an individual is not a wolf to fellow humans; the individual is another human. If principles of just war are applicable to non-Christian peoples, then the rationale, the very basis for justice and peace, could not be narrowly Christian. Human-rights violations and justification for going to war are the same for all people everywhere; they are rooted in moral realities that are unchanging and universally applicable.

While we who are perched on the cusp of the twenty-first century can scarcely appreciate how radical this idea was, in Vitoria's day it was nothing short of revolutionary.

---

[35]Ibid., art. 1.
[36]Ibid., art. 10-15, 36.

Suárez. Like Vitoria before him, Francisco Suárez taught theology at a leading university of his day.[37] Trained both as a lawyer and theologian, Suárez addressed the subject of war not unlike Augustine and Aquinas—as a duty of love. This, along with his belief that the laws of war are binding on all nations, forms the main argument of his most important work, *The Three Theological Virtues,* published posthumously in 1621. In this work Suárez asks whether war itself is evil. It is both inevitable and not always evil, he responds, even when it is utterly susceptible to abuse. Suárez follows Vitoria and previous thinkers in the just-war tradition: war is permitted by natural law and by the gospel, "which in no way derogates from the natural law."[38]

War for Suárez is a serious matter: "While war is not evil *per se*, still on account of the many misfortunes which it brings in its train, it is one of those matters which is often done in an evil manner. And therefore many circumstances are required to make war righteous."[39] Among the conditions cited by Suárez as necessary for war to be just are punitive justice (i.e., righting a wrong) and the declaration thereof by a lawful authority. At the same time he qualifies legitimate authority. While kings exercise sovereignty, that sovereignty is limited and does not extend to any and all parts of the world. Neither God nor reason grants that sort of power to an individual. Further, it is unjust to go to war if reparations have been ignored. Also, once undertaken, a war is unjust if it does not grant immunity to noncombatants. As far as is possible, innocents are to be left untouched: "For the natural law demands that no one be killed intentionally, who in fact is clearly not at fault." Those who do not bear arms are considered innocent.[40]

The overriding concern in Suárez's work is natural law and how states are to conduct themselves. Whereas civil or municipal law is alterable, based on customs and usage, the law of nature is universal and unchanging, governing how human beings as well as nations deal with one another. All aspects of justice flow from this reality. A further contribution of Suárez (and

---

[37]Suárez taught at the University of Portugal at Coimbra. Portugal, at this time, was under the domination of Spain.

[38]Francisco Suárez *The Three Theological Virtues* 3.8.1, an English translation that is found in James B. Scott, *The Spanish Origin of International Law: Lectures on Francisco de Vitoria (1480-1546) and Francisco Suarez (1548-1617)* (Washington, D.C.: Georgetown University Press, 1929), p. 77.

[39]Ibid.

[40]Ibid., 3.8.7.

Vitoria) is extending just-war thinking to additional criteria. Aquinas had identified three—just cause, right intention, and sovereign authority. They add three further conditions: proportionality, last resort, and reasonable chance of success. The latter two are best understood as prudential tests that assist the application of moral principles in particular situations.

Under the rubric of charity, Suárez scrutinizes the role of the State in both defensive and offensive modes: "A required mode and uniformity as to it [warfare] must be observed at its beginning, during its prosecution and after victory."[41] "All of the foregoing," Suárez was careful to maintain, "since it is founded upon the natural law, is common to Christians and to unbelievers."[42]

Grotius. The Dutch legal theorist Hugo Grotius, considered the father of modern international law, is roughly contemporary to Suárez. Grotius confronts the dilemma of just limits to war in much the same way as Vitoria and Suárez. The results of his work would be foundational for just-war thinking in the modern era. In his important work *The Law of War and Peace* (1625), Grotius argues that how nations relate to one another is governed by universally binding moral principles. These are "binding on all kings" and "known through reason."[43] This argument has important implications for both the church and the state; it places limitations on both. It also places limitations on whether nations may go to war justly and how warfare is to be conducted. Given the divinely instituted natural law, such rules of military engagement are valid for all people.

Grotius is remarkable both for his insight into the human condition and for his in-depth application of biblical and general revelation to the problem of peace that was so fleeting in his day. He lived and wrote in the context of the Thirty Years' War that had ravaged much of Europe prior to the Peace of Westphalia in 1648. It was the bitterness of this strife, rending church and state and leaving no international authority, that caused him to pick up the pen and write. Grotius brooded much over the horrors of war and the ways of peace. Yet, committed as he was to peace, he did not exclude the possibility of war. Rather, the ravages of war led him to refine just-war thinking in such a way that it should become the handmaiden of authentic justice, in the end securing an enduring social peace. In *The Law of War and Peace* he probes when, how and by whom war might justly be conducted.

---

[41]Ibid., 3.8.1.
[42]Ibid., 3.8.2.
[43]Hugo Grotius *The Law of War and Peace* 1.1.10; 1.3.16.

Grotius was well aware that an impartial and wholly objective understanding of justice is impossible; all efforts to apply justice are subjective. And given his abhorrence of the ravages of war, his chief objective was to prevent such in the first place. Nevertheless, in those situations where we are unable to prevent war, we must aim to minimize its devastation. Grotius self-consciously placed himself between what he called two extreme positions—militarism and pacifism. He exhorts: "For both extremes a remedy must be found, [in order] that men may not believe either that nothing is allowable, or that everything is."[44] Human reason and social necessity do not prohibit all force, only that which is morally repugnant, such as human oppression.

Early in *The Law of War and Peace* Grotius seeks to reconcile his convictions to the biblical witness. As Ambrose, Augustine and Aquinas before him, he believes that pacifist interpretations of Jesus' "sermon on the mount" err. For him several strands of biblical evidence are crucial. One is the apostle Paul's admonition to Timothy to pray for kings and those in authority (1 Tim 2:1-3). Christian piety does not abrogate political authority. Linked to this Pauline exhortation is the apostle's teaching in Romans 13. The sword by rightful authority restrains evil. Yet a third element needing explanation is John the Baptist's response to soldiers who come to be baptized. These soldiers, Grotius notes, did not renounce their military calling as inconsistent with the will of God. Rather, right motives were enjoined. Cornelius the centurion is a similar case in point. Following his baptism in Christ, the reader of Acts is not told that he was advised to leave his military commission. A further compelling argument is the manner in which Christ confirmed rather than abolished Old Testament law—and specifically that of capital punishment.[45]

Grotius does not merely acknowledge the just-war arguments by previous generations of Christian thinkers. He also interacts with fathers of the early church who were pacifist (for example, Tertullian and Lactantius). He understands that pacifist concerns about violence and idolatry were partially valid, given the circumstances surrounding early Christians. And yet he reminds the reader that reservations about military service were prudential in nature and not absolute moral prohibitions. Other evidence from antiquity indicates that Christians could—and did—indeed serve in the military. And what is striking to Grotius is that *they did so without being excommunicated* from the church.

---

[44]Ibid., 1.1.
[45]Ibid., 2.6-7.

This mediating position between militarism and pacifism, for him, is wisdom. Wisdom insofar as it recognizes that peace is not the mere absence of conflict but the fruit of a justly ordered society. And wisdom because government, with all its faults, has a critical role in restraining evil in the present world.[46] Given these assumptions Grotius sets forth in considerable detail moral criteria that are applicable to all nations in discerning whether to use coercive force *(ius ad bellum)* and how such might be applied *(ius in bello).*[47]

For a war to be just, Grotius believed, six criteria are necessary:[48]

1. Just cause. In principle, just cause is motivated by two concerns: to rectify or to prevent injustice. For it to be just a response must be proportionate to the injustice itself. It must further aim at some greater good. Not every injustice necessitates coercive force or war. Specific reasons for just cause included reclaiming stolen or occupied territory, oppressive injury or harm (even in another nation) that requires punishment or prevention of humanitarian abuses, threat to or rescue of nationals, terrorism and preventive attack. War, for Grotius, is justifiable only "to continue the work of peace."[49] We do not go to war except "with the desire to end it at the earliest possible moment."[50]

2. Sovereign authority. Three functions attend the sovereign power of a state, rightly understood: the making of laws, enforcing those laws, and appointing magistrates. All of these are public in nature and not subject to another power. Because power is so easily abused, Grotius's treatment of political sovereignty is complex. And yet not even abuse of power diminishes the fact that authority resides in the office itself.[51]

3. Formal declaration. When nations formally and publicly state their intentions, several things ensue. One is to ensure that war is removed from the private domain. Another is the possibility of the opponent's surrender. A further benefit is that a formal announcement communicates to the of-

---

[46]Ibid., 2.9.
[47]For an excellent—and quite accessible—discussion of Grotius's just-war criteria, as they apply in a more contemporary context, see Paul Christopher, *Ethics of War and Peace,* rev. ed. (Upper Saddle River, N.J.: Prentice Hall, 1999), pp. 81-103.
[48]Grotius *Law of War and Peace* 2.1-3.1. I am dependent on the English translation found in Hugo Grotius, *The Law of War and Peace,* trans. L. R. Loomis (Roslyn: Walter J. Black, 1949).
[49]Ibid., 1.1.
[50]Equally significant as his discussion of just causes is his examination of numerous unjust scenarios in ibid., 2.22-23.
[51]Ibid., 1.5.

fending nation what is to transpire. This in itself may have the effect ultimately of preventing war.[52]

4. Proportionality. The retributive response in warfare, according to Grotius, must be commensurate with the evil being redressed. Thus, for example, a draconian response to lesser abuses is illegitimate. Wisdom must cause kings to assess the cost of war, not only as it affects the enemy but also other nations and people groups. Proportionality is governed by a just political aim toward which war must be directed.[53]

5. Reasonable chance of success. Proportionality and prospects for success are related for Grotius. Hereby he understands a just response to be commensurate with the injustice caused. Such deliberation also requires a reckoning of injury but also the effects of war on one's own people as well as on other people groups. There must result from war a balance of good over evil; otherwise, the cause is not justifiable.[54]

6. Last resort. Grotius has been witness to the ravages of war. For this reason he wishes to avoid its effects at any reasonable cost. Going to war can only be justified based on "exceptional" conditions.[55] Thus, only when the previous conditions—just cause, sovereign authority, formal declaration, proportionality and reasonable chance of success—have been met without any solution is war to be undertaken.[56]

In wrestling with the particularities of justice Grotius rendered judgment on specific scenarios of intervention. Preemptive force was considered morally legitimate in cases involving, for example, commercial right of passage, punishing treaty violations, assisting an ally in a just cause and defending Christians who are being oppressed. Grotius takes pains to identify occasions that qualify and those that do not. In his work a presumption not against *force* per se but against *injustice* guides just-war thinking.[57] Grotius reminds us that preemption by a (relatively) just state is not inherently wrong, nor is defense by an unjust state inherently right.

While the average layperson may be fully unaware of the extent of Grotius's contributions to law and international relations (in fact, may never have

---

[52]Ibid., 3.3.
[53]Ibid., 2.20, 24.
[54]Ibid., 2.6, 25; 3.25.
[55]The just-war condition of "right intention" identified by both Augustine and Aquinas is met in Grotius's thinking by qualifying the justness of the cause.
[56]Ibid., 1.2.
[57]Ibid., 2.1, 25-26; 3.1, 3, 17, 20.

heard his name), his legacy is considerable. Historian Paul Christopher has sought to show that the influence of his work extends even into the nineteenth century. Among his most enduring contributions: (1) international law, grounded in the "laws of humanity," that govern international relations; (2) advocacy of universal, natural laws that impose legal and moral restrictions on nations; and (3) clearly articulated rules of international law for the conduct of war that specify *ius ad bellum* and *ius in bello* requirements.

It is impossible to overstate the significance of Vitoria, Suárez and Grotius for the development of just-war thinking as it applies to the community of nations. One commentator has aptly summarized the contribution of these early-modern just-war thinkers:

> [T]he just war theory has repudiated religious and ideological causes for going to war. . . . All people have equal rights by virtue of their common humanity. Justice insists that we treat equals equally. Religious differences and causes are therefore as irrelevant to the pursuit of justice as are differences of race or culture or economic status. Justice cannot allow for morally irrelevant considerations.[58]

It is most unfortunate that the average contemporary reader is unfamiliar with the arguments and significance of these early-modern just-war theorists. Their value lies not merely in their ability to discern the moral obligations of justice for their day but also to lay a foundation for just relations among nations that is applicable to our day as well.

---

[58]Arthur F. Holmes, "A Just War Response," in *War: Four Christian Views,* ed. Robert G. Clouse, rev. ed. (Downers Grove, Ill.: InterVarsity, 1991), p. 182.

4

JUST-WAR THINKING IN THE MODERN PERIOD TO THE PRESENT

Christian thinkers of the mid-twentieth century found themselves reacting against the overly optimistic view of human nature that had dominated the nineteenth and early twentieth centuries. The rise of totalitarian German nationalism in the aftermath of World War I—"the war to end all wars"—exposed with excruciating clarity the naiveté of this sentiment. Those committed to world peace had failed to deliver on their promise. And few critiqued this unfounded optimism more trenchantly than Reinhold Niebuhr in the 1930s and 1940s.

REINHOLD NIEBUHR

Reinhold was one of two famous brothers, both of whom taught theology and ethics. Richard, a professor at Yale, had published an essay titled "The Grace of Doing Nothing" in the March 23, 1932, issue of *The Christian Century*. In this essay Richard argued for nonintervention in the Sino-Japanese conflict of the 1930s. This inactivity, he maintained, was rooted in the conviction that the unfolding of history was the judgment of the world. This judgment, however, produced an ultimate good outcome, based on divine providence. Christians' inactivity, moreover, had a precedent. The "grace to do nothing" was the practice of the early Christians as well. This grace, as Niebuhr conceived it, is a grace that leads us to repentance. Our resultant inaction is one that refuses to judge our neighbor, since genuine contrition avoids the foolishness of self-righteousness.

Reinhold's response to his brother's essay on Christian "inactivity" came in the form of an essay titled "Must We Do Nothing?" that appeared one week later.[1] "There is much in my brother's article," he wrote, "with which I agree." He commends Richard for attempting to avoid a sentimental dilution of Christian ethics, that is, one that reduces Christian love to a lack of personal cost and sacrifice. "My brother draws the conclusion," Reinhold continued, "that it is better not to act at all than to act from motives which are less than pure. . . . He believes in taking literally the words of Jesus, 'Let him who is without sin cast the first stone.'" This sensitivity to our own sin, he conceded, was central to Christian faith.

Nevertheless, Richard's essay presents problems. "All this does not prove . . . that we ought to apply the words of Jesus . . . literally. If we do we will never be able to act. There will never be a wholly disinterested nation. Pure disinterestedness [in moral-political evil] is an ideal which even individuals cannot fully achieve." What is more, for Reinhold, justice is to be seen as the *highest ideal* for which all humans work. And justice, sooner or later, will entail "the assertion of right against right and interests against interests" until some kind of social peace and order are achieved. Love and repentance, he cautions his brother, "can do no more than qualify the social struggle in history"; they "will never abolish" the struggle, which inevitably will become violent.

The hope of attaining a moral society "without coercion," warns Reinhold, "is an illusion which was spread chiefly among the comfortable classes of the past century." Reinhold takes his brother to task for the political consequences of not confronting evil actively. For example, he cannot understand his brother's position that political-moral tyranny can be used by God, due to providence, and at the same time *require* our passivity. Yes, he concedes, God *does* work through catastrophe. And yet "ethically-directed coercion," he argues, seems the better—and moral—alternative. As long as the world is fallen, a place where real and ideal meet, human progress will depend on "the judicious use" of force in the service of the ideal. Practically, this may mean using coercion to dissuade totalitarian regimes from imposing their designs on the nations. And when we are forced to do such, we do so with a sense of tragedy and reluctance.

Niebuhr has much to say in his writings about the character of Christian love. Like Augustine, Niebuhr believes love to be "the final and highest pos-

---

[1]Reinhold Niebuhr, "Must We Do Nothing?" *The Christian Century,* March 30, 1932, pp. 415-17.

sibility of man toward man."[2] But the Christian ethic does not consist merely of love as an *ideal.* Humans, after all, live in history, and this love, properly understood, needs to be tethered to justice. Given humanity's implacable nature and stubborn capacity for "infinite regression," we need the restraints that justice of necessity imposes.[3] Niebuhr is impatient with standard Protestant notions of love and justice of his day. Many so-called Christians were prone to sentimentalize love and domesticate justice, resulting in "antinomianism" (lawlessness) of the worst kind.[4] Both of these tendencies, Niebuhr believes, are rooted in an overly optimistic, almost utopian view of human nature. And the facts, as he sees them, appear stubborn: human nature has *not* progressed.

This reality in turn has profound implications for ethics and public policy. "It is not possible to disavow war absolutely without disavowing the task of establishing justice," he wrote in the late 1930s.

> We cannot make peace with Hitler now because his power dominates the Continent, and his idea of a just peace is one that leaves him in security of that dominance. We believe, I think rightly, that a more just peace can be established if that dominance is broken. But in so far as the Hitlerian imperial will must be broken first, the new peace will be an imposed peace.[5]

Niebuhr is further convinced that "even the most chastened Germany would not be willing, except as she is forced, to accept certain provisions for the freedom of Poland and Czechoslovakia and the freedom of small nations generally."[6] For Niebuhr justice rests on an "equilibrium of forces." These forces are needed to prevent human will from degenerating into tyranny. In the end Niebuhr rejects a peace at any price. A peace without justice, he worries, delivers us into a "peace of slavery."[7]

Niebuhr is convinced that a pacifist refusal to resist evil directly, *in practice,* bestows on evil and tyranny an advantage in the present life. Pacifism, he believed, tempts us to make no moral judgments at all and thereby gives an advantage to tyranny. In his classic chapter "Why the Christian Church Is

---

[2]Reinhold Niebuhr, *An Interpretation of Christian Ethics* (New York: Harper, 1935), p. 103.
[3]This is a recurring theme in Niebuhr's writings.
[4]See D. B. Robertson, ed., *Love and Justice: Selections from the Shorter Writings of Reinhold Niebuhr* (Philadelphia: Westminster Press, 1992). This volume conveniently brings together essays by Niebuhr that consider charity's relationship to justice against the backdrop of human depravity.
[5]Ibid., p. 52.
[6]Ibid.
[7]Ibid., p. 174.

Not Pacifist," he sides with Ambrose, Augustine and Aquinas, who believe that genuine love can be called on to actively oppose the forces of evil, given the sinful will to power that is rooted in human depravity. Responding somewhat sarcastically to the pacifists of his day who, like his brother, advocate nonintervention in foreign affairs, he writes: "If we believe that if Britain had only been fortunate enough to have produced 30 percent instead of 2 percent of conscientious objectors to military service, Hitler's heart would have been softened and he would not have dared attack Poland."[8]

While Reinhold is sensitive, like Richard, to the idolatry that issues out of confusing faith and politics, there is an opposite idolatry as well. And that is to see no relevance between faith and political action. This attitude is wrong because "it denies the seriousness of political decision and obscures our Christian responsibilities for the good order and justice of our civil community."[9] Therefore, we are to resist both nationalist and isolationist politics in the name of Christ. Niebuhr wishes to preserve the Augustinian tension between our dual citizenships. On the one hand, we regard the political realm as a matter of importance, while on the other we recognize that humans are incapable of creating a purely just, moral and Christian society.

JOHN COURTNEY MURRAY

Following World War II, Roman Catholic theologian John Courtney Murray was one of the few religious thinkers to argue for the continued relevance of just-war principles. Despite the proliferation of nuclear weapons and modern warfare's inherent capacity for mass destruction, Murray believed that there is something timeless in the application of just-war criteria, even in a nuclear age.

Few religious thinkers in the twentieth century have equaled Murray in their ability to relate religious conviction to contemporary events. In both *We Hold These Truths* and *Morality and Modern Warfare,* Murray is in conversation with theologians as well as policy-makers of his day, attentive to theological faithfulness on the one hand and responsible statecraft on the other.[10]

The development of modern weapons of mass destruction gave new ur-

---

[8]Reinhold Niebuhr, *Christianity and Power Politics* (New York: Charles Scribner's, 1940), p. 6. This essay is reproduced in Robert McAfee Brown, ed., *The Essential Reinhold Niebuhr: Selected Essays and Addresses* (New Haven, Conn.: Yale University Press, 1987), pp. 102-19.
[9]Robertson, *Love and Justice,* p. 60.
[10]John Courtney Murray, *We Hold These Truths* (New York: Sheed & Ward, 1960), and *Morality and Modern War* (New York: Council on Religion and International Affairs, 1959).

gency to the moral problem of war in the 1950s. The possibility of annihilating the human race seemed for many religious thinkers and theologians to require an absolute pacifism. Murray, however, reckoned with this scenario as well as the reality of totalitarianism that made possible the political enslavement of human beings. The reality of modern totalitarianism, Murray argued, requires in principle some form of coercive response. But weapons themselves, despite their destructive potential, were not the chief problem as Murray saw it. Rather, it was a lack of clear moral reasoning.[11]

In Murray's writings, particularly those treating the problem of war, several overriding themes emerge. These themes reflect an attempt on Murray's part to think with the church through the ages. But they do more. Faithfulness to the historic Christian tradition informs us as we struggle with contemporary ethical dilemmas. War is a tragic necessity and only reluctantly undertaken; we resist the spirit of militarism and nationalism that is so readily accessible. In a democratic pluralism, theological faithfulness by Christians must combine with political prudence to inform morally responsible public and social policy, even in a nuclear age. Statecraft, Murray reminds us, is the art of making wise political decisions. For this reason, to the extent that the church removes itself from public affairs, it loses any authority to speak to society on public affairs.

Formally, Murray believes that the church has suffered from a vague knowledge of just-war principles. Practically speaking, as he sees it, the just-war tradition lies in abandon and neglect. The true relevance of the tradition today, he contends optimistically, "lies in its value as the solvent of false dilemmas." And what are these "false dilemmas"? A prime example for Murray is what he deems "two extreme positions." These two positions are "a soft, sentimental pacifism" and "a cynical, hard realism."[12] The latter assumes the need for survival and defeat of our ideological foes, unaided by any sort of moral reasoning, while the former fails to deal with the complexities of statecraft. Neither finds support in traditional Christian moral teaching, argues Murray; neither is morally acceptable.

Traditional Christian thinking about war, Murray reminds his readers,

---

[11]More recently, George Weigel has argued in the same vein as Murray, examining the last three decades of broadly Roman Catholic social thought and finding it wanting. See his important work *Tranquillitas Ordinis: The Present Failure and Future Promise of American Catholic Thought on War and Peace* (Oxford: Oxford University Press, 1987).

[12]Murray, *Morality and Modern War,* p. 15. The religious form of the latter, a "crusade" or "jihad" mentality, of course, was not highly visible in foreign affairs until the 1990s.

does not countenance such false dichotomies. It rejects—and exposes as folly—notions such as "Abolish war!" and "Better red than dead!" but also the possibility of nuclear survival that were prominent in the Cold War era. Just-war thinking, in contrast, counters the hysteria of the political left and right. It requires of us a seriousness about moral reasoning and asks us to interact with history. The church does not look in this age to abolish war. Rather, it is willing to encounter evil, all the while seeking to limit the effects of evil and as far is possible humanize the conduct of armed conflict.[13]

The work of Murray—who wrote in the 1950s and 1960s—carefully charts a course between what he believed to be two extreme positions—isolation and nationalism. As Murray saw it, much of the church, not to mention society at large, has been unduly influenced by both. The aim of responsible Christian social ethics, then, is to purify the public conscience—inside and outside of the church—and contribute to morally responsible policy considerations.

PAUL RAMSEY

The Protestant counterpart to John Courtney Murray a decade later was ethicist Paul Ramsey, who contended, against conventional wisdom, for the viability of just-war thinking, even in an age of nuclear weapons. Like Murray, Ramsey believed that the ethical principles of Christian faith were relevant to the world's economic, political and social problems. Ramsey demonstrated keen insight into the ethical dilemmas of our time. He was without equal in his ability to enter cross-disciplinary conversation with theologians, ethicists, social scientists and policy analysts of his day, and to do so in a manner that was knowledgeable and timely. Perhaps no other individual in the twentieth century has done more to link Christian ethics to public policy.

A prime feature of Ramsey's writings is to apply Augustinian thinking to contemporary ethical dilemmas. Like Augustine, Ramsey argues that Christian charity *may* be called on to manifest what he calls a "preferential ethics of protection." Part of our difficulty, as Ramsey sees it, is that we have frequently distorted the meaning of Jesus' teaching. Take, for example, the much-cited but often misunderstood admonition to "turn the other cheek" (Mt 5:39). Jesus' directive is this: "If *someone* strikes *you* . . ." The matter is *personal*—between you and someone else. Our Lord does *not* say and neither does he advocate, "If someone strikes your neighbor on the right cheek,

---

[13]Ibid., pp. 15-19.

turn to him your neighbor's other cheek [that it also might be struck]." While people are free to forgo self-defense, they are *not* free to ignore the plight of the innocent third party. Coercive force, proportionate to the offense, is a just response in the face of violent aggression. This line of reasoning is found in Ramsey's *Basic Christian Ethics*, in his important 1961 work *War and the Christian Conscience*, and in the massive volume published in 1968, *The Just War: Force and Political Responsibility*.[14]

War and the Christian Conscience might be considered Ramsey's basic statement regarding the use of military force as well as Christian participation therein. But in the years to follow, Ramsey would attempt to apply just-war principles to geopolitical challenges of his day. A central theme of *The Just War* is the importance of responsible statecraft and political responsibilities for which citizens are held accountable. Just-war thinking, in Ramsey's mind, is simply an *extension* of responsible ethics and politics. Conversant with his Protestant roots, Ramsey cites both the Augsburg Confession and the Westminster Confession as a reminder of our civic duties. So the widespread identification of just-war thinking with Roman Catholicism must be rejected, even when discussions of just-war theory are rare outside of Catholic circles.[15]

In the 1960s and 1970s Ramsey advocated various policy prescriptions that he believed were imperative for the free world's security. These recommendations were based on moral principle as well as political prudence. The United States, he argued, needed to develop a rationale for the just use of conventional military forces, given the Soviet threat. Falling prey to both pacifists' calls for disarmament and militarists' threats of mutually assured destruction was both immoral and unacceptable. Further, U.S. policy should be clear that we would not use nuclear weapons in a first strike but as a tactical response against aggression by the enemy. This response, moreover, would be governed by rules of "just conduct." Nuclear capability itself is not immoral and should be maintained for use in *counterforce* warfare, were that alternative regrettably necessary. Counterforce warfare has as its aim a just peace, not mutual destruction of societies. What is more, *intention,* and not amount of destruction, dictates what in the end is just use of force.[16]

---

[14]Paul Ramsey, *Basic Christian Ethics* (New York: Charles Scribner's, 1950); *War and the Christian Conscience* (Durham, N.C.: Duke University Press, 1961); and *The Just War* (New York: Charles Scribner's, 1968).

[15]Ramsey, *Just War,* p. xii.

[16]Ramsey's proposal regarding justified use of nuclear weapons is laid out most succinctly in *The Limits of Nuclear War* (New York: Council on Religion and International Affairs, 1963).

Ramsey's concern is with *how* people should make political decisions in the realm of foreign policy and not *what* particular decisions were made. Making moral judgments, and specifically the process by which those judgments arrive, is Ramsey's burden. Clarifying the *grounds* for using coercive force and going to war was inescapable and therefore a highest priority of civil society. And as Ramsey sees it, Christians above all people need to know how to resolve disputes over the justice of war and armed conflict. His advice is unequivocal: "Until we [learn to] do this, we have little business trying to inform the conscience of the nations."[17]

WILLIAM V. O'BRIEN

With the proliferation of nuclear weapons many religious writers during the 1970s and 1980s wrote from the perspective of nuclear pacifism. That is, while in theory they might not rule out the use of coercive force as a potential moral instrument, they assume that our present nuclear capabilities require of us a pacifist position *in practice*. An exception was William O'Brien. O'Brien was keenly aware of the shortcomings of nuclear deterrence. Most military strategists, he complained, brushed aside the morality of limited war. And yet O'Brien belonged to a minority of religious thinkers who believed that limited nuclear war is not a "dangerous heresy" but in fact a foundation for any realistic policy of deterrence and defense.[18]

O'Brien's most acclaimed work on just war, *War and/or Survival*, was published in 1969. The main argument of this book is the need for a moral realism that might counter false notions of militarism.[19] While reacting to the excesses of militarism, O'Brien also rejects any ethic that fails to take seriously the political realities of the present. In some respects he embraces the "Christian realism" of Reinhold Niebuhr. War, as understood by O'Brien, is a political given in the present order. Therefore, he argues, the elimination of war is utopian at best and wrong-headed at worst. The first order of business, morally speaking, is to limit and contain it.[20]

---

[17]Ramsey, *Just War*, p. xiv.
[18]This is the thrust of O'Brien's essay "The Failure of Deterrence and the Conduct of War," in *The Nuclear Dilemma and the Just War Tradition*, ed. William V. O'Brien and John Langan (Lexington: Lexington Books, 1986), pp. 154-97.
[19]A professor of government at Georgetown University and a Roman Catholic, O'Brien took his faith seriously, even when the language of faith in his writings is secondary to the language of politics and international affairs. See, for example, chapter nine, "War and the Christian Conscience," of his important work *War and/or Survival* (Garden City, N.Y.: Doubleday, 1969).
[20]See especially "The Laws of War" (chap. 8), in *War and/or Survival*.

The church, as O'Brien sees it, is not a pacifist church. Typical questions of his day—such as "Would Jesus submit to the draft or go to Vietnam?"— "seem to me extremely irrelevant," he wrote in *War and/or Survival.* More important for him were those questions that are theologically informed. What is justice? What does justice require of us ethically? And what does justice require when the rights of people, created in the image of God, are being denied? Theology, he believed, must condition our moral analyses of war.[21]

For this reason a major concern for O'Brien was the publication in 1983 of the U.S. Catholic Bishops' pastoral letter *The Challenge of Peace,* which served as a focal point for much debate over war in the 1980s.[22] The document, in O'Brien's view, was "seriously flawed" for two main reasons. First, it failed to acknowledge the threat that totalitarianism posed to the free world during the Cold War era. O'Brien chides the bishops for their inability to establish just cause in their deliberations and thus their inability to grasp just-war principles. Moreover, the bishops seem to believe that *no* just cause could justify going to war in *any* situation. Thus they have a dilemma. On the one hand they wish to acknowledge the threat of evil in the world. On the other hand they cannot bring themselves to say that such a threat should be deterred. They pay lip service to the just-war tradition, but they alter the tradition and render it incapable of establishing justice. Their deterrence, in the end, is "disembodied."[23] O'Brien's exhortation to the church—and specifically, to his own bishops—is to forsake idealism and aim at moral realism.[24]

In several volumes O'Brien identifies and refines traditional just-war criteria as set forth by Aquinas. First, he evaluates *ius ad bellum* requirements—just cause, competent authority and right intention—in light of the nuclear dilemma. Second, he considers *ius in bello* requirements—discrimination and proportionality—in light of the problem of nuclear deterrence.[25] Elsewhere in his work he develops the prudential implications of just-war criteria in very sensitive and relevant ways.[26] The upshot of O'Brien's argu-

---

[21]O'Brien, *War and/or Survival,* p. 265.

[22]*The Challenge of Peace* (Washington, D.C.: United States Catholic Conference, 1983).

[23]O'Brien, "Failure of Deterrence," p. 155.

[24]O'Brien's criticism of the bishops' statement is found in "Failure of Deterrence" and in "The Challenge of War: A Christian Realist Perspective," in *The Catholic Bishops and Nuclear War,* ed. Judith A. Dwyer (Washington, D.C.: Georgetown University Press, 1984), pp. 37-63.

[25]See, for example, O'Brien's first major work on just war, *Nuclear War, Deterrence and Morality* (Westminster, Md.: Newman Press, 1967); his massive volume *The Conduct of Just and Limited War* (New York: Praeger, 1981); and his important essay "Failure of Deterrence."

[26]See, for example, "Laws of War" (chap. 8), in *War and/or Survival.*

ment is to call for a limited nuclear deterrence that is guided by the moral imperatives of the just-war doctrine.

The subject of war and peace cannot be finessed, O'Brien reminds the reader in the conclusion of *War and/or Survival*. For individual Christians the crucial question is not, What would Christ do about war, deterrence, revolution or peace if he returned to earth? Rather, the question must be, What does Christ require me to do about these problems, given my station in life? In a fallen world we cannot escape the moral obligations that citizenship bestows upon us.[27]

MICHAEL WALZER

One contemporary just-war thinker who does not write from a Christian perspective deserves mention. This is so because of the moral questions he raises. In his important 1977 book *Just and Unjust Wars,* Michael Walzer inquires into the justice of particular wars of the twentieth century.[28] How can the morality of particular wars be determined? Who bears responsibility for particular acts of war? And in what dimension? The ends and means of warfare are scrutinized in this volume.

Walzer acknowledges that his book is largely the product of his own reflection on the Vietnam War. But *Just and Unjust Wars* is no manifesto of the "peace movement." Far from it. In the years that followed the war, Walzer committed himself to probing with great seriousness a basic question: What makes war—any war—just or unjust? And why? What makes this book fascinating to read—and it is not necessarily *easy* to read—is the fact that its author, a political theorist, engages in—of all things— moral reflection.

"All's fair in love and war." While this bit of conventional wisdom did not originate with Plato or Aristotle, its truth is seemingly timeless—and seemingly unquestioned. Regrettably, in Walzer's view, this proverb is typically used to justify conduct in war that is supremely unjust. When war breaks out, all laws mean nothing; only one law remains, and that is to win at all cost. Anyone who has experienced armed conflict knows what General Sherman had in mind when he first announced that *war is hell.*

Let's call this mindset political or military "realism." Realism, because war

---

[27]This is the thrust of his concluding chapter, "War and the Christian Conscience," in *War and/ or Survival.*
[28]Michael Walzer, *Just and Unjust Wars,* 2nd ed. (New York: Basic Books, 1992).

is hell. And because war is hell, the worst is inevitable.[29] But Walzer stops us at this point with a question. Is conduct in war inevitably consigned to this grim baseline reality? Is there no element of moral reasoning, of moral reckoning, that can trump—or at least inform—military strategy?

Despite his misgivings about the war in Vietnam, Walzer believes that a moral dimension to warfare does in fact exist. And despite the unwillingness of American culture to make moral judgments—indeed, despite the post-modern skepticism that pervades all of Western culture—moral arguments, Walzer is convinced, are not only possible but *must* be advocated. *Just and Unjust Wars* is about precisely that—whether and how to make basic moral distinctions. The book has become something of a classic since it was first published, in spite of the fact that it goes against the moral grain of contemporary Western thinking.

Walzer, to his credit, is deeply critical of the moral obtuseness of the academic left.[30] Certainly, the events of September 11, 2001, and since have heightened his own criticism, given the hate-mongering and America-bashing that has taken place among many fellow academics.[31] Terrorism for Walzer is a very real threat, based on its goal and method. Its aim is "to destroy the morale of a nation" or people group, while its modus operandi is "the random murder" of innocents for the purpose of sowing fear.[32] For this reason, as Walzer understands, political and nonmilitary solutions to the problem are unrealistic. Terrorists have no vested interest in dialogue or appeasement. They are only bent on indiscriminate destruction of human life.

JAMES TURNER JOHNSON

A student of Paul Ramsey's, James Turner Johnson has continued—and extended—the thinking of Ramsey to the present day, applying just-war theory to contemporary challenges. Given humankind's ability to self-annihilate through nuclear technology, is it still possible to think in terms of just-war principles? Johnson is convinced it is and presents a compelling case for the necessity of moral guidelines in the present. He applies just-war analysis to

---

[29]The renowned theorist Karl von Clausewitz remarked: "War is an act of force which theoretically can have no limits" (*War, Politics, and Power,* ed. Edward M. Collins [Chicago: University of Chicago Press, 1962], p. 65).

[30]See, for example, his more recent and extremely trenchant critique, "Can There Be a Decent Left?" *Dissent,* Spring 2002, pp.19-23.

[31]Ibid.

[32]*Just and Unjust Wars,* pp. 196-97.

several types of armed conflict. These range from nuclear war between superpowers to nonconventional terrorist activity. Like his mentor Paul Ramsey, he demonstrates an extraordinary dexterity in applying moral wisdom
to the problem of war and its moral complexities.

Johnson is the leading contemporary authority on the historical development and application of the just-war tradition. He has been nothing short of
prolific, producing a number of serious and meticulously researched works
on just war since the mid 1970s, including *Ideology, Reason, and the Limitation of War; Can Modern War Be Just?; The Just War Tradition and the Restraint of War; The Holy War Idea in Western and Islamic Traditions;* and
Morality and Contemporary Warfare. He has also been a veritable voice crying in the academic wilderness, contending for the wisdom of the just-war
tradition in an environment that has been—and today remains—"violently"
opposed to war or the use of coercive force in general.

Johnson wishes to bring just-war perspectives to bear on contemporary
perceptions of war. He believes that the issues of technology and modern
weaponry are more the symptoms than causes of moral dilemmas today.
More important, in his view, is how we understand force in political life, and
how the use of force reflects moral values. For many just-war critics the use
of coercive force is at best irrelevant and at worst immoral. This view, dominant in academic and religious circles, is the result of a divorce in our thinking between ethics and responsible statecraft. It is broadly assumed by many
people that it is not possible today to control and limit the use of coercive
force for peaceful purposes. Johnson carefully addresses this perception
head-on. He is meticulous in his review of history and adept at linking that
history to contemporary concerns. More recently, this has been extended to
his own thinking about terrorism.

While a consensus in Western culture regarding justification and limitation of war will be a surprise to some, Johnson reminds the reader that this
tradition has been remarkably consistent since the generations of the early
Christians. Just-war thinking as we encounter it today does not come to us
in a vacuum. Rather, it has been formulated and preserved in a tradition. Ac-
quainting us with that tradition and making responsible application is the
thrust of Johnson's writings.

JEAN BETHKE ELSHTAIN

In addition to Johnson, one other notable exception to the deeply entrenched pacifism of present-day academia[33] is Jean Elshtain, whose writings on the political thought of Augustine and whose more recent reflections on terrorism make her work indispensable to Christian social ethics.

Like Reinhold Niebuhr, Paul Ramsey and James Turner Johnson, she too is indebted to the cultural, moral and political wisdom that comes to us over the many centuries from the bishop of Hippo. Among her many works are *Augustine and the Limits of Politics, Democracy on Trial, Women and War* and more recently *Just War Against Terror*. Writing in a most engaging manner, Elshtain is able to weave political theory, the history of ideas and Christian moral reflection into her very astute and always timely social criticism. A prolific writer, Elshtain has that knack, so rare among academics, to engage the reader winsomely and creatively at the most profound level, whether she is considering the relevance of Augustine for understanding citizenship, placing democracy as we know it "on trial," challenging the cherished assumptions of feminism or interacting with classic just-war thinking. And she does so with moral clarity and intellectual honesty rather than bombast and a bad temper. Her most recent book, *Just War Against Terror*, published in 2003, is an attempt to discern the moral dimensions of the war on terrorism in its present application of just-war principles.

More important to Elshtain than the developmental history of the just-war tradition are the *implications for civic life* of the just-war idea. Elshtain believes that the wisdom inherent in just-war thinking is necessary not only for foreign policy but for the very ordering of domestic society. While Elshtain rejects the civic nonengagement of pacifism in its multiple expressions, she also condemns in the strongest language the moral obtuseness of *realpolitik*, with its unwillingness to be guided by any moral considerations whatsoever in the pursuit of "justice." That there are universal moral predispositions available to all for the ordering (albeit imperfectly) of a (relatively) just society means that we need not succumb to relativism. The principled reasoning that applies to just-war thinking calls us—indeed, as Elshtain sees it, forces us—to make moral judgments: judgments that distinguish between victim and victimizer, between just and unjust policies, between human behavior that is tolerable and that which is intolerable. While these are exceedingly difficult issues for postmoderns, Elshtain is convinced that they dare

---

[33]This academic form of pacifism can be religious as well as secular. Yet both varieties share common assumptions about peace (as the absence of conflict), human nature (humans should work to abolish war) and justice (coercive force is always unjust and immoral).

not be left to government or to political theorists alone to consider.

Elshtain is convinced that Augustine furnishes for us a useful model. Augustine, she writes, is a distinctly "chastened patriot." "Chastened patriots," she observes, are men and women who have learned from the past as they take seriously their dual citizenships. These two citizenships entail both earthly and heavenly stewardship; they consist of *both* civic duties *and* the pursuit of another city.[34] Elshtain acknowledges both realms, although in her writings she tends to emphasize the obligations attending the former. "Rejecting the counsels of cynicism, they [chastened men and women] modulate the rhetoric of high patriotic purpose"[35] even when they do not abandon their civic duties. These individuals do so by their sensitivity to the ways in which patriotism can shade into the excesses of nationalism. "The chastened patriot," then, is both devoted *and* detached. "A civic life animated by chastened patriotism," she writes, carries enormous implications for "how we think of war and peace and for the pitfalls in how each is construed."[36]

Regarding war, Elshtain sides with Luther in believing that the Christian is called to a moral realism: "If the lion lies down with the lamb, the lamb must be replaced frequently."[37] And yet violence must never be celebrated as it so often is in the world. Violence must always and continually be put "on trial."[38] It is the mediating nature of the just-war position that for Elshtain is compelling. Elshtain's own interest in just-war thinking is less motivated by whether or not the central criteria—which to her are exceedingly important—are met than what moral guidelines inform civil society. As such, just-war thinking

- promotes skepticism and queasiness about the use and abuse of power while not opting out of political reality altogether in favor of utopian fantasies

- requires action and judgment in a world of limits, estrangements and partial justice

- fosters recognition of the provisionality of all political arrangements

- advances respect for other peoples and nations, both in terms of autonomy as well as accountability

---

[34]Jean Bethke Elshtain, *Women and War* (New York: Basic Books, 1987), pp. 252, 268, 270.
[35]Ibid., pp. 252-53.
[36]Ibid.
[37]Ibid., p. 265.
[38]Ibid.

- acknowledges the necessity of self-defense and intervention against un-just aggression and gross oppression while refusing to legitimize imperi-alistic crusades and empire-building[39]

Just-war thinking, according Elshtain, "is not just about war." It is rather "a way of thinking that refuses to separate politics from ethics."[40] Unlike *realpolitik* and an uncritical nationalism, just-war thinking insists on fusing rather than divorcing public and private morality. Therefore, no sharp cleav-age between "domestic" and "foreign" policy should exist.

Elshtain challenges her readers to theological discernment and raises questions that both Christians and policy-makers simply cannot ignore. Her combination of philosophical dexterity, wit, ability to engage a wide range of thinkers and sensitivity to human longings make her indispensable read-ing for the person who cares about faith and culture.[41] And for the person who wrestles with the ethics of war.

ROMAN CATHOLIC SOCIAL TEACHING

Finally, any discussion of the just-war doctrine in contemporary thought requires mention of the *Catechism of the Catholic Church*.[42] Despite the mind-boggling diversity of ethical opinion that calls itself "Catholic," the *Catechism* represents the Church's official—and therefore authoritative—position on all doctrinal and ethical matters. Specifically, it reaffirms and re-mains in continuity with the classic Christian position on war: namely, in a fallen world, resort to arms and coercive force may be justified, provided that certain moral criteria have been met. Following Augustine and Aquinas, the *Catechism* cites moral as well as prudential guidelines for determining both *ius ad bellum* and *ius in bello* conditions, that is, for going to war and conduct in war.

Under the heading of "Avoiding War," the *Catechism* states: "All citizens and all governments are obliged to work for the avoidance of war." The *Cat-*

---

[39]These fundamental assumptions undergirding just-war thinking are both implicit and explicit in *Women and War,* chapters 4, 7 and the epilogue, as well as *Just War Against Terror,* chapter 3.

[40]Jean Bethke Elshtain, "Just War as Politics: What the Gulf War Told Us about Contemporary Life," in *But Was It Just?* ed. David E. DeCosse (New York: Doubleday, 1992), p. 43.

[41]Elsewhere I examine the writings of Elshtain more fully as they bear on a justly ordered so-ciety. See my "War, Women and Political Wisdom: Jean Bethke Elshtain on the Contours of Justice," *Journal of Religious Ethics* (forthcoming).

[42]Even Protestants do well to read the *Catechism,* not only to have a first-hand knowledge of Catholic teaching but also to observe the moral reasoning behind the Catholic Church's stances on particular ethical issues.

echism continues: "However, 'as long as the danger of war persists and there is no international authority with the necessary competence and power, governments cannot be denied the right of lawful self-defense, once all peace efforts have failed.'"[43]

Following in the *Catechism* are prudential tests enumerated by Thomas Aquinas that constitute "strict conditions for legitimate defense by military force" and that require "rigorous consideration." These are said to render "moral legitimacy" to the prospect of armed conflict—*ius ad bellum* and include the following conditions:

- The damage inflicted by the aggressor on the nation or community of nations must be lasting, grave and certain.

- All other means of putting an end to it must have been shown to be impractical or ineffective.

- There must be serious prospects of success.

- The use of arms must not produce evils and disorders graver than the evil to be eliminated. The power of modern means of destruction weighs very heavily in evaluating this condition.[44]

The *Catechism* also reiterates *ius in bello* requirements. These include immunity for noncombatants and the humane treatment of wounded soldiers and prisoners. Furthermore, disproportionate means of warfare, such as extermination and genocide, are decried in the strongest terms.[45] Significantly, the *Catechism* qualifies these conditions with an important statement—one that religious activists tend to ignore or disavow: "The evaluation of these conditions for moral legitimacy [of justified war] belongs to the prudential judgment of *those who have responsibility for the common good.*"[46] This statement serves as an important reminder to Christians: In the end it is *not* the task of the church to make policy decisions. Such remains the domain of political officeholders.

---

[43]*Catechism of the Catholic Church*, ¶2308, which cites a document from the Second Vatican Council.

[44]Ibid., ¶2309.

[45]Ibid., ¶2313.

[46]Ibid., ¶2309 (emphasis added).

5

CHRISTIAN ETHICS
AND THE USE OF FORCE

To struggle with the ethics of war and force is to reveal our assumptions about political power. This does not mean that all Christians need to study political theory. It does mean, however, that we must take seriously scriptural injunctions regarding authority, not least of which is the crux text of Romans 13. Our task is complicated, however, by several factors. In the Protestant tradition there has been no little controversy as to how to view the powers. Mainstream Reformers such as Luther, Calvin and Zwingli held a relatively high view of political authorities, believing that all vocations, including the soldier and the magistrate, were honorable. Radical Reformers such as the Swiss Brethren, and Menno Simons afterward, by contrast viewed the powers with suspicion, calling fellow Anabaptists to "absolute separation" from the world. These distinctions remain for the most part in the body of Christ today.

But even apart from these divisions, approaching the text of Romans 13 is difficult, given the church's speckled history. Anabaptists and other pacifists are keenly aware, and with good reason, of ways in which this text has been misused. It has been employed by regimes in the past—totalitarian and "Christian"—to justify much evil. But the fact that Romans 13 can be "misinterpreted" says nothing about its genuine meaning, provided the Christian community is rightly motivated and does not interpret the passage in isolation from the rest of the church. In truth the text of Romans 13 is relatively straightforward. And responsible interpretation, whatever the pitfalls, is not impossible. We begin by viewing these verses as part of Paul's overall thought.

THE PERSONAL AND THE POLITICAL (ROMANS 12—13)

A common tendency in teaching and preaching from these verses is to sever the material found in Romans 13:1-7 from the material before and after. This detachment, of course, permits great liberty with the text—more liberty than is warranted. This linkage must necessarily constrain our interpretation. Following Paul's theological argument up through the end of chapter 11, Romans 12 begins a listing of practical exhortations. This listing unites several smaller groupings of ethical admonitions. These groups include (1) being wholly dedicated to the purposes of God (vv. 1-2), (2) rightly appreciating various gifts and callings in the body of Christ (vv. 3-8), and (3) striving to manifest love in all relationships—to fellow Christians (vv. 9-13) and to the world (vv. 14-21).

An important part of our relationships with unbelievers is how we handle personal abuse (vv. 17-21). Several specific warnings serve to describe the contours of right response:

- Shun a retaliatory mode.
- Do what is right.
- As far as is possible, strive for peace.
- Avoid a vengeful spirit.
- Take comfort in the fact that God avenges.
- Do practical things to diffuse animosity.
- In sum, do good to those who mistreat you.

The accent in Romans 12 is on personal relationships. What does charity look like in our interactions with believers? With unbelievers? Two tendencies are typical. One, among believers, is to depreciate—perhaps take for granted—the unique gifts that are to be found among members of the body of Christ. Among unbelievers the tendency is to respond improperly to personal insult or injury. The apostle addresses both spheres—church and world—with very concrete recommendations. And if *anyone* understands the agony of personal abuse by the world, it is the apostle. After all:

> it seems to me that God has put us apostles on display, . . . like men condemned to die in the arena. We have been made a spectacle to the whole universe. . . . When we are cursed, we bless; when we are persecuted, we endure it; when we are slandered, we answer kindly. (1 Cor 4:9, 12-13)

How bad is it to be an apostle? "Up to this moment we have become the scum of the earth, the refuse of the world" (v. 13). So, the apostle *understands*.

A shift in focus goes almost unnoticed. There is no transition statement beginning the material in chapter 13. The apostle merely continues his thought, retaining several important themes. Several features unite Romans 12:17-21 and what follows: the accent on evildoing, the contrast between good and evil, and reference to vengeance and God's wrath. Catchwords that appear in Romans 13:1-7 are *servant* (literally, *deacon,* used twice in v. 4, and *liturgist* in v. 6), *wrath, evildoer* and *authority* (six times in 13:1-6). These serve as accent marks on what the apostle wishes to remind his readers.

The apostle's teaching does not remain theoretical; it is intensely practical: "This is also why you pay taxes" (v. 6). Taxes. A sore spot. But instead of adopting a Zealot platform, Paul states the authorities are *owed* something. The language that Paul is using, if we can transplant ourselves into first-century culture, is scandalous to his readers at several levels. First, the very idea that Christians *owe* society (= Rome) seems to go against the grain of Christian teaching. Are we not to *hate* the world? And what, according to the apostle, is "owed"? Strikingly, both the tangible and the intangible. We are to pay taxes as well as revenues (border taxes), and we are to pay honor and respect.

First the tangible—taxes and revenue. To bring up the subject of tax and revenue is to touch a nerve with most citizens of the empire who struggle with Roman imperialism. Historians of antiquity indicate that in Paul's day the total amount of taxation was at oppressive levels. And yet the apostle can say, "*This* is also why you pay taxes." He is maintaining, probably contrary to conventional first-century Christian thinking, that the empire actually benefits their lives in tangible ways.

Next, the intangible—honor and respect. Paul's admonition to demonstrate honor and respect to unbelievers (even those who mistreat us) and the authorities parallels the language of 1 Peter, where we find a conspicuous accent on "respect." To understand this mentality we must enter into the mindset of Greco-Roman culture. We must grasp Peter's argument, namely, that social relationships—from the Caesar to servants (so 1 Pet 2:17)—confirm or negate the Christians' testimony. That is to say, *how* we demonstrate our earthly citizenship is very important. While this may not seem remarkable to some, for many Christians—then and now—it is nothing short of radical. *Respect,* a watchword in 1 Peter, is important because faith seeks to work within the context of cultural conventions. In this sense Christian faith is not countercultural. Ethically, it may be countercultural. But socially, it is committed to live itself out in common social discourse. Christian faith then seeks to work within and through accepted social customs. It acknowledges dual responsibilities, to humans and to God, even when the one is transcendent and commands our ultimate allegiance.

Despite these similarities that unite Romans 12:17-21 and Romans 13:1-7, important contrasts are to be detected. One basic contrast is in the apostle's response to evil. At the personal level evil is to be endured. At the political level, however, it is to incur the sword wielded by the magistrate. Despite the efforts of some commentators to render *sword* in a figurative manner, a first-century audience doubtless would have understood this reference in a literal sense. Whether the implication is capital punishment or war is of secondary importance. Neither the magistrate nor the readers would have made this distinction.

The emphasis of the prior set of exhortations is this: what we might call "vigilante justice" is outlawed in the economy of God. Personal insult and injury are part of the cost of discipleship. Individuals are not permitted to take justice into their own hands. In the hands of the governing authorities, however, justice is not only permitted, it is *required*. Moral-social order depends on it, based on the propensity and social ramifications of the "evil-doer" ("wrongdoer" NIV, Rom 13:3-4). Not to wield the sword is to be delinquent in terms of the role designated by the Almighty for the magistrate.

But what disturbs many of us today is the remarkably uncritical attitude that the apostle seems to have toward government. This is especially the case when we think of sundry forms of uncritical nationalism—even hyper-nationalism—that exist in the world as we know it. Why no checks and balances? What about God-and-country types? Zealots? And irrespective of our politics, why no warnings against the apocalyptic "beast"? Why no denunciation of the Roman imperium, which, after all, waged a "cruel peace" as far as its tentacles could reach?

Two things, it seems to me, must be reaffirmed concerning the governing authorities. First, they function foremost to restrain evil and protect the commonweal. This is the clear teaching of the New Testament. This function is ordained by heaven whether or not those holding office possess any religious faith or are theists. Second, those with governing power receive authority to perform this function from the sovereign God. This authority, to be sure, is a relative authority and not to be usurped, idolized or deified;

nevertheless, it is an authority that is bequeathed by God himself. Therefore, it is unscriptural and counter to orthodox Christian belief, to maintain, as some religious pacifists and ethicists do, that power—specifically, political power—is *inherently evil*. It is not.[1]

The use of power and, by extension, force is the essence of politics and governing. Politics is not politics without power. This should not strike us as controversial. In any political economy the people are subject—some more willingly, some less willingly—to a higher power. This relationship entails both (relative) liberties and (relative) restrictions. Ideally, those liberties they enjoy are benefits that permit them to flourish in society. Those restrictions, assuming we are talking about a democracy, are tolerated in order to preserve some semblance of moral-social order. We in the West refer to this as the "rule of law."

The view that politics and government inhere in and require power is not, to be sure, shared by all. In fact, it is denied by a surprising number of people, even religious people, who nonetheless derive benefits from the system itself. Some opponents of political power are opposed on expressly theological grounds. They believe, like Tertullian in the second century, that because the business of politics and governing will not save us, it is unimportant. Or because it can be an instrument of evil, it is inherently so. Therefore, Christians should invest themselves in other pursuits that are spiritual, other-worldly and, most importantly, Christ-centered.

The second group of opponents, usually secular in their outlook, believes in the inherent goodness of human beings. These individuals invariably strive toward the goal of "world peace" and propose solutions to human pathologies—whether in the political realm or in the social sciences—that are therapeutic or rehabilitative. For these people war is merely something that must be abolished. Peace is the absence of hostility and conflict and must be secured at all cost.

What both of these visions, the "christocentric" and the "anthropocentric," have in common is a general disdain for politics and power—that is, until

---

[1]Consider, for example, some of the titles of more recent books by religious publishers making this argument—power is inherently evil: *Powers and Submissions, Engaging the Powers, Unmasking the Powers,* and *Naming the Powers.* While these books incorporate spiritual forces in the general category of "powers," their critique inevitably extends to governing powers, and alas, to the U.S. government and its purported imperialistic foreign policy. Not surprisingly, their critique is quite selective and politically partisan, bereft of any prudential considerations for responsible policy-making in civil society.

the secular opponents of power are ushered into political power, at which point there is a curious conversion of beliefs! Power politics, all of a sudden, is something to be preserved at any cost.

But I digress. The point to be made is this: society is by nature political because politics is the ordering of the *polis,* the community, toward right ends. Humans are by nature *political.* Therefore, the question to be considered is, Will political decisions and political action be guided by moral means? Will the exercise of power be subject to moral criteria? Such baseline thinking applies to both domestic as well as foreign policy. This is why most politicians, at least in the Western quasi-democratic context, take oaths upon assuming office. Why do they do this? They are thereby acknowledging that there is a proper and improper mode of governing, and that they are (at least nominally) accountable to the populace as well as to law and the principles that uphold it.

Governing authority is neutral and can be used for better or for worse, for good or for evil. While society does not *rest* on power, it needs power to subsist. By what standard then is governing power considered legitimate? To the extent that it promotes justice and seeks to counter injustice. In the end this litmus test is eminently moral. And because justice in most Western societies is increasingly defined in legal—which is to say, procedural—terms, not all laws, as we intuit, reflect justice. It then becomes the sobering responsibility of those holding office, as well as the electorate in democratic societies, to work for justice, so that over time their laws are a closer reflection of what is truly just.

But if we as citizens are convinced that politics and power are inherently corrupt, it is guaranteed that we will *not* involve ourselves at all in the political process. Rather, we will isolate ourselves from precisely those cultural institutions that need our influence. This state of affairs, however, is unacceptable, regardless of the theological justification with which it may cloak itself. "If the salt has lost its savor. . . . People don't light a lamp and put it under a bowl."[2]

RETHINKING THE "POLITICS OF JESUS"

In chapter two I noted that the lack of universal consensus among early

---

[2]On the neutrality and significance of politics and power, see chapter one, "The Uses of Power," in Paul Ramsey, *The Just War* (New York: Charles Scribner's, 1968), pp. 3-18, originally published in *The New York Times,* May 20, 1964.

Christians regarding the state. Attitudes toward soldiering and participation in war appear more varied and complex than most accounts suggest. To reconsider this evidence, while it is not the whole story, is important as we examine our own attitudes in the face of perplexing issues. There is a tendency, past and present, to oversimplify Christian perspectives on war and the military based on our particular experience or religious tradition. As one who grew up in a Mennonite home and whose father was a conscientious objector during World War II, I understand the tensions between Christians who strongly disagree.

For those believers who care to allow Christian history to inform their faith, reading classical texts can be both threatening and liberating. Threatening because to interact with Ambrose and Augustine, Aquinas and Calvin, Niebuhr and Ramsey is to put our own beliefs up to scrutiny. What has the mainstream of the church believed throughout centuries? And on what basis? But it is liberating as well, because to submit our cherished assumptions to the wider wisdom of the church's consensus is to protect us from myopic and sectarian tendencies. It is to safeguard us from adopting beliefs that depart from the witness of Scripture, from the church's consensual understanding and from the witness of reason and natural moral law.

No religious dissent toward war and soldiering has been set forth as effectively as the Anabaptist position in recent decades. While myriads of writers have adopted this view, it has been argued perhaps most eloquently by Anabaptist writers such as John Howard Yoder[3] and Myron Augsburger,[4] as well as by Methodist Stanley Hauerwas,[5] who has sought to further Yoder's Anabaptist position. The call of Yoder and company is a call for the true church to leave the world and to form communities that by their very existence are a light to the world. This call is commendable in its aim, even when its means of enactment, withdrawal, is regrettable. Their call, further-

---

[3]See, in particular, John Howard Yoder, *Nevertheless: The Varieties of Religious Pacifism* (Scottdale: Herald Press, 1971); *The Original Revolution* (Scottdale: Herald Press, 1971); *What Would You Do?* (Scottdale: Herald Press, 1983); *The Politics of Jesus,* rev. ed. (Grand Rapids: Eerdmans, 1994); and *When War Is Unjust* (Maryknoll, N.Y.: Orbis, 1996).

[4]See, for example, Myron Augsburger, "Christian Pacifism," in *War: Four Christian Views,* ed. Robert G. Clouse, rev. ed. (Downers Grove, Ill.: InterVarsity Press, 1991), pp. 79-97.

[5]See, for example, Stanley Hauerwas, *Against the Nations* (Minneapolis: Winston Press, 1985), in which he contends that all Christians should be pacifists, and his book *The Peaceable Kingdom* (Notre Dame, Ind.: University of Notre Dame Press, 1983), in which he argues that the ethic of Jesus is an ethic of pacifism and that pacifism is *the* shape of Christian conviction about God and witness to the world.

more, is to downplay the implications of Romans 13:1-7 while elevating Matthew 5:38-39 as the embodiment of Jesus' "love-ethic."

In his important work *The Politics of Jesus*, published in 1972 and reissued in 1994, Yoder argues that Romans 13:1-7 is not the center of the New Testament's teaching on the state. Moreover, he maintains that the "sword" (Rom 13:4) is merely symbolic of legal function and is not intended to bespeak the death penalty or war as (literal) punishment for temporal evil. Consistent with his Anabaptist forebears, Yoder understandably maintains that Christians are not to participate in the affairs of the state. To do so is to collaborate with evil. Where Yoder breaks with the early Anabaptists is his refusal to acknowledge that God has instituted political power and ordained the sword for the purpose of civil order and that this function is necessary.

But in what way do we "collaborate"? We are accomplices if we fail to comprehend the fallenness of the powers of this age. The "normative" understanding of the powers found in the New Testament, as Yoder sees it, is their intractable hostility toward the people of God, such as we find in the New Testament Apocalypse. In John's visions the powers are at war with the Lamb, and the Lamb is at war with the powers. But the Lamb overcomes the powers by his death and the cross. Therefore, Christian believers are to view the powers as enemies of the faith.[6]

Yoder's assumptions about government in the New Testament are extended to the early church. The reason for Christians' acquiescence to the state in the fourth century and their increasing involvement in the affairs of the state from Constantine onward is readily explained. For Yoder this development is the result of Christian "compromise." Christians became co-opted by the empire, and with the end of formal persecution the church lost its prophetic witness. Gone was the pristine beauty and purity that characterized earlier generations of believers.

There is something in the vision articulated by Yoder that is quite appealing due to its desire for purity and its idealism. And while it contains partial truth, it is insufficient at several levels. To begin, this "radical critique of Constantinianism" fails to recognize the diversity of Christian opinion among early Christians. Believers of the first centuries were not uniformly (and universally) pacifist, as we have already observed. The Anabaptist critique moreover fails to wrestle sufficiently with the responsibilities of our dual cit-

---

[6]Chaps. 6, 8, 10 and 12 of *Politics of Jesus* contain the principal parts of Yoder's argument.

izenship, as Augustine painstakingly sought to mirror them. Yes, it is true that we are called to an ultimate allegiance—that of the kingdom of heaven. But we remain citizens of the earthly kingdom, and our citizenship entails responsible "occupation," as Jesus described it. Related to this, Yoder's portrait of "Constantinian" is simplistic in that we are asked to believe that all of a sudden, without much preparation or Christian reflection, the church is now the handmaiden of the regime. Just as elections change administrations due to a change in the ruling political party, so Christians were now friends with the state. This reading of the third, fourth and earlier fifth centuries fails historically. At the very least it ignores the writings of Ambrose and Augustine themselves, who are not lackeys of the state but rather conscious of the tensions between earthly and heavenly duties.

According to the Anabaptist model, Christians may not—indeed, *must not*—serve as magistrates or soldiers. But the list does not end there. Neither should they be policy-makers or legal theorists or economists (or tax collectors) or policemen or security guards or drivers of Brinks trucks or public clerks or . . . In the end the Anabaptist call to remove ourselves from the world is interpreted rather literally, so that, for fear of being compromised by "the powers," we do not involve ourselves in mainstream institutions of society. In its place we build our "prophetic" communities on the side.

The difficulties with this way of thinking—a view not shared by mainstream Christian thinkers through the centuries—are multiple. At the most basic level this reading of the early church tends to oversimplify the ethical dilemmas that early believers faced. And it oversimplifies the data available as to the diversity of the church in various regions of the ancient world. Those ancient witnesses that do not fit the standard pacifist portrait of early Christians tend to be ignored.

A further problem with this model is hermeneutical or interpretive. At the most fundamental level this reading of the New Testament errs in its assumption that the view of the powers we find in apocalyptic literature (notably, in Revelation) is normative. But this is not the case. The powers are *both* fallen *and* in service to the purposes of God almighty. *Both* strands are represented in the teaching of the New Testament. While responsible interpretation does not argue that Romans 13 says everything about government that is true, neither do John's apocalyptic visions.

At another interpretive level the Anabaptist reading of Scripture wrongly presumes *ethical discontinuity* between the Old and New Testaments. That is, it erects a false dichotomy between judgment and mercy, between justice and love, falsely assuming that justice characterized the Old scheme while love is the benchmark of the New. This interpretive flaw, which has disastrous implications for both theology and ethics, is based on a misreading of the New Testament—and the Sermon on the Mount in particular—and needs considerable theological refinement. More needs to be said in this regard, but we will return to this concern later.

Yet a further problem, relating to aforementioned, is intensely practical, even when it has theological roots. In my opinion it will not do to remove ourselves, as Anabaptists would have it, from the messy business of tending the world. As stewards of creation we must not selectively pick and choose what we should tend in the world (*if* we choose to tend anything!). Unless a vocation clearly and expressly violates moral principles (which soldiering, politics and political science, law enforcement and policy work do not), it is appropriate for Christians to occupy these vocations, seeking to bring glory to their Creator as best they can within fallen social structures.

To illustrate: if Christians cannot in good conscience serve as security guards or policemen or soldiers or magistrates or policy analysts or judges or parole officers, then it is altogether fair to make the following demand. To the point: we *may not* in good conscience expect that *others* be required to officiate, adjudicate, protect or provide for social benefits and privileges in a free society in which we are not willing to participate and yet from which we expect to receive privileges. Something is exceedingly wrong with this picture. For after all, even Anabaptists and pacifists in general profit from law and order that serve to furnish peace and stability in society. The presumptuous (to my way of thinking) attitude of "Let the Gentiles do it!" that underlies this particular mindset of civic disengagement is simply unsatisfactory. If the messy business of protecting street corners, neighborhoods, bank accounts, buildings, cities and borders—or wrestling with policies that affect these realms—is to be left to unbelievers, as some believe, then the benefits of those services to society should fall only to those who recognize their worth.

Perhaps at this point I am guilty of overstatement. Is this judgment a bit harsh? I think not. I merely wish to argue for consistency. Very often today the pacifist position is the easy way out of civic duty. When people such as Augustine and Aquinas and Luther argued that one can be a soldier and a Christian, that one's duty may include the protection of others, that indeed one can even use *coercive force* to achieve such *and be motivated by charity,* then contemporary Christians—pacifists in particular—need to consider the moral consistency of their position. And while pacifism as self-defense is morally legitimate, pacifism as public policy is not. *Someone* must protect society. *Someone* must protect the citizenry. *Someone* must protect the neighborhood. *Someone* must perform those untidy public services that often are taken for granted. To say that Christians cannot serve in such positions or that political power is inherently evil or that force cannot serve just purposes is simply misguided and lacking support from the Christian Scriptures. Moreover, it is thoroughly out of line with mainstream Christian thinking about vocation throughout the ages, even when it is currently regnant within the academy.

Recall our discussion in chapter two of Ambrose and Augustine. One of the chief motivations behind Ambrose's tract *On the Duties of the Clergy* and Augustine's *City of God* was the concern that Christians would extract themselves from the world and not be involved in the affairs of society as they awaited the arrival of the eschaton. My hunch is that the fabulously successful Left Behind series would have been a blockbuster in Augustine's day, as dominant culture was collapsing right before his eyes.

Yet we find in mainstream Christian thinking throughout the ages a call not to withdraw but to infiltrate society in a variety of ways. This may legitimately include protecting others and safeguarding the common good. Several common features are to be found in Christian writers from the past as they reflected on just means and just ends. Virtually all of the just-war thinkers noted in this book, beginning with Ambrose and Augustine, are sensitive to the New Testament's witness regarding soldiering. And all take note of the curious inclusion by Luke of John the Baptist's encounter with soldiers and tax collectors (both of whom doubtless were despised by Christian believers). The account found in Luke 3:7-14, like the other Synoptic accounts, frames the encounter in terms of repentance. The demands of the Baptist are clearly ethical: "Produce fruit in keeping with your repentance!" "But what should we do then?" the crowd asks. Among the three categories of people being exhorted by John are soldiers. "Then some soldiers asked, 'And what should we do?'" To which John replies, "Do not extort money and don't accuse people falsely—be content with your pay."

RETHINKING THE ETHICS OF THE NEW TESTAMENT

Previously we noted the tendency among some to highlight justice in the Old Testament while emphasizing love in the New. This love as taught by

Jesus, so the argument goes, is conspicuously nonviolent and pacifist in character. Beginning with the admonition to be "peacemakers" (Mt 5:9), this view is based on a particular reading of the Sermon on the Mount (Mt 5—7) that understands Jesus' teaching as a call to nonviolence. A crux text in this narrative is Matthew 5:38-39. A frequent reading of this text renders the "eye for eye" principle obsolete and interprets the calls "do not resist an evil person" and "turn the other cheek" as flat prohibitions of forceful defense. But is this the intended meaning?

The ethics of the Sermon on the Mount is clearly one of doing. Before the specific case illustrations of his attitude toward the law (Mt 5:21-48), Jesus admonishes his disciples to be the salt of the earth and the light of the world (Mt 5:13-16). Both metaphors call the reader/listener to action—concrete deeds that verify character. Salt serves as a preservative in society, as the audience readily understood. And light exists for one purpose: to be seen by others. Jesus' call is a call to good works: "that they [others] may see your good deeds and praise your Father in heaven."

But a common misperception about the kingdom of God and Jesus' call seems to persist. "Do not think that I have come," he warns the audience, "to abolish the Law or the Prophets; I have not come to abolish them but to fulfill them. I tell you the truth, until heaven and earth disappear, not the smallest letter, not the least stroke of a pen, will by any means disappear from the Law until everything is accomplished" (Mt 5:17-18). In fact, lest there be any question, further qualification ensures: "Anyone who breaks one of the least of these commandments and teaches others to do the same will be called least in the kingdom of heaven, but whoever practices and teaches these commands will be called great in the kingdom of heaven" (Mt 5:19). An impediment to right understanding about ethics, we learn, is what religious leaders of the day are teaching and doing. Hence, this warning: "Unless your righteousness surpasses that of the Pharisees and teachers of the law, you will certainly not enter the kingdom of heaven" (Mt 5:20).

Several remarks need to be made. In the thinking of Jesus there is no ethical discontinuity between the kingdom of God and the period of the Old Testament. The words "Do not think that I have come" are filled with fire. And they are intended to address a distortion—doubtless a common distortion—in the thinking of many religious contemporaries. And what is that distortion? The idea that somehow works and judgment are the essence of the former economy but now love, grace and mercy have come and displaced them. In short, it is the view that sees the ethical demands of the law and the gospel as discontinuous.[7]

Love and justice, grace and works, mercy and judgment—these are seeming opposites. To our way of thinking they stand in tension, negating one another. The popular perception—then and now—is that Jesus dispenses with the necessity of works or that no grace existed in Israel or that the disciple's ethical standard has now changed. But this is decidedly *not* the case. Both poles in the ethical tension between love and justice, mercy and judgment, grace and works are related, representing two sides of the same ethical coin.[8] They must not be divorced; they must be held in reconcilable tension. The purpose of this prologue to the Sermon, and the material that follows, is to emphasize ethical *continuity,* not discontinuity.

Matthew 5:17-20 serves as a necessary introduction and qualification of the six case illustrations that follow—anger, lust, divorce, oaths, retaliation and love for one's enemies. Each case highlights an aspect of Old Testament law, with its ethical requirement, that is being reaffirmed. What is being set aside in each of the six cases is not the law per se as an ethical standard (recall the exhortation of vv. 17-19), rather it is contemporary misunderstandings that surround the law that require radical adjustment. And who is responsible for these misunderstandings? Much blame must be laid at the feet of the scribes and Pharisees (v. 20).

Certainly the matter of retaliation (Mt 5:38-42) challenges Christian ethics as few issues. This illustration begins with the formula that Jesus has already used four times previously—"You have heard that it was said, . . . but I tell you . . ." While some students of the Bible interpret these words as referring to Old Testament—and specifically, Mosaic—law, such a reading does not fit the context. To introduce his teaching Jesus had just reiterated that the law as revealed in the old covenant and continually reaffirmed by the prophets is not to be thought as set aside (v. 17); it is binding. Thus Jesus cannot be contradicting himself. What the context *does* require, however, is that contemporary notions—wrong contemporary notions—need adjustment. One such illustration of contemporary error concerns retaliation.

---

[7]While people such as Aquinas, Luther and Calvin distinguished between three types of law—moral, ceremonial and civil—first-century Jews who became Christians would not have thought in these terms.

[8]Elsewhere I have addressed this tendency in religious thinking to erect false dichotomies. See chap. 9 of *The Unformed Conscience of Evangelicalism* (Downers Grove, Ill.: InterVarsity Press, 2002), in which I describe an "ethics of polarity."

The words "eye for an eye and tooth for a tooth" correspond to what is called the *lex talionis* or the "law of the tooth"—a law that has parallels in most ancient cultures. According to Old Testament law, just forms of retribution (Lev 24:19-20; Deut 19:21) and restitution (Ex 21:24) were described in terms of proportionality; hence the language of "eye for eye, tooth for tooth." Much confusion surrounds our understanding of this measurement. Far from being harsh and uncivilized, it represents "the beginnings of mercy," as one biblical commentator writes.[9] That is, this measure places a limitation on vengeance. It specifies that (1) only the *guilty* may be punished, and (2) such punishment *may not exceed* certain limits.

What's more, no private citizen could exact retribution. Rather, this was the responsibility of judges, as Deuteronomy 19:15-21 makes clear. In contrast to pagan cultures, which exercised variation of the "law of the tooth," in Israel this was not carried out literally. In time, just payment of restitution for injury was assessed along financial lines. However, by Jesus' day rabbinic reinterpretation of "just rewards" for personal injury had become illegitimate in and of itself, and this misuse of "the law of the tooth" seems to lie behind Jesus' teaching on the subject.

The important point to be made is this: Jesus is not setting aside the idea of restitution itself, nor the "law of the tooth" as a standard of public justice. To the contrary, the story of Zacchaeus (Lk 19) is a reminder that our Lord affirmed the Old Testament measure for restitution. The apostle Paul furthermore implies the same in his teaching on what we "owe" others. Jesus is however challenging his listeners to consider their attitudes so that they respond properly to *personal* injustice or insult. That insult (personal injury) rather than assault (public injury) is at issue here is suggested by the mention of the right cheek being struck. And it is clarified by the further illustration "if someone wants to . . . take your tunic, let him have your cloak as well" (Mt 5:40). Handling insults and matters of clothing (a basic human need) are not the realm of the state and public policy.

The injunction not to resist evil, contextually, must be located in the realm of personal injury, not state policy. Matthew 5—7 is not intended to be a statement on the nature and jurisdiction of the state or the governing authorities. Its affinities are most closely with Romans 12:17-21, not Romans 13:1-7. In the sphere of the private, justice does not call for retribution. In

[9]William Barclay, *The Gospel of Matthew*, Daily Study Bible, rev. ed. (Philadelphia: Westminster Press, 1975), p. 163.

the sphere of the public, where the magistrate is commissioned to protect and defend the common good, justice *demands* retribution. This is the unambiguous teaching of the New Testament.

In several chapters we have already noted that the injunctions to "not resist evil" and "turn the other cheek" in Matthew 5:38-39 are widely used to justify the pacifist position. This was true of Ambrose's and Augustine's day, it was true of Aquinas's day, and it was true in Luther's day. And it continues to be cited by religious pacifists. We also noted the response by these fathers of the church. Their voice is one. All make the distinction between personal and public grievances, between matters of the heart and matters of state. While Aquinas and Luther differ with Ambrose and Augustine on the question of self-defense,[10] all agree that the Christian must resist evil to protect others, although the form of this resistance will always differ and depend on the particular situation.

In his essay "Why I Am Not a Pacifist," C. S. Lewis considers Jesus' injunction regarding "turning the other cheek." His conclusion is that this cannot be intended to rule out protecting others. "Does anyone suppose," he asks, "that our Lord's hearers understood him to mean that if a homicidal maniac, attempting to murder a third party, tried to knock me out of the way, I must stand aside and let him get his victim?"[11] If Jesus called for *absolute* nonviolence based on Matthew 5:38-39, then we would be under obligation to *turn the cheek of a third party.* Lewis prefers to contextualize Matthew 5:38-39 in the following manner. Jesus' audience consisted of "private people in a disarmed nation," and "[w]ar was not what they would have been thinking of" by any stretch of the imagination.[12] Lewis's understanding proceeds on a plain reading of the text.

Even when Jesus forbids the sword as a means to advance the kingdom of God, the New Testament does not teach absolute pacifism. Nor does it forbid the Christian from "bearing the sword" in the service of society and the greater social good. There is simply no suggestion in the New Testament that military service—*in any form*—is incompatible with Christian faith.[13]

---

[10]Forgoing self-defense is not required by biblical teaching.

[11]C. S. Lewis, "Why I Am Not a Pacifist," in *The Weight of Glory and Other Addresses,* ed. Walter Hooper, rev. ed. (New York: Macmillan, 1965), pp. 49-50.

[12]Ibid., p. 50. Significantly, Jesus does not offer "the other cheek" when struck by an official during his own trial before the high priest (Jn 18:19-24).

[13]Donald Bloesch has accurately observed that pacifism mistakenly substitutes the principle of nonviolence for divine commandment (*Freedom for Obedience: Evangelical Ethics for Contemporary Times* [San Francisco: Harper & Row, 1987], pp. 293-94).

RETHINKING PACIFISM AND THE NONVIOLENT IMPERATIVE

World War I was to be the "war to end all wars." As it turned out, this hope was premature. And yet for almost a century since, the dream of world peace has lived on. The vision of the lion lying with the lamb, so clearly indicated by Scripture as representing a *future* age, retains its appeal to the present day. For the religious believer, however, whose faith is anchored in historic Christian belief, the hope of an age of peace, in which evil has been vanquished and humankind is freed from sin's tyranny, lies in the future, following the last battle.[14]

But despite this preview of history, the alternative vision lives on with extraordinary resiliency. And it has both secular and religious proponents. Those who call us to a higher plane of nonviolence, to "war without weapons" and "world peace," would attempt to adjust our understanding of reality with their visions. Swords and spears should—nay, *must*—be given up in favor of ploughshares and pruning hooks in the present economy. According to this vision, life, liberty and communal bonds can exist without violence, without fighting, without war. And as it turns out, *without evildoing and without statecraft.*

To my way of thinking it is altogether fascinating that a non-Christian such as political scientist Michael Walzer has delivered one of the most powerful critiques of the pacifist position, which as he understands it, has been fueled by a sectarian reading of the Christian Scriptures. Listen to Walzer as he thinks through the consequences of the nonviolent position to their conclusion:

> Nonviolent defense differs from conventional strategies in that it concedes the overrunning of the country that is being defended. It establishes no obstacles capable of stopping a military advance or preventing a military occupation. . . . This is a radical concession, and I don't think that any government has ever made it willingly.[15]

Walzer wishes to follow the nonviolent position consistently to its logical end, and it seems to me that he has a point. There is as yet no evidence that this proposition—*nonviolence triumphs over tyranny*—is true. There are no

---

[14]This seems to be the implication of Jesus' statement, "You will hear of wars and rumors of wars, but see to it that your are not alarmed. Such things must happen, but the end is still to come" (Mt 24:6; Mk 13:7).
[15]Michael Walzer, *Just and Unjust Wars* (New York: Basic Books, 1977), p. 330.

cases in which civilian defense, based on nonviolence, has caused an invader to withdraw, a potential invader not to invade or a tyrant to cease and desist from his oppressive deeds. Can it be that to play the role of the lamb is *in truth* to provoke the wolf? We will doubtless never really know the hollowness of Ben Franklin's quip, "There never was a good war or a bad peace." Ask the victim of totalitarianism if there is such a thing as "bad peace."[16]

Now perhaps it might be argued that the holy war mentality of the Crusades or mistaken judgments made in World War II or the Vietnam War cancel any possibility of war being morally justified. But in response I would simply reiterate this: the just-war position, rooted in universal moral (i.e., natural) law is normative and applicable to all people in any era. That nations and kingdoms can disavow or neglect what natural law teaches is not an argument against its existence. People disobey the Ten Commandments as well, but this in no way invalidates the moral reality behind these laws. Like the Ten Commandments, the just-war ideal is universally binding, regardless of whether they are taken seriously or how well they are applied.[17] Just-war principles, properly understood, are not to be construed as immutable laws that precisely fit geopolitical events. Rather, they clarify circumstances and conditions that justify reluctantly going to war.

Or perhaps it might be argued that nonviolence discourages or abolishes war simply on the basis of its refusal to engage in violent activity. That is, nonviolence deescalates potential conflicts by transforming aggression into cautious reflection. As a result the aggressor refrains from engaging militarily. Again, intellectual honesty of the type Michael Walzer calls for requires that we verify if this sort of "transforming vision" has in fact worked.[18] Does pacifism provide governments—*all* governments, and particularly those nondemocratic varieties where its influence is most severely needed—as well as societies with the political-moral wherewithal to develop and enact wise policy decisions? Can pacifism realistically serve as a basis for criminal justice and foreign policy? What might that look like? Has pacifism helped resolve international conflict, prevent wars

---

[16]George Weigel, in his important book *Tranquillitas Ordinis* writes: "But between the peace of tyranny and the eschatological peace of shalom is the peace of dynamic, rightly ordered political community" ([New York: Oxford University Press, 1987], p. 45).

[17]Arthur Holmes has argued this point cogently in "The Just War," in *War: Four Christian Views*, ed. Robert G. Clouse, rev. ed. (Downers Grove, Ill.: InterVarsity Press, 1991), pp. 118-20.

[18]Perhaps, it might be argued, all nations should aspire to be like modern-day Switzerland.

or crimes against humanity? Has it countered or negated political totalitarianism?

What complicates matters for pacifists is the emergence since the 1960s
of two troubling tendencies. One is the conspicuously proactive attempts by
pacifist organizations to undermine the foreign policy of free, democratic
nations. Unlike my father, a Mennonite conscientious objector who served
in a Veterans Hospital as alternative service during World War II, the typical
pacifist today is less interested in serving others than in making a political
statement or sabotaging established foreign policy. This has frequently had
the effect of abetting (wittingly or unwittingly) totalitarian regimes. In fact,
in many circles wholesale criticism and denunciation of nations that defend
human rights and democratic processes is quite fashionable, even seen as a
mark of intellectual respectability. My point is not that there can be no disagreement over a nation's foreign policy; indeed, there needs to be such in
a democratic context. Rather, I only wish to point out that the character of
pacifism has changed. It has compromised itself and been co-opted by
forces other than originally intended.

A second development is related; it issues out of the first, but is more intentional in its design. Not a few pacifists have proactively defended the
moral legitimacy of Marxist, neo-Marxist or fanatical Muslim "armed struggle" and terrorism in various parts of the world. And more often than not
this moral support has translated into active support for groups and governments that are known for egregious human rights violations. Why is it that
pacifists frequently turn a deaf ear, as it were, to totalitarian regimes while
being so critical of democracy? After all, among the nations of the world it
is precisely democratic culture that has successfully and continuously demonstrated nonviolent solutions to social issues. Democracies do not go to
war with one another. Why is that? What should that suggest to the pacifist?

Tragically, both of the aforementioned developments have undermined
the integrity and original aim of American pacifism.[19] And unhappily, sympathy with both of these trends has been increasing among Protestant
churches, evidenced by some of the excesses of the World Council of
Churches and the National Council of Churches over the last twenty-five
years; in no way is it confined to historic Anabaptists (i.e., Mennonites,

---

[19]A devastating critique of these two problems in American pacifism can be found in Guenter
Lewy's important book *Peace and Revolution: The Moral Crisis of American Pacifism* (Grand
Rapids: Eerdmans, 1988).

Brethren and Quakers).[20] Is there a "moral crisis" in American pacifism? A considerable number of thoughtful social critics believe there is.[21] I am inclined to agree. What confirms my suspicion is the obsession of most contemporary pacifists with the flaws of so-called democratic nations (the United States in particular), while being indifferent to egregious and mass human rights violations in dictatorial regimes around the world. Reinhold Niebuhr properly condemned this moral inversion by noting that however serious democratic nations' failure to conform to democratic ideals might be, "it is sheer moral perversity to equate the inconsistencies of a democratic civilization with the brutalities which modern tyrannical states practice."[22]

Reinhold Niebuhr stated the truth quite succinctly during World War II. It is one thing to refuse to participate in war based on principle, even a noble thing to do so with great sacrifice. It is quite another thing to advocate "a policy of submission to injustice, whereby lives and interests other than our own are defrauded or destroyed."[23] Pacifists, in the view of writer Guenter Lewy, have "every right to avoid the moral dilemmas posed by the world of statesmanship and statecraft and to seek individual salvation through ethical absolutism and purity, but they have no right to sacrifice others for this end."[24] And any distinction between absolute pacifism and relative pacifism (which in theory *might* acknowledge some wars as justified) at this point is immaterial. Both positions are inherently flawed and deviate from the church's traditional teaching. Either we are called to be nonviolent *all the time* or we are called to act justly and discriminate between what is just and unjust use of force.

The nonviolent vision is a very appealing, if not millennial, picture, to be sure. But does it correspond to world in which we live and which we must

---

[20]It should be pointed out, however, that this commitment to political "radicalism" within mainline churches is more prominent at the level of denominational leadership and in the seminaries than among the laity. For a balanced insider's critique of these developments, pro and con, from pacifist activists as well as nonpacifists, see Michael Cromartie, ed., *Peace Betrayed?* (Washington, D.C.: Ethics and Public Policy Center, 1990). This volume is comprised of fifteen essays that emerged from a spirited (and at times, volatile) roundtable discussion in the nation's capital of contemporary pacifism.

[21]See, for example, the debate that unfolds in Cromartie, ed., *Peace Betrayed?*

[22]Reinhold Niebuhr, "Why the Church Is Not Pacifist," in *Christianity and Power Politics* (New York: Charles Scribner's, 1940), p. 17. Niebuhr called this perverse way of thinking "confused religious absolutism" (ibid.).

[23]Reinhold Niebuhr, "The Christian Faith and the World Crisis," *Christianity and Crisis* 10 (1941): 4.

[24]Guenter Lewy, "The Moral Crisis of American Pacifism," in *Peace Betrayed?* ed. Michael Cromartie (Washington, D.C.: Ethics and Public Policy Center, 1990), p. 35.

occupy? Even Mohandas Gandhi himself, lauded by pacifists the world over, leaves room for serious questioning. Consider the doubts raised by George Orwell, who spent years as a journalist in India: "It is difficult to see how Gandhi's methods could be applied in a country where opponents of the regime disappear in the middle of the night and are never heard from again."[25] Orwell, it needs to be remembered, was writing against the backdrop of communist tyranny in the 1940s. With millions disappearing into labor camps, the nonviolent vision seemed not to be working well in the Soviet Union. Correlatively, if we absolutize the distinction between nonviolent and violent resistance, as pacifism does, we arrive at the morally absurd position that Reinhold Niebuhr pointed out. That is, we give preference to "nonviolent" power that a Joseph Goebbels, Hitler's extraordinary propaganda minister, wields over that of a military officer.[26]

What is more, Gandhi's method is powerless and inefficacious against tyranny as we have known it in the last century. Consider recent estimates of the number of deaths in the twentieth century due to conventional war—around 30 million—and to *political tyranny and totalitarianism*—between 100 and 200 million. In his introduction to *The Black Book of Communism,* published in 1999 and causing an uproar in France at the time, French historian Stephane Courtois breaks down according to individuals nation-states the total numbers of victims who were sacrificed to communist ideology.[27] Truly, the stench of death surrounding Marxist-Leninist ideology is extraordinary. The total estimate in any case dwarfs Nazism's remarkable achievement within a shorter span of years of approximately 25 million deaths, based on our current reckoning. We find ourselves powerless to grasp the significance of 100 million *or* 25 million deaths. Such boggles the mind. And yet we dare not grow numb to their reality, much of which has occurred within our lifetime. They remain before us and exist for our benefit, to teach us and to humble us. The "just warrior" understands this.

---

[25]George Orwell, *The Collected Essays, Journalism and Letters of George Orwell,* ed. Sonia Orwell and Ian Angus (New York: Harcourt Brace Janovich, 1968), 4:469.

[26]Reinhold Niebuhr, *Christianity and Power Politics* (New York: Charles Scribner's, 1940), p. 8.

[27]The estimate given by Stephane Courtois et al. in the introduction of *The Black Book of Communism,* trans. J. Murphy and M. Kramer (Cambridge, Mass.: Harvard University Press, 1999) is at around 100 million. The authors' rough breakdown is as follows: U.S.S.R., 20 million; China, 65 million; Vietnam, 1 million; Cambodia, 2 million; North Korea, 2 million; Eastern Europe, 1 million; Latin American, 150,000; Africa, 1.7 million; Afghanistan, 1.5 million. The estimate of military historian Robert Conquest, *Reflections on a Ravaged Century* (New York: W. W. Norton, 2001) is in the 170 million range.

What are we to make of Gandhi's rather perverse advice to the Jews of Germany, namely, that they should commit suicide rather than fight back against Nazi tyranny? Is this the moral path? As Walzer poignantly remarks, in Gandhi's case nonviolence "collapses into violence directed at oneself rather than at one's murderers."[28] But ask the Jew who was liberated by American tanks at the end of World War II. He or she knows that force can be a moral entity.

In the end, I must admit I am not particularly drawn to Gandhi's vision. And I am inclined to agree with Walzer. Something must be done proactively to resist evil.[29] Augustine, in my view, had it right: "War and conquest are a sad necessity in the eyes of men of principle, yet it would be still more unfortunate if wrongdoers should dominate just men."[30] For this reason he was insistent on a justly ordered peace. In our own day Pope John Paul II has reminded us of the same:

> Peace requires justice, an attitude which recognizes the dignity and equality of all men and women, and a firm commitment to strive and protect the basic human rights of all. Where there is no justice there can be no peace. Peace is possible only where there is a just order that ensures the rights of everyone.[31]

A nagging possibility remains. When there is no moral code that requires of us active resistance to political-social evil when it appears, nonviolence would appear to be one of the following: (1) a way of shirking civic duties as a noncitizen, (2) a disguised form of surrender to tyranny, or (3) in the words of Michael Walzer, "a minimalist way of upholding communal values

---

[28]Walzer, *Just and Unjust Wars,* p. 332.
[29]A similar moral failure is reflected in the comments of Lee Griffith, who cannot distinguish between the criminal and the retributive act: "Once one justifies the use of violence, one should not be surprised to find that the line between just warrior and terrorist can be very fine indeed" (*The War on Terrorism and the Terror of God* [Grand Rapids: Eerdmans, 2002], p. 19). If the line between good and evil is so fuzzy, as Griffith would have us believe, then policemen are unnecessary, and to hell with criminal justice in any form. By this sort of calculus, there is simply no point whatsoever in trying to address and rectify injustice. It should be pointed out that all applications of force, according to Griffith, are "terror," an entity that Griffith would reserve for God alone. In Griffith's world criminals are to be struck dead in the very act, or to be left flourishing; law-enforcement officers are at best superfluous and at worst a negation of authentic faith. But more importantly, in Griffith's world, the use of force and not evil deeds per se constitutes the worst evil imaginable: "It is time to acknowledge that the 'just war' doctrine is one of the greatest sins that Christendom has visited upon humanity" (pp. 277-78).
[30]Augustine *City of God* 4.12.
[31]From John Paul II's World Peace Day speech of January 1, 2003 <www.vatican.va/holy_father/john_paul_ii/messages/peace/documents/hf_jp-ii_mes_20021217_xxxvi-world-day-for-peace_en.html>.

after a military defeat."[32] It is difficult to see any other possibilities, simply because of the rejection or avoidance of responsible statecraft in the paradigm of the nonviolent activist.[33] C. S. Lewis came to a similar conclusion as Walzer. In considering the assumptions of pacifism Lewis put it this way: a nation may be handed over to its totalitarian oppressor, which tolerates neither just warriors nor pacifists. Pacifism, if it does not clothe itself in martyrdom, is in the end self-defeating.[34]

But we need not dwell on a worst-case scenario such as all-out war to evaluate the morality of the pacifist position. We must examine its assumptions. Referring to the events of the Second World War, Reinhold Niebuhr reminded his audience of the need "to bear witness to the truth of Christ against the secular substitutes . . . which failed to anticipate, and which may have helped create the tragic world in which we now live."[35] Wartime experience, as he saw it, presented us with an "opportunity to bring the truth of the Word of God to bear upon the secular roots if our present predicament." Niebuhr believed that war is an expression of "divine judgment . . . visited upon men and nations."[36] The issue of war, then, forces us to reconsider our basic theological beliefs and worldview.

As Niebuhr saw it, one purpose that war serves is to show the folly of those who believe that "the sinfulness of all men" is "outmoded." Those who think that humans progress morally need only consider the entire historical process. Belief in the goodness of man turns out to be an illusion. "In a day of complacency and security," writes Niebuhr, "the Christian Church must anticipate the judgment which is to come and declare that the day of the Lord will be darkness and not light." Niebuhr wishes to torpedo any false

---

[32]Walzer, *Just and Unjust Wars,* p. 333.
[33]The Mennonite spokesperson Myron Augsburger writes that "my theology does not ask the church to tell the state how to arm itself for the fulfillment of its mandate of defending its shores" ("A Christian Pacifist Response," p. 179). In this light I do not see much merit in Stanley Hauerwas's argument that pacifists should be involved in political activity ("Will the Real Sectarian Please Stand Up?" *Theology Today* 44, no. 1 [1987]: 87-94). In fact, Hauerwas advocates that all people (universally) should be pacifists. Thus Hauerwas, contra Augsburger, would have the church "tell the state how to arm [or disarm] itself." Either Augsburger or Hauerwas is being inconsistent with Anabaptist theology or one of the two is being disingenuous. The Anabaptist tradition, which Hauerwas praises, has practiced intentional social withdrawal and separation for much of its history. For the record, however, it is the more modern version of Anabaptism that Hauerwas emulates.
[34]Lewis, "Why I Am Not a Pacifist," pp. 33-53.
[35]Reinhold Niebuhr, *Christian Realism and Political Problems* (New York: Charles Scribner's, 1953), p. 105.
[36]Ibid., p. 106.

notion of peace.[37] To Niebuhr, those who deny human depravity and insist on world peace are the new barbarians.

> The barbarian need not appear in bearskins with a club in hand. He may wear a Brooks Brothers suit and carry a ball-point pen with which to write his advertizing copy. In fact, even beneath the academic gown there may lurk a child of the wilderness, untutored in the high tradition of civility, who goes busily and happily about his work, a domesticated and law-abiding man, engaged in the construction of a philosophy to put an end to all philosophy, and thus put an end to the possibility of a vital consensus and to civility itself.[38]

What Christian thinkers from Augustine to Reinhold Niebuhr have shared in common is a Christian realism that counters the idealism of the world's ideologies. They stand on the same moral ground as the prophet Jeremiah: "'Peace, peace!' they say, / when there is no peace" (Jer 8:11).

"This, then, is why I am not a Pacifist," concluded C. S. Lewis. "If I tried to become one, I should find a very doubtful factual basis, an obscure train of reasoning, a weight of authority both human and Divine against me, and strong grounds for suspecting that my wishes had directed my decision."[39] A very troubling question in the end for Lewis was why pacifists were tolerated only in liberal societies. This seemed to suggest a moral incongruity. Lewis struggles with pacifism's incongruity, since for pacifism to be a universal moral obligation it must be prescribed for all or for none.[40]

Realists such as Niebuhr and Lewis felt constrained to counter the idealism of their day. But what is the basic character of this idealism? It is the inclination to ignore those forces within human nature that resist universal norms. Pacifists tend to underestimate—if not disavow—the extent to which sin introduces conflict in the world. As a result, they are ill-equipped to wrestle with the complexities of *applied* justice in the political context.

---

[37]Ibid., pp. 107-12.

[38]John Courtney Murray, *We Hold These Truths* (New York: Sheed & Ward, 1960), p. 12.

[39]Lewis, "Why I Am Not a Pacifist," p. 53.

[40]In addition to the empirical incongruity of pacifism that Lewis points out, Reinhold Niebuhr, in his essay "Why the Christian Church Is Not Pacifist," worries about the "self-righteous" character of much pacifism. In his view, the pacifist frequently is unable to recognize his or her own rebellion against God. It is precisely this posture of self-righteousness that is so troubling in the thinking of some deeply committed pacifists. Thus, for example, Stanley Hauerwas can insist, "I simply refuse as a pacifist to think I need any account of the state at all" ("Pacifism: Some Philosophical Considerations," *Faith and Philosophy* 2, no. 2 [1985]: 104). When the state is only conceived of as "the beast," as Hauerwas does (ibid.), one is free from any moral accountability or political obligations.

Christian realists break with their contemporaries in their acknowledging the presence of evil within the soul. As it was to antiquity, this acknowledgment is scandalous to our modern and postmodern sensibilities. Christian presuppositions about human nature lead to certain conclusions about the world. Governments necessarily will coerce, due to the presence of evil in the human heart (Rom 13:4). Strife and hostility cannot be eliminated in the present age: "It is not possible to disavow war absolutely without disavowing the task of establishing justice. For justice rests upon a decent equilibrium of power; and all balances of power involve tension; and tension involves covert conflict; and there will be moments in history when covert conflict becomes overt."[41]

World peace is a future, not present, ideal. And until the last battle, Christians must contend against evil in the awareness that *there will be* one last battle.[42]

RETHINKING NEIGHBOR LOVE

The priority of Christian charity is an important theme in the writings of ethicist Paul Ramsey (see chap. 4). Ramsey is very much concerned, like Augustine, to evaluate human deeds in terms of their intention. In his treatment of war and the use of force, we find a needed corrective to common errors—in particular, sloppy sentimentalism as well as vague humanitarianism—that so frequently pass as "Christian love."

But Ramsey is in good company with other Augustinians. Consider Aquinas, for whom "[performing] virtuous acts by reason of some outward force" could describe both love *and* the law.[43] Or closer to our time, Reinhold Niebuhr, who describes love as "the compulsion of conscience, the force of the sense of obligation, operating against other impulses in the personality."[44] Even the apostle Paul strikes us as very "Augustinian," when he writes that "Love does no harm to its neighbor" and "is the fulfillment of the law" (Rom 13:10). But whether we resort to Augustine, Aquinas, Niebuhr or

---

[41] *Love and Justice: Selections from the Shorter Writings of Reinhold Niebuhr,* ed. D. B. Robertson (Philadelphia: Westminster Press, 1992), p. 53.

[42] Nowhere in the New Testament do we find teaching to the effect that in human history good ultimately triumphs over evil. It is always conditional and provisional, requiring that we make moral judgments. Sometimes those moral judgments will necessarily be on behalf of other people or people-groups who are being victimized.

[43] *Summa Theologiae* 1-2.Q73a.1.

[44] Reinhold Niebuhr, *Justice and Mercy,* ed. Ursula Niebuhr (New York: Harper & Row, 1974), p. 39.

the apostle to the Gentiles, we come much closer to the true character of love than we would otherwise.

In a tangible sense love embodies obligations that are due God and our neighbor, whoever that may be. The "Law and the Prophets," Jesus reminds us, sum up what love entails. One of the nagging tendencies of contemporary Christianity, I have attempted to argue, is the utter divorce between love and justice, between love and law.[45] "Love" is sentimental, subjective and self-oriented; law is impersonal, objective and only to be tolerated to the extent that it enhances the self. Paul, however, fuses love and justice when he makes the twin claims that love "fulfills the law" and "does no harm to its neighbor." Hence, neighbor love, as Paul Ramsey persuasively contended, will result in an "ethics of protection." For this reason, while just war is an obscene oxymoron to some, to the Christian realist it is an expression of charity for its concern of the neighbor and its repudiation of nationalism, jingoism and militarism.

Of course, the rub for most of us seems to be the tension between the push of duty and the pull of grace. Love, God forbid, should *never* come to us in the form of "Thou shalt not . . ." Or should it? If we ponder the Pauline claim that "love fulfills the law," it would seem then that love entails a peaceful coexistence between duty and inclination, between the personal and the public. But let's be clear: any notion of love that overemphasizes duty will lean toward legalism. And on the other side, any notion of love that favors inclination will disappear into nihilism. A proper understanding of charity therefore retains a healthy tension between the personal and the public, between others and self, and between self and God (Mt 22:37-40 = Mk 12:29-31), all the while making important distinctions between the two sides.

Perhaps in this light we can begin to see how love can protect others forcefully, even to the extent of taking up arms reluctantly in the desire to help achieve a greater social good. But this eventuality can only stand on the foundation of certain biblical truths. So we recapitulate. Love frees us to serve others. Love recognizes no natural boundaries. Love considers our obligations to our neighbor. Love seeks to express to others what God has expressed to us. Love wishes for the neighbor what one wishes for oneself.[46]

---

[45]In this sense I mean by *law* that which is required of us in our social surroundings.

[46]Elsewhere I have examined the relationship of neighbor love to just-war thinking in "Justice, Neighbor Love and the Just-War Tradition: Christian Reflections on Just Use of Force," *Cultural Encounters,* winter 2004, pp. 47-67.

No discussion of love would seem complete without talking about forgiveness. What about forgiveness? And doesn't pacifism get to the heart of forgiveness as commanded by our Lord? Aren't we commanded to forgive our enemies and not resist them?

Forgiveness in the teaching of Jesus has a prominent place, without question. But any discussion of forgiveness is muddied by contemporary notions of the idea that have obscured critical moral issues. So our first order of business is to distinguish between forgiveness as inner psychological or emotional release of a party who has committed wrong and forgiveness as a declared, formal "release" of a guilty party who has acknowledged guilt, is penitent and has requested to be forgiven of the aggrieved party. This distinction is absolutely critical. While we are commanded not to harbor unforgiveness in the sense of resentment or hate toward anyone, we are *not* commanded anywhere in Scripture or the Christian tradition to forgive parties of wrongdoing who have not (1) demonstrated penitence for their actions, (2) acknowledged the guilt of their actions and (3) requested forgiveness from the offended party for wrongs they committed.

But there is a problem. Modern and postmodern culture have foisted on us a sentimental understanding of forgiveness in which mercy trumps justice, consequences for wrongdoing are denied and moral self-responsibility is absent. The religious version of the therapeutic culture is "cheap grace," though grace, it seems, has gotten ever cheaper over time. But love and mercy do not annul justice; as Paul reminds believers, they fulfill it (Rom 13:10). Sadly, there is enormous confusion in the Christian community regarding the notion of forgiveness and handling wrongs. We will need a good bit of qualification.

I *can forgive* a man who, having been caught stealing my car, is apprehended by law enforcement authorities and wishes to return or replace my car and ask for my forgiveness. That is, I release him based on his willingness to own up to his sin, evidence of which is his desire to face me directly and provide restitution. I *cannot forgive* a car thief who remains unrepentant (apprehended or otherwise). I can make sure, or struggle to make sure, that hatred does not dwell within me. Forgiveness, biblically speaking, proceeds on the prior reality of repentance and contrition.[47] Moreover, only the offended party, not a third party, can grant forgiveness, biblically speaking. Most

---

[47]Biblical teaching as diverse as Leviticus 16 ("The Day of Atonement") and Matthew 18:15-20 ("Forgiving a Brother") is predicated upon this moral reality.

significantly, forgiveness does not set aside the consequences of the ethical violation. These principles, so foreign to our modern sensibilities, are attested to by an enormous weight of biblical testimony.

In a provocative essay titled "Payback: Thinking About Retribution," Christian moral philosopher Oliver O'Donovan examines what true forgiveness entails. O'Donovan believes that there is a necessary reconciled tension between justice and mercy that must be preserved and not loosened.

> In Christian thought retribution is one pole of a dialectic with forgiveness. One reason, indeed, that Christians have insisted on retributive justice [historically] is that if one pole is lost, the opposite pole will be lost, too. The theological doctrines of forgiven sin, redemption from punishment, reconciliation of the offender with the offended God, those and nothing else are what have held the philosophical notions of desert and retribution firmly in place.[48]

Doubtless many of us are troubled by the very notion of punishment. After all, some of us grew up in less than ideal homes where less than ideal attempts to "discipline" (i.e., punish) us were implemented by our parents or guardians. And some of us are still carrying around those bruises. So why not aim for this ideal called justice in some other *less distasteful* way? Why not, say, use negotiation or moral education? Or how about community service?

If we insist on driving a wedge between justice and retribution/punishment, then we empty justice of its content and it becomes moral Silly Putty. Justice must be normative and it must be universally so. Doing what is right must be the same for you and for me, and for him and for her. Justice itself is what makes punishment retributive. And justice itself is what makes retribution a moral entity. Certain things are wrong because they are wrong universally, which means that to rectify that wrong is to believe in moral desert. People do not get—*should not* get, that is—different deserts for committing the same moral wrong. Such a phenomenon we call a "travesty of justice."

At this point, we must counter mainstream cultural thinking. Does punishment educate? Indeed it does. Does retribution have a therapeutic function? Unquestionably, *if* we understand that therapy is not merely about feelings and self-esteem but about healing the vices and moral sickness lodged within the human psyche. Punishment, alas, points us in the direction of *forgiveness.*

---

[48]Oliver O'Donovan, "Payback: Thinking About Retribution," *Books & Culture,* July-August 2000, p. 19.

Forgiveness then is rooted in moral reality. That is why, as a biblical-theological concept, forgiveness is grounded in the principle of restitution. To make restitution is to *restore* by making things right. (Any next-door neighbor of yours will be more than happy to verify this definition.)

In Old Testament law restitution is always required in proportion to the sin committed; so, for example, an ox for ox, a life for a life, a tool for a tool, property for property. In the New Testament this principle remains in effect, hence the significance of the Zacchaeus story (Lk 19:1-9), despite the fact that it is tantalizingly brief. As seen by Luke, Zacchaeus's repentance does not merely remain at the abstract level of a "change of heart." Rather, the point of the story is that he demonstrated *tangible evidence* of a profound inner change. In his situation justice meant returning fourfold what he had stolen monetarily.

Of course, in the realm of criminal justice, offenders do not always take the initiative and return to the offended party. Sometimes the initiative might be reversed, as in Jesus' teaching directed at Peter, recorded in Matthew "If your brother sins against you, go and show him his fault, just between the two of you. If he listens to you, you have won your brother over" (Mt 18:15). Several things are implied here. Sin against you has been committed. The other person is at fault. The other person has not shown repentance before you take the initiative. As a result of your initiative the other person sees the error of his ways (and supposedly repents). But notice that even if the other person does *not* receive you, you still go through a further process to confront him with his guilt. In the end, if he still refuses to accept moral responsibility, he is to be treated as an outcast. That is to say, forgiveness or "release" is *not* granted.

Following the above brief smattering of biblical evidence, we can glean several basic principles that inform forgiveness. (1) Forgiveness is preceded by contrition. This requirement before God, it goes without saying, is written on virtually every page of Scripture. Forgiveness does not do an end-run around contrition and repentance. John the Baptist makes sure that his audience does not lose sight of this reality. (2) Contrition is demonstrated when the offender returns to the offended, confessing his or her sin. Even when in the case of Matthew 18 the reverse occurs, and victim approaches the offender, the end result is that heartfelt sorrow for wrongs committed must be acknowledged. (3) Forgiveness as a result of direct dealings between victim and offender may then be imparted by the victim. (4) Forgiveness may *not* be granted by a third party—in proxy, so to speak. Only the offended party may grant forgiveness to the guilty.

But I will add one further principle that finds ample support in the testimony of Scripture. (5) Should the offending party refuse to acknowledge guilt and contrition leading to repentance, judgment rests on that party. Whether judgment is carried out sooner or later and in what manner it occurs are not our present concern.

Where does that leave us? When our therapeutic culture speaks so glibly of "forgiveness," we must be careful that we do not empty it of its moral meaning. Contrary to the teaching of many "Christian" ethicists, forgiveness does *not* stand in contradiction to retributive justice. It does not annul punitive justice. While mercy is applied to the soul of sinners, it does not set aside the ethical consequences that require "atoning sacrifice." Justice, if it is to be restorative, requires a sacrifice, a loss, a deprivation. Thus, once people who are convicted of premeditated murder have a death-row conversion, they will demonstrate the authenticity of their conversion by being willing to undergo the death penalty. Otherwise, it is fair to question whether that conversion was genuine in the first place.[49]

A final—and crucial—implication of the biblical idea of forgiveness: while individuals are required to forgive, states and nations are not. While persons receive mercy from other persons, the role of the magistrate is not to forgive and issue mercy where justice is due. Rather, the authorities function to meet out justice where justice is required. Otherwise, society falls apart and becomes ungovernable. Standards themselves become impossible. And in the end criminals thrive because there are no restraints, as evil abounds because no moral constraints are in place. In short, a world without justice is hell. Coercive force, therefore, will always be necessary as an instrument of restraining evil.

But why, you ask, this lengthy discourse on forgiveness? We began by noting Paul Ramsey's concern to broaden our understanding of charity. Charity and justice do not cancel one another. They remain wedded to each other, even when that wedding seems to be fraught with tension. This means that justice will always operate within moral limitations, within humane restraints, just as love will always seek to honor what is just, true and

---

[49]With this illustration, it is not my intention to suggest that Christians must embrace capital punishment. I merely use the example to illustrate the nature of authentic repentance in the person who has committed a capital crime.

proportionate, including the need for punishment as moral retribution.

Christian teaching throughout the ages has affirmed the morality of force that is applied for just purposes. Christian theology does *not* teach that when people do evil deeds, they are automatically struck down by God. Such, of course, is the divine prerogative, but this sort of theophany is rather rare. In most societies, evildoers are not permitted the liberty of continuing their practices in freedom. They are apprehended, usually coercively, and restrained for their own good and for the greater good of the surrounding population. This assertion should not be controversial; it is baseline Christian theology as well as common sense and political prudence.

The governing authorities serve for this express social purpose. They exist to reward the good and restrain as well as punish evil. Such is the plain and explicit teaching of the New Testament (Rom 13:1-10; 1 Pet 2:13-15). Not to resist or prevent evil deeds when they occur is to be complicit in those evil acts. This applies to individuals, who have a responsibility to their neighbor (such as the Good Samaritan did), to local and regional political structures as well as to the national and international community. To fail to respond to or prevent evil when we have knowledge or the power to do so is to be an accomplice in that very evil. Even a *religious justification for nonengagement*, namely, that God in his providence will make evil right in the end (which, in fact, he *will do*), does not release us from the obligation to resist evil.

THE MORALITY OF PREEMPTIVE FORCE

Those committed to religiously based pacifism and nonviolence, as we have observed, view their position as a necessary consequence of Jesus' purported "radical love-ethic" as taught in the New Testament. Those who rather unreflectively embrace a form of militarism, whether it is "God and country," secular or jihadist in nature, believe that might indeed makes right and view moral considerations and moral restraints as unnecessary. By contrast, those who affirm the need for moral discrimination as developed in the just-war tradition recognize both permissibility and limits of warfare. While the church does not implement policy, it plays a critical role in clarifying for society what policies are morally permissible. For those who recognize that coercive force *may* be morally legitimate, a difficult question emerges: What about preemptive action? Just-war principles lead us to examine the ethics of intervention, particularly in light of the fact that new conflicts in the world are constantly arising.

The most commonly cited just cause for going to war is self-defense. And yet many wartime situations do not neatly fit into this particular category, as Harold O. J. Brown has reminded us.[50] Hitler's invasion of Poland, from one standpoint, was unprovoked aggression that contributed to World War II. And in a perverse turn of events the Soviet Union, which was attacked by Hitler, resumed tyranny over Poland. This tyranny, of course, in a few short years was extended to other Eastern European countries, which became the property of the Soviet Empire. And while millions were disappearing, dying or being placed in labor camps during the 1930s and 1940s, many in the West were praising Stalin for his "progressive" ideas. One wonders whether pacifism as it was practiced during these years—in its religious or secular form—contributed to the expansion of this oppressive tyranny. Did it cause even greater evils?

We will never know. But this is not an idle question. Rather, it causes us to take inventory of our moral theory. Let's consider several scenarios that test the viability of our moral theory. Should we ground our preparedness to go to war *solely* on the criterion of unprovoked self-defense? Why or why not? And another troubling question: must we, from a moral standpoint, wait until an attack has begun before we respond? Or transferred to a third party, must we wait until another nation has been attacked before we intervene? These are not distant hypothetical situations. They describe the world in which we presently live.

We are quickly confronted with a difficult question, yet one that cannot be ignored. Is going to war morally justified for the purpose of preventing a greater holocaust, one that has not yet occurred? Should preemptive force have been initiated against Hitler's Germany before its "final solution" to the Jews was implemented? Why or why not? Regardless of how *we* answer, Jews who were liberated by Allied forces in 1945 know that intervening force can be moral.

Let me hasten to say that by "preventive intervention" or "preemptive war" I do not have in mind a "crusade," which attempts "to set right a past act."[51] But I do wish to pose a provocative (and pertinent) question: Are

---

[50]Harold O. J. Brown, "The Crusade or Preventive War," in *War: Four Christian Views,* ed. Robert G. Clouse, rev. ed. (Downers Grove, Ill.: InterVarsity Press, 1991), pp. 153-54.

[51]I disagree strongly with Harold Brown's conflation of "crusade " and "preventive war" in an otherwise fascinating essay previously noted (ibid.). To confuse the two notions is to collapse the distinction between "jihad" and just-war thinking. Without this necessary distinction, distinguishing between medieval crusades and modern wars of liberation in the end becomes impossible based on moral criteria.

we under obligation to prevent, if it is possible, the genocide of millions of people (Jews or otherwise) before it begins? Are we under obligation to prevent the massacre of over three-quarters of a million people in Rwanda—or in other nations for that matter—when we anticipate that bloodshed of such magnitude could be on the horizon? If not, why not? Do we deny potential victims of oppression or mass murder the same protection against gross injustice that we ourselves would want? Or going back one generation: Where were the outcries from people in the West against the mass murder of Cambodians by the Pol Pot regime from 1975 onward? Religious voices, alas, were for the most part mute.[52] The moral question then, it seems to me, looms large. Stated differently: Can nonintervention be immoral?

And where do we draw the line? Why do or don't we withhold intervention? For example, the standard response here in the United States, namely, that "the U.S. can't police the world," while it contains partial truth, is morally vacuous.[53] In the end we have two alternatives: either we are willing to involve ourselves in world affairs to promote justice and prevent injustice—in which case we must exercise moral-political prudence as to *where and to what extent*—or we isolate ourselves and not intervene in any world crisis, genocide and mass murder included. Responsible statecraft requires the former and rejects the latter. To refuse to intervene and oppose crimes against humanity—outlandish evil—is to cheapen human life and deny any morality.

At this point permit me to use an analogy. Suppose a stalker-murderer were on the prowl in your neighborhood. Would you justify getting yourself involved? Getting the police involved? Why or why not? And if you deem

---

[52]The response by Mennonite spokesperson Myron Augsburger is simply morally insufficient: "On the latter [Cambodia] it seems that so much cultural distance exists between us and the countries of Asia that we are incapable of relating to them in ways which could help change the patterns of violence" ("A Christian Pacifist Response," p. 178). Unwittingly, Augsburger tacitly acknowledges the inadequacy of the pacifist position.

[53]In considering whether to oppose evil, it is not enough to weigh the consequences, although we must do that. Morally responsible action will examine intent. At a recent university symposium (not that of my own institution), one panel member was pressed to answer why any democratic nation that had the wherewithal should not use its influence to intervene in crises around the world. His disclaimer was basically this: In how many crises shall we involve ourselves—three, twelve, thirty? This is a legitimate question if thereby we are genuinely wrestling with moral duty to others. If, on the other hand, this sort of disclaimer is merely a smokescreen to argue that free nations have no moral duties abroad, then it is disingenuous.

that a response of (potentially lethal) force is morally justified, why not extend this morality to just-war thinking at the international level? Suffice it to say this: if war is ever justifiable, then there will arise situations in which war is justifiable to prevent a greater manifestation of evil.

One of the principal fears of pacifists—indeed, many policy-makers—during the 1970s and 1980s was the nuclear first-strike scenario. But weapons and technology aside, let's think for a moment at the level of moral principle. Must we wait until the first strike is delivered before we are justified in responding? Is it morally illicit to anticipate and prevent a lethal first strike? Does moral responsibility wait until the initial blow is struck by an aggressor? Does it allow a first strike to be prevented? If so, at what point? As it applies to our stalker-murderer friend, should the police wait until he rapes, maims and kills before they intervene? Such is not a distant or improbable scenario. Law-enforcement authorities must regularly contend with this sort of situation. Foreign policy increasingly faces similar situations. At issue is the question of what constitutes "defense against aggression," the normal definition of just cause.

One of the contributions of Hugo Grotius (see chap. 3) was his application of just-war principles to the problem of multiple sovereign states. His understanding of *just cause* was similar to that of Aquinas: defense against aggression, punishment for injustice and recovery of what was stolen. But what about imminent threats that have not yet been carried through? Grotius's response, based on crime prevention, is remarkably simple: "If my assailant seizes a weapon with an obvious intention of killing me, I admit too that I have a right to prevent the crime."[54]

The upshot of this moral reasoning is that first use of force may in certain situations be morally justified. Although all defensive wars are just, not all just wars need be defensive. The degree of wickedness can be just cause itself. For this reason Aquinas does not distinguish between defensive and offensive wars.

But Grotius does not stop here; this represents only half of our moral responsibility. In addition to acknowledging occasions in which preemptive force is legitimate, he also identifies various situations in which preemptive force is *not* justifiable. What are unwarranted uses of offensive force? Precautionary killing, the attempt to weaken a foreign power and

---

[54]Hugo Grotius *The Law of War and Peace* 2.1.4.

national pride are among those that are illicit.[55]

As I write, I am reminded of the Israeli preemptive strike on an Iraqi nuclear reactor at Osirek in June 1982 that was deemed necessary. Was Israel's decision to preemptively remove (at least, temporarily) Iraq's nuclear weapons capability unjust? Why or why not? And a further question relating to Israel: Was Israel's response to its enemies' military build-up on its borders unjust in the Six-Day War of 1967?

To the point: If self-defense from aggression is justifiable, and if wisdom does not *require* that we wait until a first strike is past or already set in motion, then there may be occasions when preemptive warfare is morally justifiable. Here, of course, we are wrestling with matters of political prudence. Just-war principles, as I have tried to examine them in this volume, are very imprecise. They require prudential wisdom for their application in concrete situations. Determining at what point "imminent threat" has reached critical mass and arrived, and thereafter attack by hostile forces (whether on our soil or on a third nation), is no precise science. Political judgments will need to be made based on military intelligence, political wisdom and a sense of moral responsibility to entire populations.

Given the complex nature of international politics today, pundits and politicians frequently lecture the American people using the language of nonintervention. And nonintervention, it is fair to say, is the chief policy of the United Nations. But "peace-keeping" operations and policies do not in and of themselves remove threats to other nations. And what the U.N. lacks, based on its track record, is the ability to make nations—rogue nations, in particular—comply.

By contrast, the moral reasoning in just-war theory works both ways. It both limits and restrains the use of force, and it allows for the possibility of a just intervention. Universal justice, rooted in natural law, is the ideal that regulates justice among the nations. Any approach to nonintervention—or intervention—will need to reckon with a baseline assumption: legitimate peace is justly ordered and not merely the absence of conflict. A just peace will also be assessed by weighing both the national and international common good; neither can be ignored. If the mere absence of conflict is our goal, then enormous injustice and tyranny in a nation or people group can exist "under the radar screen," as it were, of the international community. Genocidal activities

---

[55]Ibid., 2.1.4, 17; 2.25.9.

in Bosnia, Herzegovina and Kosovo witness to this sobering possibility. And genocide in Rwanda has made this abundantly clear, even when the West was generally uninterested in mediating in this recent tragedy.[56]

Political prudence and moral obligation must merge in order to determine whether in the future we as a nation will need to intervene for humanitarian purposes. Politically responsible policies and decisions are not limited to mere reaction to events in the world. Just-war principles challenge us to consider what future contexts will require a just response to evil. Ethicist Paul Ramsey has expressed this preventive way of thinking quite admirably:

> No authority on earth can withdraw from "social charity" and "social justice" their intrinsic and justifiable tendencies to rescue from dereliction and oppression all whom it is possible to rescue. . . . This justification can never be withdrawn; it can only be limited, supplanted, or put in abeyance.[57]

Thus the possibility of forceful intervention, even if it is rare, must always remain open—a possibility that is necessarily subject to the moral restraints of justice as a cardinal virtue:

> Rescue those being led away to death;
> > hold back those staggering toward slaughter.
> If you say, "But we knew nothing about this,"
> > does not he who weighs the heart perceive it?
> Does not he who guards your life know it?
> > Will he not repay each person according to what he has done? (Prov 24:11-12)

> When justice is done, it brings joy to the righteous
> but terror to evildoers. (Prov 21:15)

No moral principle, no authority, can proscribe absolutely the possibility of just intervention.[58] No authority, that is, unless we choose isolationism both as a personal and national policy.

---

[56]While capitulation in the name of nonresistant pacifism may be noble for the individual, Reinhold Niebuhr was correct to note that it becomes "rather ignoble when the idealist suggests that others beside himself shall be sold into slavery and shall groan under the tyrant's heel" (*Love and Justice,* p. 277).

[57]Paul Ramsey, "The Ethics of Intervention," *Review of Politics* 27, no. 4 (1965): 305.

[58]A further reason that intervention can never be fully ruled out is the possibility that a third party may request our help.

6

JUST-WAR THEORY

ITS CHARACTER, CONSTITUTION AND CONTEXT

Our present cultural climate necessitates that we reorient the way in which we think about justice. Given the exaltation of rights over responsibilities in American society, the notion of justice has been severely prostituted. Some of these "rights," it goes without saying, are most dubious, to put it mildly. Today, an infinite number of cultural subgroups are making claims on the public square. Rights are no longer rooted in self-evident truths and the law of nature; rather, they extend to personal preferences, even to morally heinous acts that undermine the public good. Justice as personal rights, of course, proceeds in the name of "tolerance," that contemporary trump card that negates all moral judgments.

RETHINKING JUSTICE

Once upon a time, justice was not encumbered by such cultural baggage. Justice is developed philosophically both in the Judeo-Christian moral tradition and in pre-Christian philosophy (Plato's *Republic* is dedicated to this theme); hence, it is a cardinal virtue.[1] While Scripture agrees with the pre-Christian philosophical tradition that justice is that which is due others, it also provides the rationale for *why* this is so. In Scripture the people of God are commanded to execute justice precisely because the Creator himself does so.

---

[1]Historically, justice has been defined as that which is due each person—a definition affirmed from Aristotle (*Nicomachean Ethics* 5.1-11 [1129a-1138b]) to Cicero (*De Officiis* 1.5.15) to Aquinas (*Summa Theologiae* 2-2.Q58).

Justice in Scripture discriminates between righteousness and wickedness as well as between guilt and innocence (e.g., Gen 18:25 and Is 5:20); it erects protection for the innocent and those without a voice (e.g., Ex 23:6-9; Lev 19:9-10); it seeks to prevent injustice from arising (e.g., Lev 19:11-14); and it rectifies injustice (e.g., Is 10:1-2). It is that moral tissue by which and in which a moral society coheres.

Justice, moreover, is cognizant of the fact that humans bear the image of God. Thus the Judeo-Christian tradition, assuming the "natural moral law" (what the apostle Paul calls the "law written on the heart"), affirms certain unchanging moral realities—for example, that all people intuit justice as well as its absence, that they intuit moral accountability, and that discriminate punishment and restoration are moral entities.

Thus there can be no moral goods in society apart from justice in its non-fluid conceptualization. Otherwise, justice is not a cardinal virtue and can be manipulated by the will to power and human selfishness.

Love and mercy in no way eliminate the need for justice. They do not remove the consequences of ethical violations and the need for restoring a moral balance. Consider an illustration. While most Christians, after having been stopped for speeding on the highway, would never argue on the basis of Christ's justification and forgiveness that a highway patrolman not issue the speeding ticket they had just earned, many Christians approach ethics in precisely this manner. Such thinking, however, breeds disaster in the sphere of law and public policy. Criminal justice is impossible if standards of justice are not fixed. In the ethical realm biblical justice requires that payment always be made for a violation and that this payment be proportional to the offense; hence, the catchword *restitution* that occurs frequently in the Pentateuch. Biblically speaking, the only category of ethical offense for which no restitution exists is premeditated murder (cf. Num 35, esp. vv. 29-33).

In an important address in 1997 at the U.S. Holocaust Museum, South African Justice Richard Goldstone, who had previously been chief prosecutor of the International Criminal Tribunals for the former Yugoslavia and Rwanda, had this to say:

> The one thing I have learned in my travels to the former Yugoslavia and in Rwanda and in my own country is that where there have been egregious human rights violations that have been unaccounted for, where there has been no justice, where the victims have not received any acknowledgement, where they have been forgotten, where there's been a national amnesia, the effect is

a cancer in the society. It is the reason that explains, in my respectful opinion, spirals of violence that the world has seen in the former Yugoslavia for centuries and in Rwanda for decades, to use two obvious examples. . . . So justice can make a contribution to bringing enduring peace.[2]

Given what Goldstone has witnessed worldwide, what specific contributions can the application of bona fide justice make in a broken world? Goldstone makes four recommendations: (1) exposing the truth of specific guilt and avoidance of general collective guilt, (2) recording the truth of moral atrocity for the historical record, in order to counter attempts by the guilty (or their sympathizers) to fabricate or avoid guilt, (3) publicly acknowledging the loss endured by the victims of evil who, as broken and terrified people, want and need justice, and (4) applying the deterrent of criminal justice, since human nature and potential criminals are deterred by the fear of apprehension and punishment.

JUST WAR'S DEBT TO NATURAL-LAW THINKING

Both Luther and Calvin believed that the Golden Rule, as we know it from Scripture, was simply the restatement of another law, or norm, by which human deeds are judged. Calvin writes that "nothing is more common than for man to be sufficiently instructed in a right course by natural law."[3] It is significant that even Luther, for whom grace is so crucial, insisted that law and an uneasy conscience are the first point of contact between God and human beings. The uneasy conscience, as Luther understands it, is nothing more than the expression of an internal law.

But the Reformers are not the first to distinguish between a general as opposed to special revelation given to humankind. In their understanding they were in line with Christians of previous eras. Thomas Aquinas distinguishes between four types of law—divine law, eternal law, human law and natural law. Natural law is what Paul seems to have in mind when he speaks of a law "written on the heart." Pagan Gentiles, he notes, "do by nature the things required by the law." Thereby "they show that the requirements of the law are written on their hearts." Because of this law that is rooted in nature, unbelievers' "consciences also bear . . . witness, and their thoughts now

---

[2]Richard Goldstone, "War Crimes: When Amnesia Causes Cancer," *Washington Post,* February 2, 1997, p. C4. A full transcript of the address can be found at <www.cco.caltech.edu/~bosnia /articles/goldstone.html>.

[3]John Calvin *Institutes of Christian Religion* 2.2.22.

accus[e] . . . them" (Rom 2:14-15). Such is the language of natural law, an important part of what Christian theology calls general revelation. It is "nature" because it describes the way things are. It is a "law" because nothing can change our essential nature. The fact of sin, devastating as it is, neither eliminates our ability to choose to do good (freedom) nor releases us from the sense of moral obligation (guilt).[4]

In truth, natural law is acknowledged by the fathers of the church from Tertullian onward. In chapter three, we saw the debt of late medieval and early modern thinkers to Aquinas, who argued for just-war requirements based on Scripture as well as natural law discerned through reason.

Natural law presupposes both the existence of universal moral norms and a basic awareness of these in all humans. Natural law is assumed to exist among all peoples, not merely Christians. It is a natural system of ethics that neither depends on nor contradicts Christian revelation. It stands by itself. Something is forbidden because it is wrong and not wrong because it is forbidden. Such a moral assumption is part of the apostle Paul's argument in Romans 2. For this reason natural law is foundational to just-war theory. The just-war thinker holds certain truths to be self-evident. This applies both to individuals as well as to nations. The very premise on which just war rests is that there is a universal moral sense that informs human beings on what is good and just over against what is evil and unjust.

Natural law is an imprint made on nature itself, inscribed by the moral Governor of the universe. Justice represents the basic obligation of human beings as creatures as determined by the Creator. Nature, confirmed through conscience, reveals to all people everywhere an awareness of basic moral reality that may not be transgressed. "Thou shalt not kill," "Thou shalt not steal," and "Thou shalt not covet" are known not only through the Scriptures, which have been given to God's chosen people (Israel and the church). These injunctions are "written on the heart" (Rom 2:15) of every person alive, woven into the very fabric of creation, known and intuited by all human beings. Cain knew this, and he fled (Gen 4:1-16). The important question is this: *How* did he know this?

---

[4]Clearly there are differing degrees of sin and guilt among individuals and among nations. And these must be handled in differing ways. But milder or more extreme cases of sin are all rooted in the same inclination, the same propensity. Catholic and Protestant theology, of course, differ as to their understanding of the degree of human depravity. My position is that human beings, due to original sin, are both irredeemably fallen and capable of distinguishing between good and evil. The image of God in us has been marred, but we still retain the divine image.

But the natural moral law also makes us aware of a fundamental distinction between killing in self-defense and premeditated murder. The fact that secular law, such as is practiced in contemporary culture, even makes this distinction (unaided by "scriptural revelation") is witness to this universal fact.

Just-war thinking proceeds from this moral starting point. It distinguishes at the most fundamental level between justice and injustice, between defense and aggression. Applying political prudence, it clarifies situations and conditions in which a state might go to war and what might or might not be permissible. Just-war thinking requires that responsibility and accountability, not the lust for violence or conquest, be sufficient cause for action. Jean Bethke Elshtain describes the heart of just-war thinking in a way that deserves repeating:

> Just war argument sustains a worldview that construes human beings as innately and exquisitely social. It follows that all ways of life are laced through with moral rules and restrictions that provide a web of social order. For St. Augustine . . . God's natural law was written in human hearts; thus, unsurprisingly, all ways of life incorporate basic grammars of injunctions and prohibitions which regulate important things—the taking of life, sexual relations, the administration of justice. . . . What happens in families bears a reference to what sort of society one lives in overall; domestic peace and civic peace are related, are of a kind, rather than being entirely separate concerns. We can assess a people and a way of life by looking at what this people lifts up and loves; by what it shares in common, and by what it rejects or thrusts aside.[5]

Seen in this way just-war thinking is rooted in a certain view of reality. It understands the individual to have overlapping social commitments and loyalties. These entail family, civil society and the state. While these realms are not identical, they are nevertheless related. All need to be ordered. And all are ordered by just notions of peace that have their foundation in universal moral standards or norms. Social relations as well as political action in a just society will mirror some measure of indebtedness to those enduring values.

The natural law is the unwritten law, inscribed on the hearts of all human beings (cf. Rom 2:14-15), according to which human behavior must be ordered. It allows civil society, apart from religious conviction, to determine what behaviors are acceptable and unacceptable, what is morally just and

---

[5]Jean Bethke Elshtain, "Just War as Politics," in *But Was It Just?* ed. David E. DeCosse (New York: Doubleday, 1992), pp. 54-55.

unjust. While the relationship to God provides the highest expression and
fulfillment of human virtue, the natural law written on the heart witnesses
in all people to basic moral obligations and to the basic distinction between
good and evil. Murder, theft, lying, infidelity, harming the innocent and so
forth are readily intuited moral violations. For this reason there are basic
prohibitions against these actions that find universal expression in different
cultures. A moral order is protected "on its border," so to speak, by negative
commands; great social good arises in a society from positive motivation,
namely, from the growth of virtues in its citizens. Natural law has the function of protecting these borders. It will guard against the error of rationalism,
on the one hand, which fails to take into account the sinfulness of humans,
and the error of relativism, on the other hand, which denies the validity of
moral norms.

If natural law provides general moral guidelines for what is just and unjust, then the problem of war and the just use of force furnish a useful example of how those guidelines might be applied.[6]

THE SPECTRUM OF FORCE: JUST WAR AS A MEDIATING POSITION

Warfare can be examined according to three logically possible positions.
The first holds that war and coercive force are *always* justifiable, morally or
legally. Resort to violence, whether in its religious form (jihad[7] or crusade or
"God and country") or in its secular counterpart (often referred to as *realpolitik* or political realism), requires no justification. No moral restraints beyond political expediency or the "command of God" need be applied. We
will simply refer to this position as *militarism.* The second position, in its
pure form, is that war and violence are *never* justifiable under any circumstances. In chapter five I attempted to evaluate the basic assumptions of the
pacifist position, secular or religious.

Most people tend to think about war and force in terms of two opposing
perspectives, pacifism and just-war. However, it is more accurate to understand the just-war tradition as a *mediating* position between the two poles

---

[6]Among philosophers and political theorists there has been growing interest in natural law in
recent years, resulting in a considerable number of books being published on the subject. Two
of the more accessible ones are by J. Budziszewski, *What We Can't Not Know* (Dallas: Spence,
2003), and his *Written on the Heart* (Downers Grove, Ill.: InterVarsity Press, 1997).
[7]Here I use the term *jihad* in its more derivative sense—divinely sanctioned warfare—and not
in its narrower sense of "striving in the path of God."

of pacifism and militarism.[8] Human rights scholar David Little concurs: "It would appear that the Christian story is a story of shifting combinations of . . . three attitudes. . . . While pacifist and holy war or crusading appeals are undoubtedly mutually exclusive, the just war attitude serves to mediate between the two extremes."[9]

Let's consider the latter first, and specifically the crusade mindset, given the breathtaking growth of resurgent Islamic fundamentalism in our world today. While it may be difficult to acknowledge at the other end of the spectrum any strengths in the jihad[10]/crusade position, it nevertheless understands—in its own distorted way—that fundamentally moral and religious reasons stand behind the conflict of nations. And in its own contorted way it seeks to be integrated, understanding all of life as a whole, motivated by a zeal to honor, please or obey God. Religious convictions hereby are not privatized or separate from the daily existence; they touch—indeed, they permeate—all. War then is simultaneously a religious *and* political act. For the holy warrior the cause is just because of divine revelation or because the nationalist spirit requires such.[11]

But the strengths of the militaristic position become its most tragic weaknesses. Among its flawed assumptions are its failure to distinguish between religion and statecraft (i.e., between duties of the individual and the state),

---

[8]John Courtney Murray described the just-war position as "a way between the false extremes of pacifism and bellicism" (*We Hold These Truths* [New York: Sheed & Ward, 1960], p. 258). The important anthology edited by John Kelsay and James Turner Johnson, *Just War and Jihad,* Contributions to the Study of Religion 28 (New York: Greenwood Press, 1991), also places the just-war position as intermediate to pacifism and jihad. James F. Childress's typology of force includes five positions—nonresistance, nonviolent resistance, limited violent resistance (discrimination and proportionality), limited violent resistance (proportionality only), and unlimited violent resistance—but implies that just-war principles comprise a moderating position ("Contemporary Pacifism: Its Major Types and Possible Contributions to Discourse about War," in *The American Search for Peace,* ed. George Weigel and John P. Langan [Washington, D.C.: Georgetown University Press, 1991], pp. 109-31).

[9]"'Holy War' Appeals and Western Christianity: A Reconstruction of Bainton's Approach," in *Just War and Jihad,* ed. John Kelsay and James Turner Johnson (New York: Greenwood Press, 1991), p. 123.

[10]The religious version of this position, whether in its medieval or present-day Islamic expression, rests on the conviction that God/Allah wills its existence and success.

[11]Three volumes commend themselves to the reader in this regard. Two are edited by John Kelsay and James Turner Johnson—*Just War and Jihad* (cited above) and *Cross, Crescent, and Sword,* Contributions to the Study of Religion 27 (New York: Greenwood Press, 1990) —and the third is authored by Johnson, *The Holy War Idea in Western and Islamic Traditions* (University Park: Pennsylvania State University Press, 1997).

its inadequate and distorted understanding of God (whether through theology proper or through some skewed form of civil religion), its disregard for natural moral law,[12] its overly simplistic approach to morality by which it reduces all things to a clear conflict of good over evil, its failure to realize that justness is only approximate and not pure in the present life, and its indiscriminate attitude toward human life.[13]

At the other end of the ideological spectrum stands the pacifist. Given its appeal among people of religious faith, pacifism requires a measured critique. The strengths of the pacifist perspective are multiple and certainly compelling. To its credit, it is sensitive to the violent tendencies that permeate American culture. From our families to our entertainment habits to the streets of our neighborhoods, few would deny that our society is growing less civil and more coarse. Citizenship has become a notion that strikes many people as almost quaint. In addition, the pacifist perspective recognizes diverse—and in many respects, creative—avenues for political and social action. It is sensitive to the effects of violence that all too often pervade the human experience, and in time, express themselves in society. In the words of Jean Elshtain, pacifism puts "violence on trial" in that it views social life from the perspective of the potential victim and not the victor.[14]

In its religious form pacifism takes seriously both the commandment to love and the demands of Christian discipleship. At least for a previous generation of conscientious objectors like my own father, it has shown a willingness to self-sacrifice, counting the cost of one's convictions, even when it means paying the price of alternative service to others.[15] Further, it is keenly sensitive to the distortions of faith that come with an uncritical view of the state—a continual problem throughout the history of the church. Pacifists help sensitize nonpacifists to an all too human tendency to rationalize violence in the service of nationalism, reminding us of the relative norms of politics and "social justice."

The weaknesses that attend the pacifist position require a measure of cri-

---

[12]By disregard for natural moral law, I mean that it does not accept that some actions are wrong in themselves, not right or wrong as God wills it. For example, the killing of the innocent is always wrong; therefore, God will never order it.

[13]A very thorough examination of the militaristic position—in both Christian and Muslim history—is Kelsay and Johnson, eds., *Just War and Jihad*.

[14]Jean Bethke Elshtain, *Women and War*, rev. ed. (Chicago: University of Chicago Press, 1995), pp. 123, 132.

[15]Conscription, of course, was the reality of World War II. Such does not apply today, since soldiering in our culture is voluntary, which renders pacifism as policy all the more dubious.

tique. In its refusal to resist evil directly through action, *in practice* it bestows on evil and tyranny an advantage in the present life. This, of course, was the burden of Reinhold Niebuhr, who noted somewhat caustically that had Christians demonstrated more love in his day, Hitler would not have invaded Poland.[16] Indeed, there did come a point at which Nazi evil reached a critical mass and warranted retribution by the nations. To deny such is ethically untenable.

In fairness it should be said that being gullible or naive vis-à-vis totalitarian regimes and mass murder is not a feature that is solely confined to pacifism. Truth be told, much of democratic culture in the last eighty years has been guilty of this. Nonetheless, precisely how pacifism is able to counter or negate totalitarianism has not yet been sufficiently demonstrated. Justice without force is a myth, because there will always be bad men.

Another weakness is that pacifism tends to have an excessively apocalyptic view of governing authorities. As a result it is unable to contribute meaningfully to statecraft and specifically to national security issues, much less to political philosophy (where, one would think, it needs to be). But if political authority is *inherently* evil, then our state and local governments, not to mention school boards, unions and all political interest groups, are vessels of corrosion and tyranny as well. Thus the pacifist will have to concede that the municipalities in which we live, self-governing as they are, have no redeemable features whatsoever, structurally speaking.[17] But the reality is that society without coercive powers is an impossibility, whether locally, nationally or internationally. Coercive power, however, as we have been arguing, need not be corrupt. And if coercive powers belong to the governing authorities, they cannot simultaneously be legitimate in domestic affairs but illegitimate in foreign policy. The same authority that restrains internal enemies of society also opposes external enemies.[18]

Pacifism overestimates the effectiveness of nonviolence and nonresistance at the same time that it underestimates—if it does not fully deny—the fact that an ethics of protection issues out of Christian charity. If we are to

---

[16]Reinhold Niebuhr, *Christianity and Power Politics* (New York: Charles Scribner's, 1940), pp. 1-32.

[17]In fact, one could argue that the family unit itself is oppressive.

[18]One of the best arguments for the necessity of coercive powers of government is found in Elizabeth Anscombe, "War and Murder," in *War and Morality,* ed. Richard A Wasserstrom (Belmont, Calif.: Wadsworth, 1970), pp. 42-53. Anscombe is perhaps best known for having "won" a debate with C. S. Lewis while teaching at Oxford.

remain nonviolent, what is the alternative to force? The only other option is rational persuasion. That is, we must attempt to persuade people, people groups or nations out of violent or criminal behavior. But what if violent or criminal people have no interest in being reasonable? As it is, criminal types are rarely reasonable. It is impossible to engage in rational persuasion unless the enemy is willing to stop, be reasonable, talk and be persuaded to desist from criminal activity. Here, pacifism suffers from a lack of realism.

But we must examine the flip side of this problem—the pacifist's underestimating charity as an *ethics of protection*. The real test of pacifist morality is its willingness to protect others in need. Without question, the pacifist is permitted to forgo self-defense. But is he or she permitted to forgo a defense of other people? And can the pacifist legitimately argue that *we all* have a moral obligation not to defend the third party? And wherein lies this obligation to refrain from defending others with force?

Yet another problem is pacifism's tendency to create a nonexistent divide between the sacred and the secular, between monk and magistrate due to its emphasis on separation from the world and abstaining from worldly vocations. Consequently, it contributes, wittingly or not, to a withdrawal of the church from the world. It prevents among its adherents, or those who are sympathizers, responsible Christian involvement in cultural institutions. Such was a valid concern of Reinhold Niebuhr, who worried that "an ethic of pure non-resistance can have no immediate relevance to any political situation" whatsoever.[19] A related defect, in my opinion, is that religious pacifists give too little attention to the church's rich and broad history, which affirms, rather than negates, the worth of the soldier and the magistrate alongside all vocations. Many pacifists are content to view themselves as a beleaguered (though superior) minority, unwilling to allow the authority of the church's consensual tradition to adjust their minority views, and they do this by donning a "prophetic" mantle. While this mindset will not always lead to an attitude of self-righteousness and prophetic posturing, very often, sadly, it does. This attitude in turn prevents honest and fruitful dialogue with Christians who disagree.

Pacifism in its religious expression is also weak at the theological level. In particular it is inadequate in helping us reconcile two important features of God's divine nature: God as warrior and God as the crucified one. Rec-

---

[19]Reinhold Niebuhr, "Why the Church Is Not Pacifist," in *Christianity and Power Politics* (New York: Charles Scribner's, 1940), pp. 9-10.

onciling these two divine attributes is no small point and needs to be confronted, as Darrell Cole has persuasively argued in his important recent book *When God Says War Is Right.*[20] Scripture alas is *filled* with allusions to the divine Warrior and his activity. What are we to make of this? Merely to spiritualize God's warring nature will not do. Neither will it suffice to say or imply that God evolves from an Old Testament conceptualization to that of the New Testament. The divine nature does not change. To argue that the New Testament has different ethical foundations than the Old will also not do. What we have here is a theological problem, and this problem will not go away.

Finally, pacifism fails to distinguish between homicide and murder—a distinction recognized by natural law, Scripture and church tradition. But we cannot ignore the social problem that confronts us on a continual basis: what to do about thieves, rapists and murderers, whether they operate as individuals or in gangs. In democratic societies we take for granted the norm that law backed by adequate force keeps evildoing in check. Not all killing is outlawed by Scripture and the Christian tradition. The sixth commandment applies to the killing of innocents, not moral retribution against those who do evil.

But let's pause for a moment to consider the alternatives if we are to assume that force and killing are *always or never* morally unjustified. Basically, we are left with two attitudes toward criminal behavior. One is to see the world as a jungle and unqualified brute force as the necessary means by which to keep an upper hand. In such a world, might *does* make right, and moral considerations fall by the wayside. The other response is to allow crime to occur, without any forcible restraints. We ride out all levels of social decay in the hope that people will become better (the secularist myth) or God will intervene and set things right in the eschaton (the religious version). The point is this: we are not limited to the two choices. Applied to the realm of crime and criminal justice, we are not confined to police brutality on the one hand or tolerating crime on the other. There is a third choice that is located somewhere in the *middle;* that is why we must get our hands dirty, as it were, and work for justice, whether in domestic affairs or foreign policy.

But when the issue is actual war, the pacifist seems to have a legitimate point. Aren't all wars inherently unjust, exuding the worst degree of brutish

---

[20]Darrell Cole, *When God Says War Is Right* (Colorado Springs: Waterbrook Press, 2002). See especially chapter two, "Why Christians Use Force," pp. 27-51.

violence that humans can know? As Augustine worried, warfare does breed the temptation to unleash unjustified violence. And the most common temptation for those engaged in battle is the killing of the innocent. Yet noncombatant immunity is one of two nonnegotiable moral criteria in the just-war tradition. Just-war thinking maintains the distinction between homicide and murder, a distinction that is affirmed in Scripture.

Much contemporary pacifism is grounded in a basic horror and revulsion at the notion of violence and bloodshed. While these are unquestionably horrible, policemen and emergency medical technicians, to their credit, voluntarily engage horror and bloodshed as a public service every day. Violence and bloodshed, hence, are not the worst of evils. The worse evil is not to engage social-moral evil when it manifests itself and innocent people are its victims. By analogy, just-war thinking applied to criminal justice leads us to a choice *between* crime and police brutality, between "softer" and "harder" forms of idealism.[21]

In addition, for decades pacifists have argued that because of the sheer destructive potential of modern weaponry and technology, war in the modern context is a moral absurdity, incapable of being justified in any circumstances or situation today. Even if war were not intrinsically evil, present circumstances and technological developments render war as obscene and morally indefensible.

But this objection does not let pacifists off the hook. They will need to offer some rationale for public policy, even when they themselves do not involve themselves in those policy debates. While pacifism may be the dictate of the private conscience, as it was in my father's faith, it cannot be *public* policy. The use of the police force and the military is a matter of social policy, and we citizens ultimately bear moral responsibility for enacting policy. Christians—motivated by charity and a sense of justice—must be involved in the process of policy-making, even when it is not the church that enacts policy.

THE MORAL CRITERIA OF THE JUST-WAR POSITION

In chapter two I attempted to show that both pacifist and nonpacifist strains were present in the early church. Those who argue that early Christians were uniformly pacifistic contend that just-war thinking represents a compromise

---

[21]Inis L. Claude Jr. argues convincingly for this via media in "Just Wars: Doctrines and Institutions," *Political Science Quarterly* 95, no. 1 (1980): 83-96.

of the church in its relation to the state. These Christians, once they began soldiering and going to war, were said to be "doing ethics for Caesar," as one prominent pacifist theologian has described it.[22] But in addition to ignoring evidence of Christians serving in the military in the first several centuries, this portrait is both inaccurate and unfair. One simply cannot read Augustine's *City of God* and still maintain that this Christian theologian was encouraging fellow Christians to do "ethics for Caesar."

The just-war tradition, it needs to be emphasized, is not merely about military tactics and strategy; it is much more. Just-war thinking, properly viewed, is a *theory of statecraft* that views peace as not only possible but morally obligatory as a byproduct of just relationships. Peace, however, is not to be understood as the absence of conflict; it is rather the fruit or byproduct of a justly ordered society. At its best, as one student of just-war theory writes, the tradition has worked to forge moral and political links between the limited use of armed force and the pursuit of peace, security, justice and freedom. This linkage rests on a foundational assumption, that is, that morality and politics "do not exist in hermetically sealed compartments of life. Rather, the tradition insists that there is one indivisible human universe of thought and action, a universe that is . . . inescapably moral and inescapably political."[23] Just war, then, is an account of politics that places politics

> within an ethically shaped framework and commits its adherents—by definition, all citizens who share some sense, however loosely defined, of just and unjust, fair and unfair—to debates of a particular kind whenever and wherever a resort to force is contemplated.[24]

Unlike both militarism and pacifism, which sever morality and politics, and encourage a false dichotomy between private and public morality, just-war thinking weighs motives and takes into account the realities of human nature. It understands that while might never makes right in and of itself, it *can* find moral applications that serve what is right.

The average layperson might be surprised to learn of the high profile that just-war thinking has in American military life and policy. Just-war theory is a significant component in the ethics curriculum of our service academies.

---

[22]This is the view of Anabaptist theologian John Howard Yoder in *The Politics of Jesus* (Grand Rapids: Eerdmans, 1972), and *The Original Revolution* (Scottdale: Herald Press, 1971).

[23]George Weigel, "From Last Resort to Endgame: Morality, the Gulf War, and the Peace Process," in *But Was It Just?* ed. David E. DeCosse (New York: Doubleday, 1992), pp. 19-20.

[24]Elshtain, "Just War as Politics," p. 46.

My appreciation for this has deepened as a result of a dear friend, a commander in the U.S. Navy, who teaches a class titled "Faith and Force" at the Naval War College in Newport, Rhode Island. And at a recent ethics conference at the University of Notre Dame, I listened with gratitude as an ethics professor from the U.S. Air Force War College described the nature of ethics instruction required of officers in his branch of the service. Perhaps no other nation agonizes over the morality of war and warfare as does ours.

To be sure, there are secular versions of the just-war tradition, notably in the modern era. What's more, secular thinkers and institutions at times have been the chief transmitters of the tradition, more so than Christian influence per se. The frequently unacknowledged debt to Christian moral reflection nevertheless has been astutely pointed out by James Turner Johnson:

> Today we have versions of just war thinking in international law . . . in military codes of conduct, in the thought of political philosophers like Michael Walzer, and even in the language of policy. But there are reasons to maintain a specifically Christian perspective on this issue, not only for informing the behavior of individual Christians who may be involved in the use of force as ordinary police or soldiers or in commanding roles, up to the highest level of government, but also as a way of contributing to a rigorous public debate aimed at understanding the justifications and limits of the use of force in the nation and the world today.[25]

What are those norms that help determine the *relative* justness or rightness of a cause?[26] Two groups of criteria, already alluded to in chapters two and three, serve as guidelines for just-war thinking. These criteria help in deciding whether to go to war (the historic *ius ad bellum*) and how to conduct war (the *ius in bello*). Although many discussions of just war contain longer lists of *ius ad bellum* criteria that are probably familiar to us, there are three core criteria from which all others derive. These three were identified by Thomas Aquinas and have served as a basis for all subsequent just-war theory up to the present: just cause, proper authority and right intention.[27]

Ius ad bellum. *1. Just cause.* A nation or people group must be able to identify an injury or injustice inflicted. When a nation invades and an-

---

[25]James Turner Johnson, "Can Force Be Used Justly? Questions of Retributive and Restorative Justice," the 2001 Kuyper lecture, delivered November 1, 2001, at Gordon College, Wenham, Massachusetts.

[26]Strong nationalists and crusader types lose sight of the reality. With Augustine we must remember that no earthly order is wholly just or good.

[27]Thomas Aquinas *Summa Theologiae* 2-2.Q40.

nexes as its own another nation, people group or territory, the most basic human rights to sovereignty are violated. Military intervention is just in restoring those inalienable rights.[28] Just cause wrestles with an appropriate response where gross injustice and moral culpability are established. It defends the basic order of justice that has been violated. Sufficient justification for war, according to Grotius, also arises from humanitarian abuses, that is, when another state "inflicts upon his subjects such treatment as no one is warranted in inflicting."[29] Grotius, it must be emphasized, developed a lengthy list of unjust causes alongside those situations that were deemed just.[30]

Do all people possess certain rights that are self-evident and inalienable? What are these? How has basic justice been violated or withheld? And from the standpoint of the party considering war, are there certain things that are worth sacrifice, worth risking death, even worth dying to preserve or defend? A weakness of the pacifist perspective is that it does not consider certain rights of others as inalienable and worth defending.

2. Proper authority. War, according to Aquinas, can only be waged by sovereign authorities. In a day when private wars, piracy and vandalism were justified, Thomas's emphasis on order and proper authority is not misplaced. Once private warfare becomes normative, all matters degenerate into revenge. The magistrate, he argued, represents the people and thus is responsible for protecting the commonweal against anarchy and tyranny. Public goods require public authority to act on behalf of the community. This burden is the heart of politics—a necessity that Aquinas grasps. Inherently modern questions such as the process by which governing authorities come into power are not a concern of Thomas in his discussion of war. However, his emphasis on protecting the common good presupposes that those authorities are not despotic in nature. Also ruled out are public offi-

---

[28]Significantly, Aquinas does not distinguish between offensive or defensive wars, although later just-war thinkers do.

[29]Hugo Grotius *The Law of War and Peace* 2.25.7.

[30]While Grotius lays a theoretical foundation for military intervention, there exists no present consensus in just-war doctrine supporting a right to military intervention not narrowly considered "self-defense." Nevertheless, William V. O'Brien writes that "the substance of the just cause in just revolution is to remove a government that is *intolerable to its subjects* . . . [and] this just cause is a kind of self-defense of the people." In such a scenario, according to O'Brien, "resistance to a *violently oppressive or genocidal* . . . government may literally be justified as self-defense" ("Just War Doctrine's Complementary Role in the International Law of War," in *Legal and Moral Constraints in Low-Intensity Conflicts,* ed. Alberto R. Coll et al. [Newport, R.I.: Naval War College, 1995], p. 189, emphasis added).

cials who have no duly constituted governing authority.[31]

The sword in the hand of the magistrate, moreover, is to be wielded against both internal and external enemies, against criminal individuals as well as unjust states. Both can undermine justice at the elementary level. Coercive force will be necessary if a justly ordered peace is to be preserved. Force is neither to be misused through indiscriminate application nor considered inherently evil. Political scientist Russell Hittinger has expressed well the necessary moral sentiment: "there are [certain moral] goods worth the risk of war and . . . 'peace at any price' is unacceptable."[32]

The ability to declare and go to war is not merely a legal formality. It is rather the meeting place of morality and political prudence. Both militarism and pacifism miss the essence of political responsibility. The former rides roughshod over any moral considerations, focusing purely on what it believes to be military necessity. By its ignoring of moral considerations it undermines the very legitimacy of politics. The latter devalues the political realm, either by its disengagement or by its attempts to undermine policy. Its failure is a failure to recognize the role that politics plays in preserving the peace. The former abuses political power; the latter negates it.

3. Right intention. Unjust war is perhaps best illustrated by what does *not* constitute right intention. Such scenarios include a sovereign's pride or reputation, national aggrandizement, blood thirst and territorial expansion. For war to be just its aim must be a greater good, and that greater good is a justly ordered peace. Where the magistrate or political sovereign is acutely aware of the responsibility to protect the commonweal of his or her population or another, chances are greater that just criteria have been met for going to war. The establishment of a just peace rules out the possibility of territorial domination, revenge or other wrong motives. Within just-war thinking the goal of war is to *stop* the strongman, not killing. Therefore, killing in war is not murder. A just response acknowledges the greater goal of a just peace and

---

[31]More recently, discussions of proper authority have been focused on the United Nations. While working with the U.N. is politically prudent, there is no moral obligation on the part of a nation contemplating war to receive consent from this body since (1) the U.N. does not technically "wield the sword" as a national government does, and (2) due to its commitment to avoid war it runs the risk of fostering unjust peace. As did its predecessor, the League of Nations, it also runs the risk of being irrelevant to the concerns of justice, particularly when rogue nations have (potentially) greater representation in its process than democratic ones.

[32]Russell Hittinger, "Just War and Defense Policy," in *Natural Law and Contemporary Public Policy,* ed. David F. Forte (Washington, D.C.: Georgetown University Press, 1998), p. 342.

goes beyond sentiments of hatred and vengeance that are so typical of human behavior. It is cognizant that anything apart from just cause negates the morality of the response.

These three core conditions represent the heart of just-war thinking. Together, however, they give rise to other related conditions. While these latter tend to be the focus of most contemporary discussions of just war, they are secondary to the core conditions, being foremost prudential considerations. That is, they express political prudence, are eminently imprecise and derive from the core criteria discussed above:

Last resort. Have all *reasonable* efforts to utilize nonmilitary (e.g., diplomatic, economic and political) alternatives been exhausted?[33] Last resort reflects the gravity of acts of force, even though it is a factor only when the other principle conditions have been weighed.[34]

Reasonable chance of success. Based on projected losses and inherent dangers, is there a reasonable chance of victory? Is the cause hopeless and thus politically and militarily unwise?[35]

Proportionate means. The principle of proportion lies at the heart of justice in general and military necessity in particular. Does the just goal desired equal or surpass the losses that war will produce? What is the ultimate cost of war and loss imposed on both sides? Does the cost indicate that the war effort was worth the endeavor?

Peace as ultimate aim. Does going to war proceed with the ultimate goal of establishing a just peace and political-social stability? Does the likelihood of achieving a greater good guide the prospects of going to war?

Ius in Bello. *1. Discrimination (= noncombatant immunity).* The same moral reasoning that leads to determinations about going to war contributes to conduct in war. Ends and means are related. This linkage is particularly relevant for the militarist, who can justify war but fail to apply any restraints in prosecuting war. The most basic moral prohibition, even in war, is the taking of innocent life. This proscription is part of the natural

---

[33]The qualifier *reasonable* is important, since those who oppose all war in principle will never see diplomatic possibilities as having been exhausted.
[34]The operative word here is *reasonable*. It is immoral—and counterproductive—when "last resort" stalls just response to the extent that it becomes too late to defend the just cause.
[35]Although frequent situations arise that cry out for just intervention, some will hold little likelihood of success. While there may be a moral justification for a seemingly hopeless intervention of resistance, just-war reasoning seeks to balance a potential greater good against the costs and losses of war incurred.

moral law and confirmed in legal codes ancient and modern. Guilt is predicated on intention. The noncombatant—inclusive of civilian populations,
wounded soldiers, prisoners, women, children and males—cannot be held
guilty. Because of human dignity, respect for life is not to be forgotten.
Inflicting suffering or injury that is not directly related to morally legitimate
strategic purposes is strictly prohibited.[36] A fundamental flaw of both militarism and totalitarianism is an indiscriminate attitude toward human life.
Accordingly, all and any may be sacrificed for the greater political end.[37]

2. *Proportionality.* Just-war thinking distinguishes itself from crusading or
militarism by its commitment to *limit* war. This is a moral stricture that is all
but ignored by the religious or secular militarist, who is willing to enter into
total war. The motivation behind this warring spirit is either nationalist or,
as in the case currently, religious. Doubtless it can be both. Any necessary
means is justifiable to obliterate the enemy. But the principle of proportionality rests on several basic assumptions. Force is an entity that can be regu-
lated, and the degree of force applied is not to be greater than what is
needed to render the enemy compliant. In principle, all-out war would be
counter to the very reason for being of the armed forces in nontotalitarian
nations. To wrestle with proportionality of response is to discern what is
"reasonable" in terms of economy of force in a given situation.

Because just-war criteria give an *approximate* account of what is just,
we are forbidden from giving an absolute or definitive answer to the question, Was this war just? There will be differing opinions, even among those
who adopt just-war principles. This is not to say we cannot work for justice; it means only that justice will be less than perfect in this life. The duty
of justice, one student of American law has observed, rests on the entire
population, not merely politicians or the military: "All bear the full weight
of these duties: the political authorities, the citizens who elect them to
power, and the military personnel who must implement such policies."[38]

But the alternative is to allow injustice free rein in this world.[39]

---

[36]Russell Hittinger cites as an example the battlefield code of the U.S. Air Force containing strict
guidelines that are required of its pilots ("Just War and Defense Policy," p. 347).

[37]O'Brien observes: "The principles of proportion and discrimination are difficult to apply at all
levels of the spectrum of military force." Some wars, for example, are fought "where the bellig-
erents and civilians are closely intermixed" ("Just War Doctrine's Complementary Role," p. 194).

[38]Ibid., p. 349.

[39]For helpful discussions of just-war criteria that are not overly technical, see Jean Bethke Elshtain, *Just War Against Terror* (New York: Basic Books, 2003), and Darrell Cole, *When God
Says War Is Right* (Colorado Springs: Waterbrook, 2002), esp. chapters 4 and 5.

THE JUSTICE OF DETERRENCE

We have observed thus far that the just-war tradition both permits *(ius ad bellum)* and limits *(ius in bello)* the use of coercive force. In this way it shows itself to be a mediating position between militarism and pacifism. Human beings should neither assume that everything is always permissible nor believe that nothing ever is. Implicit in this way of understanding war and force is that reprisal *can* be morally justified. William O'Brien has expressed this sentiment well:

> Few rights are more solidly established in the law of nations than the right of reprisal. . . . This exceptional right applies to all the laws of war. It is supposed to serve two purposes: it provides a sanction for the law and it tends to restore the balance upset when one belligerent uses illegal means.[40]

The ethics of the just-war position can be summarized in its two basic assumptions. The very moral tradition that sanctions the use of coercive force also establishes moral limits as to what is a just response. Together these two assumptions raise the important question of deterrence. As anyone working in the criminal justice system knows, fierce debates have been raging for some time, at least among social scientists, about the morality and utility of deterrence. Does deterrence really work? People are sharply divided. Those who are skeptical generally have a more secular understanding of human nature: humans are basically good, not flawed, and punishment is injurious to the person's psyche.

By contrast, Christians and religious people in general intuit that punishment and retribution deter human beings from doing evil. These are necessary instruments for restoring a just peace and social order. Just ask any parent. Does punishment deter? The only case in which it does not deter is the child who has never known moral restrictions. For that individual few things short of death will inhibit evildoing.

That punishment and retribution do have a deterrent effect on people is strongly suggested in various biblical texts. One such text is Deuteronomy 19, with a parallel account in Numbers 35. Deuteronomy 19 happens to serve as a preface to instructions on going to war (chap. 20). Cities are to be designated in Israel as places of refuge to which a killer might flee. If the killing was accidental, "the judges must make a thorough investigation"

---

[40]William V. O'Brien, "Nuclear War and the Law of Nations," in *Morality and Modern Warfare,* ed. William J. Nagle (Baltimore: Helicon, 1960), p. 140.

(Deut 19:18). Based on the evidence of multiple witnesses, a verdict is to be given. If the person is found to have intended the killing, he or she is to be put to death. If it is found to be an accident, the killer lives. The purpose of this procedure is stated unambiguously: "You must purge the evil from among you. The rest of the people will hear of this and be afraid, and never again will such an evil thing be done among you" (Deut 19:19-20). This is the language of deterrence.

If we assume from the outset that retribution or just reprisal does deter, the question then becomes: Should we deter evil? And if so, in what manner and to what degree?

Just-war principles as they have developed in the Christian tradition proceed from charity. When an injustice has occurred, the just response is a response *in kind*. This accent is present among just-war theorists from Ambrose and Augustine to Paul Ramsey and James Turner Johnson. For this reason, then, we might speak of a "law of reprisal"—an all-embracing and unchanging rule of conduct that has retribution and restoration in view. Just retribution distinguishes itself from revenge or retributivism in fundamentally important ways. The Christian moreover views the obligations of justice to issue out of love, even when such a notion seems absurd to many religious people and certainly to society at large. Again, I cite Augustine in this regard: when "men are prevented, by being alarmed, from doing wrong, it may be said that a real service is done to them."[41] And not only to them but to society as well.

Just reprisal then is more than a legal concept; it is a moral good. And yet laws at any given time in a society may not be a reflection of justice and the greater good; they may abet injustice. In a cultural climate where laws do not in fact mirror justice, where legality and morality do not correspond, it is the task of its citizens—and foremost of Christians—to contend for notions of justice that over time will contribute to a change in legal climate. Perhaps we presently live in such a cultural climate.

Just reprisal is rooted in natural moral law—that universal bar of justice known through reason to which all people and all nations are held accountable. Where natural law is ignored or eclipsed, social and legal dilemmas abound, and moral rot eventually sets in, yielding catastrophic consequences where spiritual renewal does not intervene. The two most likely

---

[41]Augustine *Epistle* 47.

scenarios following moral decay in society are a softer or harder form of totalitarianism.

Most contemporary observers, and not a few Christians, assume that American society—and, for the moment permit me to write as an American—could never become "totalized" and oppressive. After all, we convince ourselves, democratic government has built-in checks and balances. What is more, we have never known the dark side of statist rule and oppression that have visited other societies. While these balances do potentially retard the speed with which a society degenerates, they are foremost procedural and do not affect the moral foundations of a people. When a whole people—and everything in that culture—is full of putrefaction and moral rot, it is only a question of time as to when the system collapses and a "new elite" must step in to fill the power vacuum that has resulted.

But my interest here is not to engage in apocalyptic gloom. The point to be made is this: there is a qualitative difference between *legality* and *morality*. Laws will inevitably be a reflection of the values of a particular society. This is why Christians—religious conservatives especially, at least in the American context—need to be saved from the folly of trying to change laws and enact legislation without simultaneously seeking to change the way people think. The laws of the land will follow the engine of values and principles that a people holds dear. If a people's highest values are self-interest and autonomy, its laws will become utilitarian. If a society has a low regard for the value of human life (whether at the beginning or at the end of the life spectrum), then its laws will reflect that view of human personhood.

To attempt to change culture by merely changing its laws is at best cosmetic. Our priority is to change the hearts and minds of people. This is slow, arduous work. That is why evangelism proper (in the narrow use of the term), while important, is only a small part of what Pope John Paul II has called "evangelization" of culture. That is, we must begin to reseed culture from the ground up, as it were, training and educating our own in terms of broader Christian worldview thinking so we are prepared to impart values to broader culture. If we resist or ignore long-term efforts to educate and penetrate culture by changing the way people think, no amount of "godly legislation"—or evangelism, for that matter—will ever be able to change culture at the root. It will be the equivalent of pouring Roses Lime Juice on cancer.

What does this have to do with deterrence? Contemporary Western culture generally holds punishment, all punishment, to be cruel, absurd and ir-

rational. Retribution is frowned on if not outright rejected by the social sciences. Strangely and somewhat ironically, not a few criminologists oppose
punishment more vehemently than many of their fellow social scientists.[42]
For this reason we speak today of prisons as "correctional facilities" rather
than "penitentiaries." And sentences for crimes committed, resulting in incarceration, are understood to have a *rehabilitative* rather than *penal* goal.
Justice to contemporary society is foremost *therapeutic* in character, not *retributive*.[43] So to argue today for the morality of punishment and retribution
in our present social climate is nothing short of scandalous.

But an inconvenient question presents itself: How is the moral balance in
society restored in the event that one of its members acts illegally? What happens when heinous crime or crimes against humanity occur? In what manner
does any restoration transpire (if it does at all)? Is "restoring the moral balance" reserved for the next life? Is the unpleasant business of retribution as
restoration reserved only for God?

To the point: Today there are not a few Christians who stubbornly maintain
that retribution—whether in the criminal justice system or among the nations—
is unjust and immoral. But it will not do merely (or chiefly) to argue that Jesus'
teaching is nonviolent in nature, and therefore, prohibits us. Nor is it morally
responsible to relegate the messy matter of justice (in either domestic or foreign
policy) to unbelievers. Both of these solutions fail to do justice to justice itself.
Both transfer back to God and God alone what providence has already commissioned to the magistrate and the magistrate alone as a temporal obligation.

But is just reprisal really necessary? Don't we thereby play God? The answer
need not elude us: *only* if and when the governing authorities, or the state, are
placed above God. The fear among some that Romans 13 will be misused as

---

[42]A graphic example of this absurdity is found in a symposium published in June 1994 issue of
the journal *Criminal Justice Ethics*. Here a number of political scientists, philosophers and
social scientists (including one criminologist) were invited to evaluate James Q. Wilson's recently published book *The Moral Sense* (New York: Basic Books, 1993). Wilson had argued
that there is a universal moral sense within all people, irrespective of culture, customs and
time. Such a moral sense shows itself in the fact that all people everywhere denounce murder,
child molestation, theft, adultery and so forth while cherishing community, honesty, reliability
and so on. The symposium member who most vehemently objected to Wilson's argument, at
it turned out, was the criminologist, who grew livid that Wilson condemned cannibalism. Wilson's "moralism" and Christianity in general, added the criminologist, "spoil" pagan feasts that
are a rich part of cultures other than ours. This objection, recall, came from someone who
teaches future law-enforcement officers, political scientists and social scientists.
[43]I do not deny that punishment has a restorative or therapeutic element. I only wish to point
out that the punitive is scandalous to our contemporaries.

it has at times in history is to be taken seriously. This can be a legitimate concern. But politics and government will always run the risk of overstepping their bounds. This is because human beings (i.e., fallen creatures) inhabit the world in which politics and government live. As an institution, political office is no more intrinsically flawed than any other human institution, whether the work place or education or entertainment or the arts or the scientific laboratory. Humans will always be tempted to displace the Sovereign of the universe. This we call idolatry. And indeed political idolatry is a temptation in every era, not merely in the form of 1930s National Socialism.

But even this blasphemous recurring tendency does not remove the fact that the Lord God Almighty has given the magistrate a role to play in human affairs, and that is to reward good and punish evil. What humans fail—or refuse—to do, the governing authorities are under obligation to constrain. It matters not where one lives or when one lives in human history. The magistrate performs the role of a divine servant; *diakonos* (deacon) is the language used by Paul in Romans 13 to depict governing authorities' chief function. And whether the authorities possess faith or not is irrelevant to the question of how the authorities function in civil society. The civil and the salvific are unrelated in the economy of God.

Years ago while doing criminal justice work, I came to understand the force and salutary effect of deterrence. Ironically, this awareness grew as I was doing research on capital punishment. At the time (early 1990s), law enforcement authorities in Washington, D.C., were finding it increasingly difficult to find witnesses to corroborate evidence against murder suspects. Many of these cases, as it happened, were drug-related. Why was it getting so difficult to find witnesses to testify against murder suspects? Were the crimes all occurring with no one present? Not necessarily. The real problem was that potential witnesses were terrified to testify, because if they did, they did so under the threat of death.

Now consider, for the moment, conventional thinking among social scientists. Increasingly, there have been calls to abandon the traditional notion of criminal justice, with its retributive core, for a more "medical" or biological model.[44] Some criminologists, correlatively, have been repeatedly telling

---

[44]See, e.g., W. Wayt Gibbs, "Seeking the Criminal Element," *Scientific American,* March 1995, pp. 100-107. I assess this growing consensus in "Blame It on the Beta-Boosters: Genetics, Self-Determination and Moral Accountability," in *Genetic Engineering: A Christian Response,* ed. T. J. Demy and G. P. Stewart (Grand Rapids: Kregel, 1999), pp. 241-58.

us that punishment—and capital punishment, in particular—*does not* deter. Moreover, study after study is said to demonstrate that punishment does not deter.[45] Meanwhile, out on the streets of D.C. (not to mention other major cities around the United States), drug dealers know whether or not punishment—and specifically, threat of death—deters. They threaten to kill any potential witnesses who might rat. And guess what? Those potential witnesses invariably clam up.

My argument is simple, although I do not wish to be simplistic. We deceive ourselves if we think that we can hand over to God our civic, moral or filial duties, under the justification that (1) Christians should not involve themselves in these duties, or (2) unbelievers should perform these duties. Can punishment be draconian and unjust? Indeed, it can. Can justice be perverted? Of course. Do we humans err in our feeble attempts to work for justice? Without question. And let us be honest: retribution is not the only dimension of justice. This goes without saying. But to understand justice fully apart from its retributive function, which has a restorative component, is to empty it of its major constitutive element. For that reason parents do not cut off the hands of their children when their kids are caught stealing from the cookie jar. But neither do we—if we value justice—slap people on the wrist who have plotted to murder innocents in cold blood. Justice demands both permission and limits. And those limits have upper as well as lower restrictions.

Will all evildoers be deterred? Certainly not. And if that is the end of the argument, we can stop right here. However, simply because some individuals or people groups demonstrate a pathological and incorrigible tendency does not therefore mean that the threat of punishment has no deterrent effect on human beings. It simply means that in particular cases, evil has been so normalized that nothing, or at least very little, will deter them.

Now the reader at this point might say "Well and good. I have no problem with your argument as it applies to the criminal justice system. But war is a different matter." Fair enough. The potential for deception in the politics of war is great. And who is morally astute enough for such matters? Depending on our perspective, no one. All humans are in the same boat; all fall short of perfect justice, and all fall short of perfect construals of justice. And what politician can be trusted to take us—or any nation—into armed conflict?

---

[45]In fairness I should note that social scientists tend to produce studies "demonstrating" the ineffectiveness of the death penalty, whereas economists routinely publish studies that "prove" the opposite: capital punishment does deter.

Without question, the responsibilities of government are supremely daunting. Which is why we are commanded to pray for our leaders (1 Tim 2:1-6). But the *politics of justice* in all its forms, whether domestic or foreign policy, in matters ranging from incarceration to the death penalty to war, is always susceptible to error. Which is why political decisions are removed from the private domain, as Aquinas insisted, and reserved for public officials. In our culture this process typically unfolds through consensus. We do not trust individuals who are unaccountable. We do not trust only one political party, whatever our own political affiliation. For better or worse we operate in plurality, through representative government, in (relative) consensus. And in the long run, provided democracy does not collapse from within (which *may* happen where moral reasoning is bleached from the process), we all are responsible to work for justice.

For this reason any interpretation of the Bible or mandate for the Christian community that calls us away from the cultural mainstream and that breeds civil disengagement is inconsistent with the teaching of Scripture and is to be rejected as sectarian. Even those interpretations that don the mantle of "prophetic" authority.

RETRIBUTION OR REVENGE?

A common objection, both in foreign policy and in criminal justice, is the following: Isn't justice as retribution merely a pretext for vengeance? Clearly, revenge is not rooted in love of one's neighbor. Pacifists conclude that because of the human tendency toward vindictiveness, we should not enter into conflict with a foe. How might we respond?

The Christian moral tradition distinguishes the retributive act from revenge, vindication from vindictiveness, in important and unmistakable ways. At the most fundamental level it understands punishment or retribution to be established by divine agency, manifesting itself both in this life and after death, "often visibly, always invisibly."[46] A letter written by Augustine to his friend, Marcellinus, who is a Roman official in Carthage, is instructive in the way it addresses the subject of punishment. Marcellinus had previously written Augustine to ask for help in answering common objections to Christian faith raised by influential pagans. One of their charges was that Christianity is incompatible with sound political rule and civic responsibility.

---

[46]So Augustine *City of God* 20.1.

You added that they say that the preaching and teaching of Christ are not at all suitable for the morals of a republic. They have in mind the precept that we should not return evil for evil to anyone, but turn the other cheek to anyone who strikes us, give our tunic to anyone who takes our coat, and walk a double journey with anyone who would force us to go with him (Mt. 5:39-41). They assert that all of these things are contrary to the morals of a republic.[47]

Augustine begins his response by asking a rhetorical question. The question sounds something like this: How is it that those who supposedly overlook evil rather than punishing it are able to govern the republic? Is this the way a republic is really maintained? What is a republic if it is not a *public* affair? Is it not a multitude of people who have joined together and made mutual commitments to one another?

Augustine initially attacks the popular distortion that is widespread. He explains that Jesus' teaching in the Sermon on the Mount is intended to address *personal* attitudes: "these precepts refer to a disposition of the heart." The effect of Christ's teaching is that "a man is freed from an evil that is *not external and foreign* but *inner and personal.*" At the private level Augustine reminds his friend, overcoming evil with good may be quite effective in changing human behavior. A godly person, therefore, "ought to be prepared to endure patiently the malice of those whom he seeks to make good."[48]

So far, so good. However, "with respect to those who, contrary to their own will, need to be set straight" (in other words, with those who are a public menace), we take up very different measures, even though these measures are rooted in the same right intention. And how do we respond? Augustine has this to say: "[M]any things must be done with a certain *benevolent harshness.*" And his rationale? "*Their welfare rather than their wishes* must be considered. . . . He whose license for wrongdoing is wrested away is usefully conquered, for nothing is less prosperous than the prosperity of sinners, which nourishes . . . and strengthens the evil will."[49] Thus charity—if it has moral backbone and is not sloppy sentimentalism—will want what is best for the criminal and for the public at large.

At its base the moral outrage expressed through retributive justice is first

---

[47]Augustine *Epistle* 138. I am relying on the English translation provided by Michael W. Tkacz and Douglas Kries, in *Augustine: Political Writings* (Indianapolis: Hackett, 1994), p. 205.
[48]Ibid., pp. 206-7 (emphasis added).
[49]Ibid., pp. 208-9 (emphasis added).

and foremost rooted in moral principle, not mere emotional outrage and hatred. Recall Augustine's words to Marcellinus: retribution is a form of "benevolent harshness." The governing authorities, by punishing criminal behavior, mirror a concern for the welfare of the population and for those doing the wrong. Any parent knows the truth of this principle. Indeed, not to act against the will of a wrongdoer, in the words of Augustine, is to "nourish and strengthen the will toward evil." It needs reemphasis, especially in our culture, that *it is virtuous and not vicious to feel anger at moral evil.* In truth, something is very wrong with us if we do not express anger and moral outrage at evil. And yet moral outrage alone is not enough.

But in what specific ways are retribution and revenge different? There are several critical distinctions. Whereas revenge strikes out at real or perceived injury, retribution speaks to an objective wrong. Whereas revenge is wild, insatiable and not subject to limitations, retribution has both upper and lower limits, acknowledging the moral repugnance both of assigning draconian punishment to petty crimes as well as light punishment to heinous crimes. Vengeance, by its nature, has a thirst for injury and delights in bringing further evil upon the offending party. The avenger will not only kill but rape, torture, plunder and burn what is left, deriving satisfaction from its victim's direct or indirect suffering. Augustine described this inclination, rooted in the flesh, as a "lust for revenge."[50] Retribution has as its goal a greater social good and takes no pleasure in punishment.

Finally, whereas revenge, because of its retaliatory mode, will target both the offending party as well as those perceived to be akin, retribution is both targeted yet impersonal and impartial, not subject to personal bias. For this reason Lady Justice is depicted as blindfolded. The difference between retribution and revenge is the difference between Romans 13 and the end of Romans 12. In the latter the apostle describes and prohibits what renders justice illicit: the private sphere. "Vigilante justice" is justice that is enacted apart from the governing authorities. In another context, the public sphere, justice becomes legitimate and, indeed, divinely instituted. The governing authorities are commissioned to "bear the sword," and they do so "not in vain."

The pacifist argument then against revenge is partially flawed on two levels. It ignores the fact that capitulation to our foe may well subject us—*and*

---

[50]Augustine *City of God* 14.14.

our neighbor—to a *worse* brand of vindictiveness, and it fails to make the critical moral distinction between revenge and retribution, which is the basis of our criminal justice system. Understood properly, retributive justice serves a civilized culture, whether in domestic or international context. It isolates individuals, parties or people groups who endanger the community—locally, nationally or internationally—for their wanton disregard for the common good and a just peace. It controls the extent to which a citizenry is victimized by criminal acts. It rewards the perpetrator proportionately with consequences befitting the crime. And it forces both the offender(s) and potential offenders to reflect on the grievous nature of the crime. Each of these elements is critical in preserving the social order.

Augustine is not naive about political realities. He does not turn a blind eye toward the injustices of the Roman Empire. But he does seem to have little patience for the notion that Christianity will passively tolerate evil based on a particularly distorted understanding of Jesus' teaching. Even pagans, he notes, are capable of displaying extraordinary civic virtue without religious faith. How much more will Christian faith make us good citizens?

Pacifists will frequently argue that retribution constitutes an uncivilized or barbaric response by society to crime or moral evil. But is this the case? Our answer depends fundamentally on how a society perceives the moral difference between the criminal and the punitive act. If society refuses to make this moral distinction, which the cardinal virtue of justice is committed to do, then it is impossible to denounce moral evil—anywhere, in any form, at any time.[51]

Seen in this light, the Nuremberg trials were wrongheaded, since Nazi war crimes—indeed, any crimes against humanity—cannot in principle be denounced, much less can mass murderers be put on trial and sentenced. In the end, one person's torture was another person's good time.

Our society's deeply entrenched moral evasiveness begins with its relative indifference to the marker, "Thou shalt not murder." The Torah, it must be remembered, does not forbid taking the life of a human being; rather, it forbids premeditated murder. Indeed Jewish and Christian moral traditions concur in acknowledging justifiable forms of homicide, such as self-defense, protecting civilians and resisting insurrection. In a morally courageous society this list would be extended to include waging a just war in a morally justified scenario.

---

[51]At this point pacifists, in order to be consistent, will need to advocate the abolition of the *entire* judicial and criminal justice system.

The impulse toward retribution is innate in human beings, not because it is a lower or primitive impulse; rather, it is because of the divine image within us. To treat people or nations, however severely, in accordance with the belief that they should have known better—and they *do* know better—is to treat them as responsible human beings, endowed with human dignity and moral agency. A society unwilling to direct retributive justice toward those who murder in cold blood is a society that has deserted its responsibility to uphold the sanctity of human life. Civilized society will not tolerate murder at any level; an uncivilized one, however, will.[52]

To affirm retribution, which is integral to the history of Judeo-Christian moral thinking and foundational to any self-governing society, is not to abandon our belief in mercy and forgiveness. But it does acknowledge the difference between the criminal and the punitive act as well as between private and public recourse. In the end mercy does not release the public demands that justice imposes.[53]

Retributive justice then is a moral necessity for a civilized culture. In responding retributively to moral evil, we channel our energies in several directions. We respond to victims who have been wronged; we respond to wider society that has been scandalized by the wrong done in its midst; we respond to the actual offending party by declaring that moral evil will not be tolerated; and we respond to future offenders who might be tempted to engage in the same evil. Understood correctly, retributive justice performs a multifaceted moral good.[54]

---

[52]The fact remains that despite its flaws, we cannot dispense with criminal justice, whether at the domestic or international level. And in the end, the "root cause" of the criminal's or terrorist's pathology becomes relatively immaterial, since neighbor-love requires that we punish and incarcerate. This, alas, is just cause.

[53]A most helpful and succinct examination of the difference between retribution and revenge is found in David A. Crocker, "Retribution and Reconciliation," *Philosophy and Public Policy,* winter/spring 2000, pp. 1-6.

[54]Elsewhere I have sought to underscore the critical distinction between retribution and revenge/retributivism in the context of criminal justice. See J. Daryl Charles, "The Sword of Justice," *Touchstone,* December 2001, pp. 12-16.

7

JUST-WAR THEORY AND
THE PROBLEM OF TERRORISM

It has been said that policy is the hand of practical reason. And indeed it is. But let's go a step further. Policy, rightly understood, is the meeting place of politics and morality.[1] For this reason an important subtheme in this volume has been that Christians must be culturally engaged. To the extent that our culture wishes to remain civilized rather than barbarian, to the extent that we tolerate moral discourse and wrestle with the obligations of justice to our neighbor, Christians have opportunities to make significant contributions to our times.

Debates about war and the ethical use of force are, properly, the domain of the military. But they also belong in the public square, to which we all have access. One of the great challenges for Protestant churches today—and I write from within the Protestant evangelical tradition—is to expand our vision of Christian faith beyond mere devotional and inspirational concerns. While personal piety is important, and while God does bless our personal lives, our current focus (if I am to go by religious publishing trends) is extremely self-centered. We risk neglecting the weightier matters of religious faith—matters such as justice and mercy and social concern. We risk being ethically irrelevant.

What are implications of Christian faith as they touch not just my heart but broader society? What does Christian social ethics look like? How might Christian conviction apply to public policy concerns? Is it possible that

---

[1]This basic insight belongs to John Courtney Murray and forms the basis of his book *We Hold These Truths* (New York: Sheed & Ward, 1960).

Christians, particularly those in the West, might use their influence to re-
lieve oppression and great injustice around the world without succumbing
to the temptation of being nationalistic? What about the persecuted church?
Are we concerned at all that foreign policy might be directed to help alle-
viate the conditions under which our brothers and sisters in nondemocratic
states are suffering?

THE NATURE OF THE TERRORIST THREAT

If war confronts us with difficult issues, contemporary terrorism throws them
in our faces, and with a vengeance. And yet although the word *terrorism*
seems to describe a fairly recent phenomenon, the systematic terrorizing of
populations as a strategy of warfare, whether conventional, guerilla or private, is not new. Its purpose, very simply, is to destroy the morale of a people group, class or nation. Its method? Very simply, harassment or murder—
random murder, that is, of innocent people. As Christopher Harmon has reminded us, terrorism never loses its essential nature, and that is the abuse
of the innocent in the service of political goals.[2]

Reflecting a bit on the derivation of the word *terror* tells us much about
its character. It comes from the Latin *terrere,* "to cause to tremble," and as
Timothy Demy and Gary Stewart helpfully remind us, as a political (and at
times religious) act it has been with us for centuries in a variety of forms.[3]
In the varied attempts to try to define what terrorism really is, Demy and
Stewart suggest two working definitions that capture the spirit of the terrorist
threat:

- the deliberate and systematic murder, maiming and menacing of the innocent to inspire fear for political ends[4]

- the unlawful use of—or unthreatened use of force or violence against individuals or property to coerce or intimidate governments or societies, often to achieve political, religious, or ideological objectives

With these basic definitions in mind, let's consider, for the moment, what
is implied in these words. Terrorism, by the above description, is deliberate.
There is much to be said about this word.

---

[2]Christopher C. Harmon, *Terrorism Today* (London: Frank C. Cass, 2000), p. xv.
[3]Timothy Demy and Gary P. Stewart, *In the Name of God* (Eugene, Ore.: Harvest House, 2002),
   pp. 30-33.
[4]This definition is borrowed from Christopher C. Harmon, "Terrorism: A Matter for Moral Judge-
   ment," *Terrorism and Political Violence* 4, no. 1 (1992): 2.

All of criminal justice, of course, is based on the fundamental distinction between *intention* and *effect*. Mosaic law is meticulous in drawing this line as well. If you killed a person by accident and the judges so determined this in the presence of witnesses, your flight to the city of refuge prevented the avenger from slaying you. If, on the other hand, witnesses confirmed that the act was premeditated, your own life was required (Num 35:6-34; Deut 4:41-43; 19:1-21; Josh 20). Murder and homicide are not the same. Criminal negligence is always less offensive than intended criminal acts. Terrorism, by its very nature, is intended violence against innocent human beings. For this reason it is a moral abomination.

Regardless of its garb, terrorism is the deliberate violation of established moral norms. Victims are sometimes targeted, although very often they remain impersonal. To the terrorist way of thinking, there is no immunity granted to the innocent; all by virtue of association are guilty. This indiscriminate method of killing delivers a powerful psychological message, implanting fear in others who are just like those assassinated. In some policy circles it has been debated, particularly since 9/11, whether terrorism is most akin to criminal activity or war. My position is that it is both, thus requiring responses that are informed by both definitions.[5]

But what separates terrorists from "gangsters," at least as we have come to know them, is their randomness, their political code and the global scope of their activity. For this reason they are frequently defended by propagandists and apologists as reputed representatives of oppressed minority peoples. By virtue of these peoples' marginalization in the world—no fault of their own, of course—many in Western culture who are bereft of moral reasoning choose to identify with the marginalized and by extension the terrorists. As the saying goes, one man's terrorist is another man's freedom fighter.[6]

The moral response to this, however, is not to view terrorism as the natural and somewhat "unfortunate" result of a people who have been marginalized and therefore who are not to be held accountable for their crimes against humanity. In truth, terrorism is a very shrewd and calculated exploitation of this perception among those in Western culture.

---

[5]Therefore, whether or not we refer to the battle against terrorists as a "war" is immaterial; it obscures the moral issues at hand.

[6]It is important that we debunk the shallow relativism that hides behind the "freedom fighter" mentality while at the same time taking it seriously, since many academics and not a few journalists embrace this nonsense. Is Osama bin Laden a terrorist or a freedom fighter? And what of the many suicide fighters who share bin Laden's vision?

I must go further in parsing terrorism's basic definition. Terrorists set out
to "murder, maim and menace." But why not resort merely to political statements or negotiation or political dissent or debates? Replies Christopher Harmon: "body counts do not matter so much as the fear generated by the violence and threats."[7] And it is hard to argue with the facts. Terrorists seem
to have remarkable success in producing their desired effect. They will not
engage in mass combat. Indeed, there is no need for such since "a few well-
planned, highly public murders may be more politically useful."[8]

In recent times we have witnessed firsthand the effect of maiming by Islamic fundamentalists with the release of videotapes intended to serve as ag-
itprop for other extremist Muslims. The initial of these "performances"
showed a *Wall Street Journal* reporter who had been taken hostage and who
was treated to slaughter as a lamb, as it were, when he was slit at the throat.
A videotape of this event was used to encourage fellow jihadists and other
warriors sympathetic to anti-Americanism. Several like "performances" have
followed. Similarly, though less gruesomely, some might recall, with Christopher Harmon, the knee-capping tactic used by Red Brigade radicals during the 1970s in Europe:

> This tactic requires real hatred, but something else is more noteworthy: a knee
> is harder to hit than a chest, and then the bullet does not have a lethal effect.
> It is the maiming that's wanted, not the murder. The Red Brigades wanted a
> cripple, a living proof of their own ability to inflict pain. . . . The ugly little
> tactic . . . thus has a strategic purpose.[9]

There is something profoundly psychological at work here. Once the reputation for cruelty has been established, mere threats begin to have their intended effect. Though largely forgotten today, we saw glimpses of this a
generation ago in Cambodia where the notorious Pol Pot terrorized villages
in his own country. A decade earlier the Vietcong also practiced tortures
with considerable effectiveness during the Vietnam War. Locals can be paralyzed into inaction and thoroughly dissuaded if they sense that they or their
families are next.

But it is not merely the *fact* of menacing that intimidates. The *timing* is
also important, and specifically the unknown element is so crippling. Not
surprisingly, then, a crucial aspect of terrorist activity is the randomness with

---

[7]Harmon, "Terrorism," p. 3.
[8]Ibid.
[9]Ibid.

which it strikes. Randomness, as Michael Walzer has observed, is a significant and identifying characteristic of terrorist activity. If the aim is to spread fear among a population, then death must visit by chance, as it were. The result? People paralyzed by a morbid fear of random death will demand that their government negotiates for their safety.[10]

The power of "menacing" that is unleashed in terrorism is exemplified by hostage-taking. During the late 1970s and throughout the 1980s we were witness to this seemingly on a continual basis. Perhaps the most visible hostage incident was the debacle created by the Carter administration as it tried unsuccessfully to free U.S. hostages from Iran. In a kidnapping, the psychological element is maximized because of the fears that spread to the victim's family, friends and community. Needless to say, this is a politician's worst nightmare.

At the heart of the definition of terrorism is the word *innocent*. At first glance the distinction between innocence and guilt seems rather cut-and-dried. And yet certain qualifications need to be made. Who is innocent and on what basis?

Terrorism is an indirect form of engaging the enemy. And because of this indirectness, it is not typically viewed as war.[11] In modern times it is not merely random murder but the assassination of innocent noncombatants that distinguishes terrorism. It deliberately crosses the line, demarcated by just-war thinking, between combatants and noncombatants. Gone is any distinction between soldiers and nonsoldiers, between innocents and those fighting in a conventional (wartime) sense.

Hugo Grotius, the father of international law, argued persuasively that foreign ambassadors were to be granted diplomatic immunity, a determination that was confirmed at the Peace of Westphalia in 1648 (the formal end of the Thirty Years' War). Today this custom continues. But for the terrorist, the ambassador as well as the citizen traveling abroad are fair game; there is no such thing as immunity, diplomatic or otherwise. All citizens are agents of the state. Thus, all are guilty by virtue of their association with the enemy. What unifies all terrorists is the conviction that they are engaged in a form of vigilante justice. All who represent this battle are guilty, even innocent

---

[10]Michael Walzer, *Just and Unjust Wars,* rev. ed. (New York: Basic Books, 1992), p. 197.

[11]Walzer writes that the random murder of innocent people, as a political strategy, "emerged as a strategy of revolutionary struggle only in the period after World War II. . . . The increasing use of terror by far left and ultranationalist movements represents the breakdown of a political code first worked out in the second half of the nineteenth century" (ibid., p. 198).

bystanders, since *all* are representative of the enemy. The agents of terrorism might well be described as gangsters in political or ideological dress, though this would be too kind.

But what about weapons? Neither the ambassador nor the civilian traveling abroad is armed. Shouldn't they therefore be immune from attack? Up until recently, as Christopher Harmon has observed, neither the diplomat nor the civilian had been considered a legitimate military target.[12] Until recently, that is.

Which leads to the question of armed representatives of the (enemy) state. What is problematic is that terrorism is not a declared state of war in the conventional sense. The terrorist can use this state of affairs to his or her advantage and operate behind a double standard. The terrorist can utilize and maneuver within peacetime conditions, while at the same time carrying out crimes against humanity as if it were a wartime scenario. Policemen, soldiers, ambassadors and civilians are fair game. But the list does not end. Journalists, judges, businesspeople, indeed *all* qualify as potential victims as terrorists live as parasites from the very system that they are out to destroy.

Before I suggest just-war's response to terrorism, the words "for political ends" in our definition require comment. Question: Which of the following crises may be legitimately considered "terrorism"?

- A domestic crisis that leads to a hostage stand-off with police?
- The bombing or sabotaging of an abortion clinic to prevent business?
- A religious sect that practices common-law marriage and stockpiles weapons in the event that the world will end soon in cosmic conflagration?

By our definition, none of the above, to the extent that none was intended "to inspire fear *for political ends.*" Terrorists live in a clandestine world, much like organized crime, though with markedly political and not merely economic goals. But is terrorism perhaps a legitimate political struggle? After all, not all political struggles are immoral.

Indeed, some political struggles *are* legitimate. In fact, it is probable that most current political struggles around the world are legitimate and deserve our attention as well as our sympathy. Humans, regardless of where they live, possess the rights to political dissent. And this dissent can express itself in a variety of ways. Christians, for example, have displayed different tech-

---

[12]Harmon, "Terrorism," p. 4.

niques in China from those in Solidarity-led Poland fifteen years ago. And Christians in southern Sudan will of necessity utilize different strategies to survive than those employed by Christians in the former Soviet Union. Conversely, tyrants and despots around the world have claimed revolution as their moral justification for setting up ruthless regimes, both past and present. So, what is morally and politically justifiable?

People who suffer oppression have numerous forms, short of martyrdom, by which to express dissent. These include, but are not limited to, forming political movements, forming secret organizations, organizing political rallies, publishing political views, creating information and intelligence networks, influencing opinion abroad, cooperating with political dissidents abroad and protests.[13]

What they do not have recourse to is *attacking innocent people,* wherever such may be found. The justice of the cause of an oppressed people can never excuse crimes against humanity and killing of the innocent. Period. Listen to the words of Christopher Harmon, as he asks us to reflect on the plight of Eastern European peoples before communist tyranny ended in 1989-1990:

> Had the Lithuanians turned to terror, does anyone imagine that they would have done better? Solidarity won in Poland with all . . . [possible] means *except* terrorism. In Lithuania, as in Poland, terrorist tactics might have paid limited dividends but the vital battle for public opinion would have been utterly and perhaps instantly lost. The communist governments would have had field days—quite literally, with military operations against the unarmed populace. If the Baltic peoples wanted to take their fight beyond political resistance, if they decided to use violence, they should have fought Soviet Army officers and soldiers.[14]

While particular and varied expressions of political dissent are valid and in many ways necessary, terrorism never is. It is there that we must draw the line.

TERROR IN THE NAME OF GOD

Up to this point I have made no distinction between religiously and politically motivated acts of terror. From the moral standpoint, terrorism is terrorism, regardless of what inspires it. But no discussion of the phenomenon can fail to take account of its chief form as we enter the twenty-first century.

---

[13]I am indebted to Harmon's very useful discussion of political protest in ibid., pp. 14-17.
[14]Ibid., p. 16.

The year 2002 saw the publication of numerous works on Islam and its relationship to the contemporary world. Few were more significant than Philip Jenkins's *The Next Christendom*.[15] Jenkins examines a religious-cultural fault line that is currently emerging both in the Middle East and on several continents. He believes this to be the twenty-first-century equivalent of the Iron Curtain. This development raises complex questions for both Christianity and American foreign policy. While no one, least of all Jenkins, is calling for a return to the Crusades, Jenkins, along with many thoughtful observers, believes that the political boundaries of the new century will be determined above all by religious matters. Therefore, according to Jenkins, it is in America's interests to ensure that vibrant Christian communities throughout the Third World are not crushed or snuffed out by the forces of militant Islam.

Jenkin's thesis raises an important question—one that is not unrelated to the burden of this book: What is our obligation to these oppressed Christian communities worldwide? Given the worldwide eruption of militant Islam, *what are the requirements of neighbor love to these third parties?*

The dilemma is amply illustrated by simple demographics. Missiologists have been telling us for years that the most explosive growth of Christianity has been and will continue to be in Africa, Asia, Latin America and Eastern Europe. Consider Africa alone. One hundred years ago Christians comprised roughly 9 percent of the continent's entire population. Today, it is approaching 50 percent. By the year 2025 it is projected that there will be approximately 2.6 billion Christians worldwide, with half of these in Africa and Latin American and another 18 percent living in Asia.

By 2050 Jenkins predicts that Christians will outnumber Muslims by roughly three to two, with some growth occurring in Muslim countries. Although many pundits, politicians and policy-makers are content to ignore this remarkable sociological and demographic development worldwide, Islam has not. It is Jenkins's conviction that the triumph of Islam in the coming decades is no more inevitable than the communist triumph of the last century just concluded. At the same time we should not be ignorant of the fact that a growing number of Muslim extremists are calling for a new jihad (struggle) against the West worldwide, the principle actor of which is the United States.

My concern in this chapter, however, is not that of many policy discus-

---

[15]Philip Jenkins, *The Next Christendom* (New York: Oxford University Press, 2002).

sions. I do not care to challenge the reader to a renewed interest in the study of Islam (although that is important) or to get us to understand why Muslims resent us. Rather, my burden is to ask what might be our moral obligation, in the realms of prayer *and* policy, to oppressed Christian communities—indeed, any oppressed community, regardless of nationality—in Islamic societies, where human rights violations are both growing and flagrant.

The growing "Talibanization" of nations in Africa, the Middle East and Asia has served notice to many Christians in these regions: *neither their faith nor their basic rights as human beings will be tolerated.* We are growing accustomed to calls by religious extremists for the establishment of purely religious states, supported by the full apparatus of Islamic law. And recall, again, Muhammad and Jesus take drastically different approaches: Jesus acknowledges both religion and political power while keeping them distinct; Muhammad readily fuses the two.

The persecution of Christians in southern Sudan has become well known, thanks to organizations like Freedom House and the Center for Religious Freedom. Perhaps the single most significant example of the fault line is the country of Nigeria, whose population is expected to be near 300 million by the year 2050. Nigeria currently produces as much oil as Kuwait and the United Arab Emirates combined.[16] Given the nation's size, location and natural resources, Nigeria could well be a major spot of conflict. In fact, it already is.[17] What makes Nigeria particularly volatile is its current population; presently, the nation is almost equally divided between Christians and Muslims. Increasingly, Muslim-Christians rivalries are leading to violence. Thirty years ago the predominately Christian eastern part of the country attempted to secede. The attempt, however, was unsuccessful, triggering a bloody civil war that claimed about one million lives.

Since the end of a military dictatorship in 1999, Nigeria has sought to reinstall democracy. At the same time a new degree of Islamic militancy has emerged. The plight of Nigerian Christians today is a difficult one, and it is growing worse. Currently, about one-quarter of the nation's thirty-six province-states have imposed Islamic Shari'a (God's law), and others are considering the same.[18] The level of oppression of Christians is nearly intolerable,

---

[16]Philip Jenkins, "The Next Iron Curtain," *American Outlook,* winter 2002, p. 27.
[17]See, for example, Paul Marshall, "Radical Islam in Nigeria," *Weekly Standard,* September 15, 2002, pp. 15-16.
[18]Ibid., p. 28.

especially for women. Repression, bloodshed and retaliation are constant problems that Christians face.

These issues—and Nigeria is representative, not alone—raise important questions both for Christians in the West and for U.S. foreign policy. Philip Jenkins poses the challenge in this way: Does it matter whether Christians are persecuted in great numbers and whether nations like Nigeria or Sudan fall to militant Islam, losing their pluralistic character as well as basic human rights?

Up to now U.S. foreign policy has been reticent to adopt a particular political course of action, given the fear of appearing pro-Christian. But in practice we have tended either to favor the Muslim side of the conflict or ignore Christian persecution. The result? The establishment of international terrorist bases in these regions, leading to even less tolerance of Christians and far greater brutality.

We have heard repeatedly that the war on terrorism is not a war against Islam, and as a nation we are understandably resistant toward a religious bias in our foreign policy. Yet there are strong prudential reasons for giving serious consideration to intervening for the purpose of defending governments or Christian populations or other minorities who are being oppressed by fanatical Islam. Time will tell whether we resist terrorism by our commitment to neighbor-love or whether an "ethics of protection" that lies at the heart of just-war thinking will be smothered by an "ethics of ignoring."

It is one of history's ironies that although religion has been used to justify violence, it counsels us and guides us morally in a proper response to violence. In the words of one student of terrorism, it "provides a beacon for moral order."[19] Is it possible that Christians can help temper the wild, irrational spirit that animates religious terrorism? To the surprise of many, precisely that inclination toward moderation is lodged in the moral-political wisdom of the just-war tradition.[20]

---

[19]Mark Juergensmeyer, *Terror in the Mind of God* (Berkeley: University of California Press, 2000), p. 248.

[20]Important resources for understanding the ethos of resurgent Islam, written at a more technical level, include Bernard Lewis and Mark Juergensmeyer. See Bernard Lewis, *Islam and the West* (New York: Oxford University Press, 1993); *What Went Wrong?* (New York: Oxford University Press, 1992); and "The Roots of Muslim Rage," *Atlantic Monthly,* September 1990, pp. 47-60. See also Mark Juergensmeyer, *The New Cold War?* (Berkeley: University of California Press, 1993); and *Terror in the Mind of God*. A more lay-friendly treatment of terrorism and Islamic fundamentalism is Demy and Stewart, *In the Name of God*. Jean Bethke Elshtain's *Just War Against Terror* (New York: Basic Books, 2003) is also indispensable reading.

JUST WAR'S RESPONSE TO TERRORISM

Just cause. Is a response to terrorism necessary? Terrorism, by nature, seeks to destroy public goods and people's lives. It constitutes a radical undermining of the social order. It wishes to destroy the very foundations of civil society. Terrorism is injustice. Just cause, by contrast, is predicated on punishing evil as well as defending and restoring what has been injured. A just-war response serves the good of the perpetrator(s), the victims, the population and future terrorists. A response is both morally necessary and pedagogically necessary. Just cause does not limit us to after-the-fact responses, for it is not morally responsible to anticipate evil and then not seek to prevent it. Religious terrorism, in contrast to just-war, automatically assumes just causes without moral considerations; terrorists' "justice," at least in its religious form, is thought to have been divinely validated.

Proper authority. The United States is said to be "at war" with terrorism. At the same time, those using this expression believe the nature of the conflict presents moral and political problems. They believe that because the principal players in this international drama are nonstates, operating apart from or beyond territorial sovereignty, the morality of a tactical military response is dubious. What about this problem? Does this scenario then technically not constitute a "war" since these are nonstates?

First, let's recall the discussion in the opening chapter about presumption against justice. A presumption *against war* is not part of the classic just-war tradition. But neither is the existence of territorial sovereignty, for that matter. What is more, a little bit of national and military history here is instructive. The initial exercise of U.S. military power beyond its borders in the eighteenth century was not directed against any particular nation-state; it was to repress the Barbary Pirates on the high seas.[21] Did this response qualify as just?

Piracy is a useful illustration since it shares many features of terrorism, even when it seeks to make more of an economic statement than political. To the extent that ideological, religious or political beliefs of contemporary terrorists, who murder, maim and menace, lie beyond our reach, our main responsibility is not ideological so much as it is moral. While there is an ideological element in countering terrorism and planning the future, the priority is to seek justice. For this reason I disagree with the viewpoint that a

---

[21]I am indebted to Martin L. Cook, a professor of military studies and ethics at the U.S. Army War College in Carlisle, Penn., for this reminder.

war against terrorism "requires winning the battle for the hearts and minds of potential terrorist recruits." While this sort of statement sounds noble and contains a fraction of truth, it is not the business of governments to "win the hearts and minds" of people; it is to protect society by rewarding good and punishing evil.

The decision to use force or go to war is a public act. Fighting terrorism is a public act—on behalf of a political community that has been wronged and injured in extraordinary ways. There is no higher authority to which one might appeal than government. Both national sovereignty and international law permit a nation to respond to armed conflict and mass murder. As James Turner Johnson notes, "Any country targeted by terrorist acts is justified in a military response, both morally and by the terms of international law."[22] By contrast, religious terrorists understand themselves as needing no validation by any political authority, since revelation has validated their claims.

Right intention. Right intention carries both positive and negative obligations. Viewed negatively, it refuses to respond out of wrong motives, such as implacable hatred, blind rage or nationalistic pride. Positively, it has as its ultimate goal the establishment of a just peace, an ordered society, stabilizing what has been destabilized. For religious terrorists, on the other hand, the goal is destruction of the enemy at all costs. Hatred must lead to annihilation. Nonviolence, for the terrorist, is a sign of cowardice and dishonor.

Discrimination. When we do respond to terrorists, we commit ourselves to take the moral high ground. We target not the innocent, rather the slayers of the innocent. Unlike terrorists themselves, we seek not to spread fear and dread throughout the population. We rather intend—and we make those intentions clear—to end the reign of terror and liberate those who are oppressed. We never lose sight of the moral distinction between guilt and innocence, between offender and victim, between hunter and hunted. Nor do we fear the potential retaliation, simply because we act justly. The type of enemy who intends to strike our innocent, in the shadows, for political ends is an enemy of the most despicable sort. This terrorist must be resisted to the utmost and defeated soundly. To the extent that terrorists hide among civilians, our task is complicated. However, when a thug or stalker invades my neighborhood or my city, and then my house, I marshal sufficient force and tactics and I use prudential wisdom. To be sure, I am not idle.

---

[22]James Turner Johnson, "In Response to Terrorism," *First Things,* February 1999, p. 12.

Proportionality. To respond or preempt justly, we use force that is proportionate to the evil intended. We use no more and no less than is minimally necessary. Just force is measured. All-out warfare or scorched-earth policy is not inevitable, despite the complaints of many. Religious terrorists, by contrast, assume that the enemy has no rights—to protection, to life, to mercy, to anything. Restraint is not virtue, only a sign of cowardice. Excess is a sign of devotion.

But let's stop and reflect at this point. It is useful to ponder what might be the result were humans as responsible moral agents *not* to respond to terrorism when it surfaces. What happens in the minds of citizens when governing authorities fail—or refuse—to respond to outrageous evil and moral atrocity? How is the relationship between government and the people affected? Clearly, there is a severing of the bond that unites them. People grow discouraged, disillusioned and cynical; they also rely more and more on vigilante justice. Since the authorities, invested with the power to protect society, are not performing their chief function, it is left to the citizenry itself to protect and safeguard its interest. Is it just and proper to fail to take preemptive action or to fail to protect the innocent or to punish those who commit crimes against humanity? It is morally inexcusable. In responding, we distinguish between innocence and guilt. The innocent are not targeted, rather the murderers of the innocent. Nor is our goal in responding to foment political and social unrest or to destabilize. Quite the contrary. It is to end aggression and oppression and bring a justly ordered peace. No one can legitimately argue that a policeman and a criminal are morally equivalent. The same holds true regarding terrorists.

Terrorism, as I have tried to argue, stems not from purported victimization or marginalization in the world; neither is it to be understood as some sort of benign repressed idealism. It is a form of nihilism, a moral abomination in that it violates the universal moral standard of natural law. It transgresses justice at the most fundamental level for its wanton disregard for human sanctity. In addition to breaking the law at multitudinous civil and legal levels—violations of territorial sovereignty, theft, kidnapping, piracy, to name but a few—it transgresses natural moral law in its degraded and deliberate attacks on innocent human life. It is fueled not by idealism but by hatred. As one commentator has aptly stated, it is a wrecking ball, not a blueprint, for building society.[23]

---

[23] Ibid., p. 17.

For this reason terrorism challenges us at the most basic level. It challenges amoral Western culture to engage in moral reasoning, to make moral judgments, and then act on those judgments. Because it is politically and morally illegitimate, it confronts us with issues that simply cannot be evaded.

To be sure, part of the confusion surrounding the use of force that exists among people of religious faith stems from the advice and pronouncements by certain Christian ethicists, denominational spokespersons or religious leaders who themselves are extreme pacifists. Perhaps I am not the only person who still remembers pious statements by some clergy, religious leaders and academics (at least in the American context) that were foisted on us in the aftermath of September 11. Their intonations—and these were Protestant, Roman Catholic as well as Orthodox—went something like this:

"We must forgive our enemies."
"Love covers a multitude of sins."
"Whoever is perfect, let him cast the first stone."
"America got what it deserved."
"We must seek to understand Muslim rage."
"Islam is a religion of peace."

Alas, these were not the voices of prophets speaking, however well intended or pious-sounding. Neither were they offering responsible theology or policy recommendations. Doubtless the more extreme among these pacifist voices will continue to express their anger in the days ahead, and they will assuredly continue to decry America's "imperialistic" tendencies.

Such individuals, an extremely vocal minority, will decline the invitation to wrestle with the political-moral complexities that confront us. They will insist, in their peculiar mix of self-righteousness, distorted theology and resentment, that the Christian should not respond in retribution when terror strikes, since judgment and vindication belong to God alone.[24]

To that highly vocal and extreme pacifist minority, we may respond. What really does happen when we cannot or do not bring ourselves to resist social-moral evil, whenever and wherever it strikes? Does charity indeed *require* that we not actively respond? And while we are free to forsake self-defense, can we justify not protecting the innocent third party who is being

---

[24]There are, of course, plausible theological reasons for embracing a "grace to do nothing," as Richard Niebuhr called it. Anabaptist theologian John Howard Yoder affirms providence in this way: we wait in the historical moment and allow vengeance to be executed eschatologically by the Lord of history.

victimized by oppressive evil? Martyrdom and murder are not the same ethical category.

Something profound, I believe, is lost—something that is exceedingly tragic—when we adopt, even for religious reasons, the conviction that retribution cannot be a moral enterprise. Like the righteous who falls, like the hero who waxes cowardly, like the virtuous who commits graft, something immeasurable is lost when we do not "rescue those being led away to death" (Prov 24:11). And if we say:

> But we knew nothing about this [and, by implication, did not act],
>> does not he who weighs the heart perceive it?
> Does not he who guards your life know it?
>> Will he not repay each person according to what he has done?
>> (Prov 24:12).[25]

And when we deny that the magistrate executes retributive justice as a divinely ordained function (Rom 13:1-4), are we not then complicit with the evildoer? The argument that the magistrate or political power can be corrupt is not a valid argument at all. It in no way eliminates the need for justice to be mediated through the authorities when evil appears. Indeed, when we deny the need to resist evil actively, this loss, at the political level, can be described as one social analyst has done:

> The citizen looks to his government and says "you cannot protect me." When leadership is not in evidence, and cannot guide, the citizen loses confidence, politically and personally. A true democracy has a robustness, a quality which can lapse, or fade altogether, if it is not ever exercise.[26]

However, the great majority of religious people do not reject the use of force absolutely, as does the ideological pacifist. Rather, for most of us the source of confusion and consternation comes from not knowing precisely *how* to respond or *in what measure*. And this makes the principled pacifist position very attractive.

But let it be said that when we *do* respond, and do so with measured (i.e., proportionate) force (a matter of political prudence), we have not engaged in what is immoral. Very much the opposite. We are responding in accor-

---

[25]The wisdom of this proverb is that it calls the listener to react—to rescue, to resist, yes, even to fight—in the present context. This in no way sanctions vigilante justice, as Rom 12:17-21 makes clear. It does, however, sanction people to act justly, even if this means violent rescue or resistance.

[26]Harmon, "Terrorism," p. 18.

dance with the intuition of justice. We are reacting in accordance with natural moral law. It is not wrong to be enraged by evil. Indeed, something is radically wrong with us if we fail to be enraged by evil when it manifests itself.

Consider how any child responds when evil strikes. Does a boy want his father to intervene when there is a neighborhood bully out of control? Does a daughter really care that Dad will stand with her and protect her when a neighborhood stalker has been on the prowl? Notice that it is not children who call us to nonviolence; it is always adults. Why is this? Is it that children's intuition is flawed? Hardly. Children know when they are threatened, and their need for security, for a right ordering of their world, is legitimate. "When justice is done, it brings joy to the righteous / but terror to evildoers" (Prov 21:15).

This brings me to a final reason why we must respond to terrorism. We must do so *for the sake of our children,* the next generation. To do the right thing has pedagogical value. It teaches. And what does it teach?

- that evil exists
- that people must be able to tell right from wrong
- that wrong must be constrained
- that we hate evil and not people
- that justice is virtuous
- that fairness matters and is to be cultivated
- that in acting morally we become wiser, more discerning

The history of just-war thinking and the Christian moral tradition serve as important and indispensable moral guides as we travel through this world of woe. It is the source of enduring political-moral wisdom. "Resist not evil" does not mean that we should not attempt to prevent it, when such is within our power. Just as "Turn the other cheek" is not intended to apply to innocent third parties.

EXTENDING JUST-WAR THINKING BEYOND WAR AND TERRORISM: POSTBELLO CONSIDERATIONS

Just-war thinking is not limited merely to questions of whether to go to war (whether conventional or nonconventional forms such as terrorism) and how to conduct war. Its moral principles extend to the realm of postwar and nonwar activity. Even when discussions of just war do not typically spill over to political-military activity following war (postbello), this third realm is crucial and needs further consideration.

War crimes and justice. External sanctions are necessary to invoke for those nations or leaders unwilling to observe any moral restraints. These sanctions not only hold such parties accountable, they also serve as a deterrent to potential evildoers. In addition, for justice to be confirmed, the extent to which individuals in war are guilty of war crimes must be verifiable and publicly identifiable. Sanctions are necessary to prevent mere ideals of justice from disappearing into mere ideal or diplomacy. The regulations found in the Geneva, Hague and Nuremberg Conventions prohibit certain actions, based on international law, that are not required by military necessity. These accord roughly with the *ius in bello* tradition.

Humanitarian intervention and justice. Can coercive force be used for the purpose of peace-keeping missions? Can humanitarian intervention be achieved through armed forces? Just-war thinking lends itself to these complex situations as post-Cold War crises around the world have shown. While such situations are difficult and evade any precise guidelines, and thus generate enormous national debate, they nevertheless raise serious questions of morality and justice. Just-war principles are applicable on the basis of several criteria already discussed.

Given the commitment of justice and love to defend and protect the third party, serious human rights violations and crimes against humanity in another nation or people group require a measured response. Recall one of the sufficient justifications for war identified in chapter six: egregious humanitarian abuses that arise when another state "inflicts upon his subjects such treatment as no one is warranted in inflicting."[27]

But what about a nation's sovereignty? After all, there exists within the international community a bias against interfering in the internal affairs of other nations.[28] While this presumption against interference is present, international law as developed by Hugo Grotius takes account both of national sovereignty *and* natural law. A nation's right to persecute or oppress its people does not have precedent over the law of nature. Thus Grotius:

> The fact must also be recognized that kings, and those who possess rights equal to those of kings, have the right of demanding punishment not only on

---

[27]Hugo Grotius *The Law of War and Peace* 2.25.7, in *Grotius, Law,* trans. F. W. Kelsey (Indianapolis: Bobbs-Merrill, 1962).
[28]So article 2 of the United Nations Charter.

account of injuries committed against themselves or their subjects, but *also on account of injuries which do not directly affect them but excessively violate the law of nature or of nations in regard to any persons whatsoever.*[29]

Human decency then obligates forceful intervention in cases where egregious human rights violations are taking place: "If the wrong is obvious, in cases some [tyrant] should inflict upon his subjects such treatment as no one is warranted in inflicting, the exercise of the right vested in human society is not precluded."[30] And what acts constitute moral atrocities worthy of intervention? Only those, he cautions, that are "very atrocious and very evident"— for example, cannibalism, piracy, abuse of the elderly, rape and castration.[31]

In his important work *Just and Unjust Wars,* Michael Walzer thoughtfully treats the subject of humanitarian intervention. His line of reasoning is similar to that of Grotius: "the violations of human rights within a set of boundaries is so terrible that it makes talk of community or self-determination . . . seem cynical and irrelevant."[32] What are specific reasons that warrant humanitarian intervention? These might include disaster relief, protection of refugees, prevention of genocide, curtailment of human rights violations or other forms of like human suffering. What is the factor that unites all of these circumstances? According to Paul Christopher, it is that "the intervening nation(s) uses its armed forces in a coercive role to cause some effect in the internal affairs of another nation and, after this humanitarian objective is achieved, the intervening force withdraws."[33]

Christopher issues two cautions. He warns us, on the one hand, to relativize the rights of national "sovereignty" in discussions of intervention. Nations should not be permitted to conceal human rights violations under the guise of sovereignty. On the other hand, the legitimacy of the need to intervene must be critically examined and found morally compelling. Different modes of governing and different religious or social customs are to be tolerated. Crimes against nature are not.

The issue of humanitarian intervention is a growing concern among policy analysts and policy-makers. Doubtless, as the last decade demonstrated, the years ahead will afford new opportunities to test the viability and endur-

---

[29]Grotius *Law of War and Peace* 2.20.40 (emphasis added).
[30]Ibid., 2.25.8.
[31]Ibid.
[32]Walzer, *Just and Unjust Wars,* p. 90.
[33]Paul Christopher, *The Ethics of War and Peace,* rev. ed. (Upper Saddle River, N.J.: Prentice Hall, 1999), p. 193.

ing value of just-war principles. In the geopolitical configuration of today's world, it is imperative that we debate and refine moral criteria for such situations. Who better to help inform these debates than thoughtful and engaged Christians who desire justice for the nations?

Postwar nation-building and justice. Regardless of our differences over the justness of the U.S. intervention in Iraq, the Iraqi people illustrate the importance of extending just-war thinking to postwar scenarios. Twenty-five years ago, remarkably, Iraq's per capita income was $3,600 annually, roughly that of Spain at the time. Per capita income as of October 2003 barely reached the $600 mark. Between 1980 and 2001, Iraq tumbled fifty places in the United Nations Humanitarian Development Index.[34]

Civil society, utilizing diplomatic efforts (the "extended hands" of the military, the private sector, nongovernment organizations, even the church), plays a crucial role in reconstructing any semblance of a civil society in war-torn or politically decimated regions. And in Iraq, despite the great challenges it poses, there is great hope. The reconstructive task, however, begins with education.

Education has something of a humanizing effect, particularly in cultures that have known totalitarian tendencies and repressive rule. Thus basic exposure to ideas, to history, to other cultures, to literature, to law, to science and technology are critical. At a very practical level job skills will need to be learned in order that Iraqis can be productive, utilizing their remarkable creativity. A future generation of leaders must be educated—leaders who will not simply emigrate to the West where they might live the rest of their lives.

The legal system is all but nonexistent in these countries. Of course, this is due to monarchical or dictatorial practices. Similarly, the rule of law is meaningless, and law has been entirely arbitrary; graft and injustice have largely been the norm. Overcoming the past in this regard is particularly challenging yet essential if a people is to become self-governing.

All of the important components in a nation's rebirth—education, learning job skills, the rule of law, self-government and so on—will contribute to the overall development of that people. Very often socialist practices were the nearest thing to official policy in the past. Learning to be self-motivated, to serve others, to make basic wise economic decisions—these require a fundamental change in the way people think. Government restricted what

[34]Ana Palacio, "The Rebirth of a Nation," *Wall Street Journal*, October 27, 2003, p. A22.

jobs were available, where citizens could work, and how much they could earn. And in the end government siphoned off from the people what resources they had in order to maintain power.

All of these and more considerations are rooted in a fundamental notion of justice. That is, all human beings have been endowed with certain inalienable rights—rights that in many regimes are denied. Nothing less than justice is required to allow formerly oppressed people to flourish. To be sure, we must be careful not to foist our culture on them. They must learn to flourish in theirs. We do, however, facilitate what is due all people—the choice to be free from social-political tyranny.

8

THE CHURCH'S
WORLDLY MISSION

What responsibility does the church have for the world? This is a difficult question to answer. And with no lack of wildly divergent responses. I
write with a fundamental bias, and that bias is this: the church is *morally*
responsible for the world. "But isn't *God* in charge?" the reader might rightly
object. Yes. But there is the matter of stewardship, tending the Garden, as it
were, that confronts us immediately in Scripture (even when it is absent
from Protestant evangelical theology).

CHRIST AND CULTURE REVISITED

How Christian faith is reconciled to cultural values, of course, is not a new
question. From the beginning, Christians have struggled with the tension between heavenly and earthly allegiances. Tertullian, in the second century,
may have been the first to frame the matter formally—What does Athens
have to do with Jerusalem?—but Christians certainly agonized over this relationship long before Tertullian.

And ever since, the question has been continually restated: How are we
to understand the relationship between Christian faith and culture? Are they
friends? Enemies? Both? Perhaps something in-between? Compounding our
dilemma is the fact that Christians seem to be in perpetual disagreement
about the correct answer. And no wonder. Scripture can be cited as evidence
for any of the possible positions. Which led Richard Niebuhr (the *other* Niebuhr!) several generations ago to identify several possible explanations.[1]

---

[1]H. Richard Niebuhr, *Christ and Culture* (New York: Macmillan, 1951).

And despite George Marsden's recent complaint that Niebuhr's typology "could be near the end of its usefulness,"[2] I think not. Does it need recasting in the language of the day? By all means. But it is nowhere "near the end of its usefulness," contrary to Marsden's protestations. Niebuhr's categories are still supremely useful; indeed in the last fifty years, since the publication of *Christ and Culture,* they have not been improved on as a means by which to evaluate how Christians should relate to their surrounding culture.

One explanation is that Christian faith is always and irrevocably *against* culture. The world and our faith are diametrically opposed. A radical antithesis exists between the two realms, and never the twain shall meet. At all times, in every circumstance and with regard to all matters, faith and culture are at odds. With notable exceptions, this attitude tends to look somewhat condescendingly at those who have not resisted the social system in the same manner.

At the opposite end of the spectrum are those who understand Christ as working *through* culture. In contrast to the pessimism of this first model, this perspective is quite optimistic about society and its achievements and about faith's comfortable place within society. As a result, Christian faith embraces and assimilates cultural values. It flourishes in—and therefore participates readily in—the various institutions of mainstream culture. While doing so it marvels at others somewhat disdainfully who divorce themselves so readily from mainstream culture.

And then, Niebuhr notes, there are alternative viewpoints, *mediating* positions, that are neither absolutely opposed to culture nor uncritically adopting of the cultural climate. Those who opt for a mediating stance are content (or resigned) to live with a tension, a certain unrelenting tension. This is a tension stemming from the realization that the kingdom of God is "already but not yet." It is the tension that understands our dual citizenship in the present life.

Doubtless not all will be willing to live in this tension. And different answers to resolving the tension between faith and culture can be given, depending on where one is located in the church's history. And if this does not complicate things enough, the American experiment itself, so diverse and so different from other cultures, may give rise to any of the above possibilities,

<hr/>

[2]Marsden's critique of Niebuhr was initially delivered as a lecture on February 2, 1999, at Austin Theological Seminary. It was subsequently published in *Insights: The Faculty Journal of Austin Seminary,* fall 1999.

depending on one's upbringing and social location.

Nevertheless, Augustine's understanding of dual citizenship seems to preserve the necessary tension between faith and culture. That is, we have responsibilities as citizens of *both* the heavenly kingdom *and* this world. The easy way out of this uncomfortable tension, of course, is to choose absolutely between one or the other—between religion or culture. Some of us opt for the heavenly city, choosing to withdraw from society in which we are placed. With Tertullian we remind ourselves that nothing in this life can add to our basic salvation through Christ. We wait for Christ's return and the inauguration of the eschaton. Civic duties, to say the least, are the least of our worries. And some of us even do this with a prophetic edge.

Others of us, reacting against the extremes of sectarianism and religious fundamentalism, move in the opposite direction. We are bound and determined not to become narrow and rigid; we embrace culture whole-heartedly, becoming enmeshed in and ultimately absorbed by our cultural surroundings. In the final analysis, truth be told, our lives are scarcely discernible from culture itself.

Niebuhr's position, after a generous description of each possible model, is that *in the main* Christian faith and wisdom call us to a mediating position. There may be times, circumstances and issues that require of us opposition to culture, but there may be times, circumstances and issues that require of us a more friendly relationship to culture. Generally speaking, however, we do well to emulate Augustine's attitude. We have been entrusted with a dual citizenship based on creation and providence, and this twin responsibility, based on creation, entails certain moral obligations.[3]

For this reason, then, we "render to Caesar the things that are Caesar's," while we "render to God the things that are God's." Given our periodic discomfort, it is quite easy to release the tension in this dual citizenship by denying either pole—Caesar or God. Christian faith, however, does not let us off the hook. We must embrace the world *without* becoming identified with it. Stated otherwise, we must be citizens of heaven first, *without* removing ourselves from the world.

Of course, there may arise situations in which we must choose between the two. And in those situations faithfulness requires that we demonstrate our ultimate allegiance. But this state of affairs (in which we must choose)

---

[3]In my view, Richard's brother Reinhold does a better job of preserving the necessary tension between our dual citizenships in the present life.

is not always and everywhere the case. Sometimes, many times, we experience ambiguity. And unless we have thought a lot about culture, unless we
have developed a theology of culture, we will be inclined to opt for either
opposition or uncritical acceptance.

ADJUSTING OUR ESCHATOLOGY AND ETHICS

For the readers of this book who are predominately Protestant evangelical or
broadly orthodox, many of us, though not all, have been nurtured in the faith
with a relative contempt for culture. Why is this? Chances are we have been
molded by teaching, preaching and church life that, wittingly or unwittingly,
has devalued (1) the life of the mind, and (2) Christian responsibilities to society. This has been done, of course, in the name of Christian spirituality and
with all good intentions. And if we do not come from denominations and traditions that display a relative contempt toward culture, many of us are frus-
trated if not clueless as to how to relate our faith meaningfully to culture. And
keenly aware that the chief temptation comes in the form of cultural accom-
modation, we maintain an abiding contempt toward our environment
throughout our Christian pilgrimage that lies just under the skin.

   But our problem is not only practical or dispositional, it is theological.
If Christ is indeed is returning in our lifetime, as we have been taught to
fully anticipate, then it is supremely difficult—nay, nonsensical—to pursue
other matters over the long term that require considerable energies, strategies, finances and personal investment. I have in mind, for example, education or certain types of vocational careers. With Tertullian we answer
the question, What does Athens have to do with Jerusalem? with firm resolve: Well, absolutely nothing. No wonder, then, that evangelical Protestants (for example) tend not to be found among social scientists, economists, educational theorists, political scientists, legal theorists, policy
analysts, politicians (football players excepted), ethicists and so on. Why?
Because such endeavors require a vision that takes culture seriously and
views "occupying" (Jesus' word) as *both a Christian mandate and a high
calling*. All of these vocations require a long-term perspective, and at min-
imum, an interest in society.

   The perspective that we end up choosing is decidedly short-term. We
comfort ourselves that as things "grow worse" in society around us, we will
"meet the Lord in the air" and not have to wrestle with social, economic or
political repercussions of current trends. After all, if culture is "going to hell

in a hand-basket," as our bestselling Christian novels drum into us, why attempt to save it? Why attempt to rearrange the chairs on a sinking ship? And while we await the rapture, we blissfully forget, of course, that other generations assumed the same—though not with such a strong publishing arm as we (who are closet entrepreneurs) have developed!

And so it goes. We remain immune to long-term vision and forsake long-term projects as we convince ourselves that long-term occupying will not be necessary. At the very least this sort of myopia (not to mention, theological shallowness) bears directly and distinctly on how we educate our own—both in the congregation and in the academy (although that is a topic for an entirely different volume!).

Do we need any proof of what I am describing? Visit a Christian bookstore. What do you see? Chances are high that you will be bombarded with (1) novels and pronouncements about the end times (passing under the guise of "biblical prophecy"), (2) Christian historical fiction (a euphemism for religious romance novels), and (3) Christian inspirational and "breakthrough" literature (allowing readers to "break through" to their untapped potential and untold personal "blessing"). These three genres comprise the bulk of religious publishing today. That we are now up to the twelfth installment of the Left Behind series and that books like *The Prayer of Jabez* have become bestsellers while spawning a veritable subculture (cult?) speaks volumes about the state of American religious faith—Protestant evangelicalism in particular (permit me again to write as an American Christian). Either we have checked out of culture or we are wholly self-absorbed in a quest to obtain personal blessing and find significance. Something, alas, is very wrong with this religious picture. It is the unhappy—though exceedingly necessary—task of pastors, teachers and prophets everywhere to decry this unfortunate state of affairs and take the task of theology seriously. And this must happen before we can expect to make any meaningful contribution in the public square.

But Christian vision must keep one eye on our future hope—which is Christ himself and not some sort of rapture from responsibility—while we focus sharply on the task at hand. It is a vision of "already and not yet." Our calling is not monastic, with a bloated eschatology. It is in the direction of the world, even when the world is not our home. It is, in a word, incarnational. Christianity, after all, by its very nature calls us into the world, with its diversity and humanity, much like the Son of God himself.

INCARNATIONAL WITNESS AND CIVIC DUTY

At the center of this reconstructive project are the primary threads of Christian theology—creation, fall and redemption. But beware. Despite the familiarity of these three terms, there is more to plumb in these basic Christian doctrines than we have heretofore imagined. Significant attention will need to be directed toward creation and redemption, since Protestants—to their credit as well as their discredit—have largely majored on human depravity while ignoring the wider implications of creation and redemption.

One theologian of two generations removed demonstrated the close relationship between creation and redemption when he spoke of "incarnational humanism."[4] By incarnational humanism he meant that human beings, transformed by the redemptive work of Christ, aim not merely to save souls but also transform culture around them. That Scripture promises "a new heaven and new earth" is indication that all of our efforts are not destined for some cosmic or eternal ash heap; rather, fueled by the grace of God, we seek to bring all things—*all things*—captive to the obedience of Christ. We are to witness to the consummation of *all things*—things heavenly and things earthly, things visible and things invisible. For by Christ *all things* were created; and they were created both through him and for him. He is both agency and end. Christ then is the goal of everything in life, in existence, in our awareness. Which is to say, nothing exists that is not potentially the possession of the Lord.

It is this extraordinary reality that the apostle Paul declares to the Colossian Christians: "He is before all things, and in him all things hold together" (Col 1:17). Similar cosmic language is applied to redemption in Ephesians as well: it has been God's purpose to "bring all things in heaven and on earth together under one head, even Christ" (Eph. 1:10). Imagine, just for starters, what education becomes when we are possessed by a vision of the cosmic scope of Christ's redemptive work! Education takes on an incarnational cast; it becomes a gateway into previously unrecognized domains of awareness, into realms of knowledge that heretofore were unacknowledged. Through our study and through our work we begin to restore what was marred by the Fall. We work toward the redemption and consummation of what Christ purchased on the cross. All things are the goal of that redemption, not merely the "soul" in the narrow sense. By expanding the scope of

---

[4]I am indebted to John Courtney Murray in this regard, who develops the notion of "incarnational humanism" in *We Hold These Truths* (New York: Sheed & Ward, 1960), pp. 175-96.

redemption, we undo, as it were, the effects of sin in the world. In a word, we *integrate,* and we do this in the fullest and best sense. We thereby become people of integrity. We begin to discover what loving the Lord with all our heart, soul, mind and strength fully entails. It entails *all things;* it involves *every dimension* of human existence.

Needless to say, if we only plan for the near future and do not develop sufficient vision that will enable us to occupy culture responsibly, then we have no right to complain when that very culture, into which we have been placed, refuses to take us seriously. To be sure, the implications of what I am saying affect all believers, but they challenge separatist Christians in particular. Incarnational humanism, by contrast, seeks to bring redemption to all that is natural, all that is human and all that is earthly (though not confined to the earthly). The heavens and earth, as Scripture reminds us, are *not* destined to become a cosmic ash heap; they are destined for transformation; thus the fruit of our efforts remain. This also helps explain, in my opinion, why we will be judged according to our works (2 Cor 5:10). It infuses the present with meaning and purpose.

> You see that a person is justified by what he does and not by faith alone. (Jas 2:24)

> Do you see a man skilled in his work? / He will serve before kings. (Prov 22:29)

The dangers of a perspective that is chiefly eschatological, as I have suggested, are that we abrogate our earthly citizenship. To be incarnational is to wrestle with how to manifest the eternal in the midst of the temporal, how to mirror redemption in its breadth, how to work for the transformation of all that is called "creation."

THE MORAL NECESSITY OF POLITICS: RENDERING TO CAESAR WHAT IS CAESAR'S

As a moral dilemma, war and the use of coercive force are ultimately a matter of policy. And policy, in the end, is determined by society, through its representatives serving in government. For this reason citizens bear the moral responsibility for the policy that comes into being. This, of course, implicates Christians since they are part of society, whether they wish to be or not.

And because war raises inherently moral issues, American society at present is at a loss. Given the twin challenges of radical individualism and pervasive moral skepticism, we are prevented from entering into responsible moral discourse. Consumed by issues of the self (which is perfectly normal in a therapeutic culture) and having entertained ourselves to death, we are ill-equipped to engage in basic moral reasoning, much less to recommend whether or not to go to war and offer a rationale.

If policy, as I have argued, is the "meeting-place of the world of power and the world of morality," it is the duty of those who wish to uphold moral principle to work for justice. That duty may find expression locally, in the neighborhood or the city where one lives. But if we are morally sensitive, duty will also beckon us to work for justice at the national and international level, at least as long as representative government, basic freedoms and basic resources are still ours. In this sense redemption and transformation have political implications.

There is no "Christian political agenda" per se. Such thinking borders on the theocratic heresy. But the church's contribution to the world entails contributions in the political sphere. These contributions are basic, but no less significant: freedom that is political (from tyranny and oppression) and religious (to worship) and participatory (permitting us to involve ourselves in public life).

Laypeople are the primary links of the church to the world. Therefore, while our corporate presence in the world (through word and sacrament) is important, we must strengthen our vision of why these links are so strategic. Vocations that are very public in nature are quite strategic, affording us opportunities that we might not have had otherwise.

The issue of war and peace confronts us with an important question: What is the appropriate role of the church in public moral debates? We have noted throughout the book that neither the vision of the jihadist (religion = politics) nor that of the isolationist (politics and force = evil) is adequate. What is appropriate will differ for everyone, depending on our callings and our theological outlook. How we enter and participate in the public arena, then, will vary. However, on the matter of war, the Catholic *Catechism* reminds us of an important truth: evaluating whether to go to war and how to conduct war is a matter of political prudence and therefore belongs to the realm of the state. In the end, after the church has participated in debate, it is the task of office-holders, not the church, to make policy decisions. Up to that point, however, we involve ourselves in the political process, working for justice, as far as it is within our power.

Now this is not to suggest that we all should enter politics or work for the government. It is to underscore, however, the fact that power, wherever it is utilized, must be harnessed to the forces of good. Power in some situations will need to be forbidden. In other situations it will need to be limited. In all situations it will need to be guided. The questions that remain then are these: *Who* will exercise those restraints on power? And by what standard?

A recurring theme in this book, even when it has been standing in the shadows, has been the relationship between the Sermon on the Mount and public policy, between the personal and the political. It is here that most of us feel tension. Not long ago I sat in on a student discussion of war at Baylor University, where I served a visiting fellowship for the 2003-2004 academic year. Students attending this seminar were thoughtfully reflective about the issues that perennially torment us. The instructor was patient, allowing the students to stumble, however painfully, through the difficult terrain of moral dilemma.

One particular issue, however, that wholly evaded any resolution was the seeming contradiction between Christian love and the demands of the state. In frustration one student confessed: "I just cannot accept the tension between *not resisting evil and turning the other cheek,* on the one hand, and *having to obey the governing authorities,* on the other hand, especially when the authorities must wield the sword."

That student spoke for many of us. Aren't the two spheres in conflict? Don't the personal and political clash? That seems to be the rub.

Recall our earlier discussion of Romans 12—13. There was no contradiction for the apostle Paul, who knew personal abuse as an apostle and yet calmly and with surprisingly little qualification could say that while justice in the *private* realm is illegitimate, in the *public* realm it is not only legitimate but required. When it comes to handling personal insult, we are to "turn the other cheek" and "not resist evil." Giving people our cloak and walking an extra mile are not issues of statecraft and public policy, however much they might inconvenience us personally. When it is a matter of defending others, however, then we are required to act on their behalf, and on occasion this will entail coercive force—whether at the local, national or international level. We do not turn their cheek, for to do so would be to assist in evil itself, and hence, to commit a moral abomination.

For this reason, then, force can be a valid expression of Christian charity. It is not a contradiction of Jesus' purported love ethic, as some would vigorously maintain; rather, it is consistent with love's demands.

For some of us the urgent need is to adjust our assumptions about political power. Power is not inherently evil, despite the fact that human nature is inexorably corrupt. Jesus admonished his disciples that both God *and* Caesar require of us certain obligations. Some Christians, truth be told, would interpret the New Testament in such a way as to make it read that nothing is owed Caesar. But this is false, and very often our bias against the powers serves as a smokescreen for our pride and autonomy. We would have no authority over us—heavenly or earthly. Such an attitude, it must be said, is a denial of the spirit of Christianity.

Consider Jesus' own view of power. While he desacralized political power by relativizing its claims over him, he did not deny it. Nor did he attempt to fuse religion and political power, in contrast to Muhammad, with whom he is often compared. Rather, Jesus acknowledged their coexistence while keeping the two realms distinct. The difference between Islam and Christian on the nature of political power is radical and should be pondered. Not for nothing is Islam known as "the religion of the sword." Writing as a Christian and a political scientist, Jean Bethke Elshtain puts the sword in proper perspective when she writes:

> Not that Christianity has no knowledge of the sword. But within Christianity the sword always has to justify itself. The arguments within Islam begin in another place, asking . . . what is honorable in fighting rather than whether fighting in itself is forbidden (it is not).[5]

The state, then, is necessary, our protestations notwithstanding. Political power is not an inherent evil that is merely to be tolerated, even when it has the potential to be perverted.

But against the wishes of the militarist, power must be bridled and channeled. Christians should particularly resist the theocratic tendency and not make the mistake of Islam or of God-and-country nationalism. The political order and the religious order are to be kept distinct. The teaching of the New Testament is that *the sword must justify itself.* Caesar and God are not the same.

Politics then can be viewed in two ways. The pacifist option, because it loathes political authorities—viewing them as intrinsically unjust—and eschews civic engagement, has the potential to create a tyranny of a false peace. It is a tyranny of peace without justice, such as we have witnessed in the totalitarian movements of the twentieth century. In sheer irony, militarism and

---

[5]Jean Bethke Elshtain, *Just War Against Terror* (New York: Basic Books, 2003), p. 159.

the crusade mindset also tilt in the direction of an oppressive peace. Moral considerations that place restraints on force are thrown to the wind. Vanquishing the enemy at all costs must be achieved. Neither approach, however, finds sanction in the just-war tradition. Already forty-five years ago John Courtney Murray pressed the argument that a necessary defense against generic "barbarism" is the blend of force and moral intuition. Responsible policy, he maintained, issues only out of such a mix. We must be on guard against the ideologies of the age, he warned, that pull us toward one extreme or the other. And so, some of us as Christians will need—somewhat painfully—to adjust our assumptions about political power, whether we be patriots or pacifists.

For others of us, the pressing need may be to adjust our understanding of love. Not a few of us have grown up thinking—or been duly instructed by Christian mentors—that coercive force can never be a moral enterprise. In this vein the illustration of the Good Samaritan is a helpful reminder, raising both provocative and ethically significant questions: Would Christian love have impelled the Samaritan to stop the mugging, were he to have encountered it in process?

I conclude, then, with the question that opened the chapter. What responsibility does the church have to the world? *Moral* responsibility was the answer. And morally, what ought the church be doing about the world? An infinite number of creative possibilities belong to the answer. These are limited only by our imagination. But in broader terms we should be living and speaking in such a way that (1) God's character is reflected by his people, and (2) we are used by God to redeem what is hopeless, darkened and affected by the Fall; in short, all things. To fulfill this mandate our ethical foundation, confirmed by rightly-ordered reason and natural moral law, is what is expressed in the "Ten Words," the Decalogue—a summary of fundamental moral obligations toward the Creator and fellow human beings. These words serve both to protect us and cause us to flourish.

TAKING THEOLOGY SERIOUSLY

In the final analysis our foundation for acting ethically is as strong or weak as our grasp of Christian theology. Held in mysterious tension are attributes of God's nature such as his holiness, righteousness/justice and wrath with other divine attributes such as lovingkindness, mercy and peace. Is his holiness any less in the New Covenant? Does his wrath burn any less today at human wickedness than in times past? Has the moral foundation of the New

Covenant changed? Is it different from that of the Old? Are justice and love diametrically opposing aspects of God's nature? Aren't all humans forgiven through the peace of the cross? And at what price, we might ask, is "peace with God" ultimately secured?

Peace, regardless of its form, *always* comes with *a price*. And that peace is only authentic peace when it has been ordered by justice or righteousness.

We see this priority—justice bearing peace—suggested in the New Testament in a tantalizing allusion to the figure Melchizedek. The writer of Hebrews notes what is an important theological lesson as he makes comparisons between this Melchizedek and Jesus. Of the former he writes: "First, his name means 'king of righteousness'; then also 'king of Salem' means 'king of peace'" (Heb 7:2). Melchizedek, so mysterious to the reader, is said to be "like the Son of God" in the exercise of his priesthood (Heb 7:3).

For the biblical author, this order is not incidental. First, righteousness or justice (*righteousness* and *justice* are interchangeable in both the Old and the New Testaments). Second, peace. The one is a byproduct, a fruit, of the other. The order is important in both the spiritual and the political realm: first, justice; then, peace. First, right order; then, right relationship. Without the former there is no authentic latter. And what is true in the theological realm applies to the political.[6]

Christians live in the constant awareness that our sins are covered by the Lamb of God. But that Lamb, behold, is also a *Lion*. He is simultaneously the sacrifice *and* a warrior. The vanquished *and* the Vanquisher. The conquered *and* the Conqueror.

Christian theology, and with it Christian ethics, will need to hold these two realities in tension. Justice and peace—and in that order. One is prior; the other follows. It is our confession of this reality—justice with God resulting in peace with God—that brings us into relationship with God.

In living out our lives we must faithfully give witness to the world of this One who is simultaneously the divine warrior and the divine sacrifice. And it is the mystery of this wonder for which we bow before the Lion-Lamb on bended knee. This mystery brings him eternal praise.

---

[6]The biblical concept of shalom, the peace of the kingdom of God established in its fullness, is that future eschatological reality to which various images point—for example, lions and lambs coexisting, swords becoming ploughshares (see Is 2:2-4). The establishment of shalom is God's work, however, and not humankind's. This realization will prevent us from utopian thinking that is at once unbiblical and unattainable in the present life.

SELECT BIBLIOGRAPHY

Abrams, Elliott, ed. *Close Calls: Intervention, Terrorism, Missile Defense, and "Just War" Today.* Washington, D.C.: Ethics and Public Policy Center, 1998.

Adeney, B. T. *Just War, Political Realism, and Faith.* Philadelphia: ATLA, 1988.

Allen, J. L. *War: A Primer for Christian.* Dallas: Southern Methodist University, 2001.

Ambrose. *On the Duties of the Clergy.* In *Nicene and Post-Nicene Fathers of the Christian Church.* Edited by Philip Schaff and Henry Wace. Vol. 10. Grand Rapids: Eerdmans, 1955.

―――. *Select Works and Letters.* In *Nicene and Post-Nicene Fathers of the Christian Church.* Edited by Philip Schaff and Henry Wace. Vol. 10. Grand Rapids: Eerdmans, 1955.

Anscombe, Elizabeth. "War and Murder." In *War and Morality.* Edited by Richard A. Wasserstrom. Belmont: Wadsworth, 1970.

Aquinas, Thomas. "On Princely Government." In *Aquinas: Selected Political Writings.* Edited by A. P. d'Entreves. New York: Barnes & Noble, 1959.

―――. *Summa Theologica.* Vol. 2. New York: Benziger, 1947.

Augustine. *The City of God.* Edited by Vernon J. Bourke. Translated by G. G. Walsh et al. Garden City, N.Y.: Doubleday, 1958.

―――. *Contra Faustum.* In *Nicene and Post-Nicene Fathers of the Christian Church.* Edited by Philip Schaff. Vol. 4. Buffalo: The Christian Literature Co., 1887.

————. *The Free Choice of the Will.* In *Nicene and Post-Nicene Fathers of the Christian Church.* Edited by Philip Schaff. Vol. 5. New York: The Christian Literature Co., 1887.

————. "The Confessions and Letters of St. Augustine." In *Nicene and Post-Nicene Fathers of the Church.* Vol. 1. Buffalo: The Christian Literature Co., 1886.

Bainton, Roland H. *Christian Attitudes Toward War and Peace.* New York/Nashville: Abingdon, 1960.

Barber, Benjamin. *Fear's Empire: War, Terrorism and Democracy in an Age of Interdependence.* New York: W. W. Norton, 2003.

Bergen, Peter. *Holy War, Inc.* New York: Free Press, 2001.

Berger, Peter, and Richard J. Neuhaus, eds. *Movement and Revolution.* Garden City, N.Y.: Doubleday, 1970.

Berry, LaVerle B. *Bibliography on Future Trends in Terrorism: A Report.* Washington, D.C.: Federal Research Division, 1998.

Best, Geoffrey. *Humanity in Warfare.* New York: Columbia University Press, 1980.

Boot, Max. "Who Says We Never Strike First?" *New York Times,* October 4, 2002.

Brock, Peter. *Pacifism in the United States.* Princeton, N.J.: Princeton University Press, 1968.

Brown, Robert McAfee, ed., *The Essential Reinhold Niebuhr: Selected Essays and Addresses.* New Haven, Conn.: Yale University Press, 1987.

Burns, J. P. *War and Its Discontents: Pacifism and Quietism in the Abrahamic Traditions.* Georgetown: Georgetown University Press, 1996.

Cadoux, C. John. *The Early Christian Attitude to War.* New York: Seabury, 1982.

Cady, D. L. *From Warism to Pacifism: A Moral Continuum.* Philadelphia: Temple University Press, 1989.

Cahill, Lisa S. *Love Your Enemies: Discipleship, Pacifism, and Just War Theory.* Minneapolis: Fortress, 1994.

Calvin, John. *The Institutes of Christian Religion.* Translated by F. L. Battle. Philadelphia: Westminster Press, 1960.

Campenhausen, Hans von. "Christians and Military Service in the Early Church." In *Tradition and Life in the Early Church.* Philadelphia: Fortress, 1968.

Capizzi, Joseph E. "On Behalf of the Neighbor: A Rejection of the Complementarity of Just-War Theory and Pacifism." *Studies in Christian Ethics* 14, no. 2 (2001).

The Challenge of Peace: God's Promise and Our Response. Washington, D.C.: United States Catholic Conference, 1983.

Charles, J. Daryl. "Between Pacifism and Jihad." *Touchstone,* November 2003.

———. "The Character of Justice in the Just-War Tradition." *Logos,* spring 2005.

———. "'Do Not Suppose That I Have Come . . .': The Sermon on the Mount Reconsidered." *Southwestern Journal of Theology,* summer 2005.

———. "Justice and Neighbor Love in the Just-War Tradition: Christian Reflections on the Just Use of Force." *Cultural Encounters,* winter 2004.

———. "Presumption Against War or Presumption Against Injustice? The Just War Tradition Reconsidered." *Journal of Church and State* (forthcoming).

———. "The Sword of Justice." *Touchstone,* December 2001.

———. "War, Women and Political Wisdom: Jean Elshtain on the Contours of Justice." *Journal of Religious Ethics* (forthcoming).

Childress, James F. *Moral Responsibility in Conflicts.* Baton Rouge: Louisiana State University Press, 1982.

Christiansen, Drew, and Gerald Powers. "Economic Sanctions and the Just-War Doctrine." In *Economic Sanctions: Panacea or Peacebuilding in a Post-Cold War World?* Edited by D. Cortright and G. Lopez. Boulder, Colo.: Westview, 1995.

Christopher, Paul. *The Ethics of War and Peace.* Rev. ed. Upper Saddle River, N.J.: Prentice Hall, 1999.

Clancy, William, ed., *The Moral Dilemma of Nuclear Weapons.* New York: Council on Religion and International Affairs, 1961.

Claude, Inis J., Jr. "Just Wars: Doctrine and Institutions." *Political Science Quarterly* 95, no. 1 (1980).

Clausewitz, Karl von. *On War.* Edited and translated by M. Howard and P. Paret. Rev. ed. Princeton, N.J.: Princeton University Press, 1984.

Clouse, Robert G., ed. *War: Four Christian Views.* Rev. ed. Downers Grove, Ill.: InterVarsity Press, 1991.

Cole, Darrell. *When God Says War Is Right.* Danbury: Waterbrook, 2002.

Coll, Alberto R., et al., eds. *Legal and Moral Constraints on Low-Intensity Conflicts.* International Law Studies 67. Newport, R.I.: Naval War College, 1995.

Cordesman, Anthony H. *Terrorism, Asymmetric Warfare, and Weapons of Mass Destruction.* Westport: Praeger, 2002.

Cromartie, Michael, ed. *Peace Betrayed? Essays on Pacifism and Politics.* Washington, D.C.: Ethics and Public Policy Center, 1990.

Culver, Robert D. *The Peacemongers.* Wheaton, Ill.: Tyndale House, 1985.

Deane, Herbert. *The Political and Social Ideas of St. Augustine.* New York: Columbia University Press, 1963.

Defarri, Roy J., et al., eds. *The Political Writings of St. Augustine.* Chicago: Regnery, 1962.

Demy, Timothy, and Gary P. Stewart. *In the Name of God: Understanding the Mindset of Terrorism.* Eugene: Harvest House, 2002.

Dwyer, Judith A., ed. *The Catholic Bishops and Nuclear War.* Washington, D.C.: Georgetown University Press, 1984.

East, John P. "The Political Relevance of St. Augustine." *Modern Age,* spring 1972.

Elshtain, Jean Bethke. *Augustine and the Limits of Politics.* Notre Dame, Ind.: University of Notre Dame Press, 1995.

———. *Democracy on Trial.* New York: Basic Books, 1995.

———. *Just War Against Terror. The Burden of American Power in a Violent World.* New York: Basic Books, 2003.

———, ed. *Just War Theory: Readings in Social and Political Theory.* New York: New York University Press, 1994.

———. "Politics Without Cliché." *Social Research* 60, no. 3 (1993).

———. *Women and War.* Rev. ed. Chicago: University of Chicago Press, 1995.

Emerson, Steven. *American Jihad: The Terrorists Living Among Us.* New York: Free Press, 2002.

Eppstein, Joseph. *The Catholic Tradition of the Law of Nations.* Washington, D.C.: Catholic Association for International Peace, 1935.

Etzioni, Amitai. "An Old-Fashioned War." *Weekly Standard,* June 10, 2002.

Fortin, Ernest L. "Augustine's City of God and the Modern Historical Consciousness." *Review of Politics* 41 (1979).

———. "Reflections on the Proper Way to Read Augustine the Theologian." *Augustinian Studies* 2 (1971).

Fortin, Ernest L., and Douglas Kries, eds. *Augustine: Political Writings.* Translated by M. W. Tkacz and D. Kries. Indianapolis: Hackett, 1994.

Friesen, Duane K. *Christian Peacemaking and International Conflict.* Scottdale: Herald Press, 1986.

Griffiths, Paul J., and George Weigel. "Just War: An Exchange." *First Things,* April 2002.

Grotius, Hugo. *De Jure Belli ac Pacis Libri Tres.* Oxford: Clarendon, 1925.

———. *The Law of War and Peace.* Trans. L. R. Loomis. Roslyn: Walter J. Black, 1949.

Hallett, Bruce. *Engulfed in War: Just War and the Persian Gulf.* Honolulu: University of Hawaii Press, 1991.

Hamilton, Bernice. *Political Thought in Sixteenth-Century Spain.* Oxford: Clarendon Press, 1963.

Harmon, Christopher C. "Terrorism: A Matter for Moral Judgment." *Terrorism and Political Violence* 2, no. 1 (1992).

———. *Terrorism Today.* London: Frank Cass, 2000.

Hartigan, Richard S. "Saint Augustine on War and Killing: The Problem of the Innocent." *Journal of the History of Ideas* 27 (1966).

The Harvest of Justice Is Sown in Peace. Washington, D.C.: United States Catholic Conference, 1993.

Hauerwas, Stanley. *Against the Nations.* Minneapolis: Winston Press, 1985.

———. *Should War Be Eliminated?* Milwaukee: Marquette University Press, 1984.

Hehir, J. Bryan. "Just War Theory in a Post-Cold War World." *Journal of Religious Ethics* 20, no. 2 (1992).

Helgeland, John. "Christians and the Roman Army, A.D. 173-337." *Church History* 43, no. 2 (1974).

Helgeland, John, Robert J. Daly and J. Patout Burns. *Christians in the Military: The Early Experience.* Minneapolis: Fortress, 1985.

Hittinger, John P. "Just War and Defense Policy." In *Contemporary Public Policy.* Edited by David F. Forte. Washington, D.C.: Georgetown University Press, 1998.

Hoffmann, Bruce. *Inside Terrorism.* New York: Columbia University Press, 1998.

Hoffmann, Stanley. *Duties Beyond Borders.* Syracuse, N.Y.: Syracuse University Press, 1981.

———. *The State of War.* New York: Praeger, 1965.

Holmes, Arthur F. *War and Christian Ethics.* Grand Rapids: Baker, 1983.

Hogue, James F., Jr., and Gideon Rose. *How Did This Happen?* New York: Council on Foreign Relations, 2001.

Hunter, David G. "A Decade of Research on Early Christians and Military Service." *Religious Studies Review* 18, no. 2 (1992).

Jenkins, Philip. "The New Iron Curtain." *American Outlook,* fall 2002.

————. *The Next Christendom: The Coming of Global Christianity.* New York: Oxford University Press, 2002.

Johnson, James Turner. "Aquinas and Luther on War and Peace." *Journal of Religious Ethics* 31, no.1 (2003).

————. "The Broken Tradition." *National Interest,* fall 1996.

————. *Can Modern War Be Just?* New Haven, Conn.: Yale University Press, 1984.

————. "Historical Tradition and Moral Judgment: The Case of Just War." *Journal of Religion* 64, no. 3 (1984).

————. *The Holy War Idea in Western and Islamic Traditions.* University Park: Pennsylvania State University Press, 1997.

————. *Ideology, Reason, and the Limitation of War.* Princeton, N.J.: Princeton University Press, 1975.

————. "In Response to Terrorism." *First Things,* February 1999.

————. *The Just War Tradition and the Restraint of War.* Princeton, N.J.: Princeton University Press, 1981.

————. *Morality and Contemporary Warfare.* New Haven, Conn.: Yale University Press, 1999.

————. *The Quest for Peace: Three Moral Traditions in Western Cultural History.* Princeton, N.J.: Princeton University Press, 1987.

————. *The Restraint of War: A Moral and Historical Inquiry.* Princeton, N.J.: Princeton University Press, 1981.

————. "Toward Reconstructing the *Jus Ad Bellum.*" *The Monist,* October 1973.

Johnson, James Turner, and David Smith, eds. *Love and Society: Essays in the Ethics of Paul Ramsey.* Missoula: Scholars Press, 1974.

Johnson, James Turner, and George Weigel, *Just War and the Gulf War.* Washington, D.C.: Ethics and Public Policy Center, 1991.

Juergensmeyer, Mark. *The New Cold War? Religious Nationalism Confronts the Secular State.* Berkeley: University of California Press, 1993.

————. "Religious Nationalism: A Global Threat?" *Current History,* November 1996.

————. *Terror in the Mind of God: The Global Rise of Religious Violence.* Rev. ed. Berkeley: University of California Press, 2003.

Kagan, Donald. "Terrorism and the Intellectuals." *Intercollegiate Review* 37, no. 2 (2002).

Kelsay, John. *Islam and War: A Study in Comparative Ethics.* Louisville:

Westminster John Knox, 1993.

Kelsay, John, and James Turner Johnson, eds. *Cross, Crescent, and Sword.* Contributions to the Study of Religion 27. New York: Greenwood Press, 1990.

———. *Just War and Jihad: Historical and Theoretical Perspectives on War and Peace in Western and Islamic Traditions.* Contributions to the Study of Religion 28. New York: Greenwood Press, 1991.

Kennedy, Thomas D. "Can War Be Just?" In *From Christ to the World: Introductory Readings in Christian Ethics.* Edited by Wayne G. Boulton et al. Grand Rapids: Eerdmans, 1994.

Kramer, Hilton. "Reflections on the End of History." *The New Criterion,* December 1999.

Langan, John. "The Western Moral Tradition on War: Christian Theology and Warfare." In *Just War and Jihad: Historical and Theoretical Perspectives on War and Peace in Western and Islamic Traditions.* Edited by John Kelsay and James Turner Johnson. Contributions to the Study of Religion 28. New York: Greenwood Press, 1991.

Laqueur, Walter. *A History of Terrorism.* New Brunswick: Transaction, 2001.

———. *The New Terrorism: Fanaticism and the Arms of Mass Destruction.* New York: Oxford University Press, 1999.

Lavoy, Peter R., et al. *Planning the Unthinkable: How New Powers Will Use Nuclear, Biological, and Chemical Weapons.* Ithaca, N.Y.: Cornell University Press, 2000.

Levere, George J. "The Political Realism of Saint Augustine." *Augustinian Studies* 11 (1980).

Lewis, Bernard. *Islam and the West.* New York: Oxford University Press, 1993.

———. "The Roots of Muslim Rage." *Atlantic Monthly,* September 1990.

———. *What Went Wrong? Western Impact and Middle East Response.* New York: Oxford University Press, 2002.

Lewis, C. S. "Why I Am Not a Pacifist." In *The Weight of Glory and Other Addresses.* Edited by Walter Hooper. Rev. ed. New York: Macmillan, 1965.

Lieber, Robert J. "The Folly of Containment." *Commentary,* April 2003.

Lloyd-Jones, Martin. *Why Does God Allow Suffering?* London: Hodder & Stoughton, 1939.

Long, Edward LeRoy, Jr. *War and Conscience in America.* Philadelphia: Westminster Press, 1968.

Lovin, Robin. *Reinhold Niebuhr and Christian Realism.* Cambridge: Cambridge University Press, 1995.

Luther, Martin. "On War Against the Turk." In *Luther's Works,* 46:161-205. Edited by Jaroslav Pelikan and Helmut Lehmann. Philadelphia: Fortress, 1967.

——. "Temporal Authority: To What Extent It Should Be Obeyed." In *Luther's Works,* 45:81-129. Edited by Jaroslav Pelikan and Helmut Lehmann. Philadelphia: Muhlenberg Press, 1962.

——. "Whether Soldiers, Too, Can Be Saved." In *Luther's Works,* 46:91-129. Edited by Jaroslav Pelikan and Helmut Lehmann. Philadelphia: Fortress, 1967.

Lynch, Christopher. "Making War." *Weekly Standard,* November 3, 2003.

Marshall, Paul. "Keeping the Faith: Religion, Freedom, and International Affairs." In *Politics and Public Policy: A Christian Response.* Timothy J. Demy and Gary P. Stewart, eds. Grand Rapids: Kregel, 2000.

Miller, R. B. *Interpretations of Conflict: Ethics, Pacifism, and the Just-War Tradition.* Chicago: University of Chicago Press, 1996.

MacCormick, Neil. "Natural Law and the Separation of Law and Morals." In *Natural Law Theory: Contemporary Essays.* Edited by Robert P. George. Oxford: Clarendon, 1992.

Murray, John Courtney. *Morality and Modern War.* New York: Council on Religion and International Affairs, 1959.

——. "Remarks on the Moral Problem of War." *Theological Studies* 10 (1959).

——. *We Hold These Truths: Catholic Reflections on the American Proposition.* New York: Sheed & Ward, 1960.

Niebuhr, H. Richard. *Christ and Culture.* New York: Harper Torchbook, 1951.

——. "The Grace of Doing Nothing." *Christian Century,* March 23, 1932.

Niebuhr, Reinhold. *Christian Realism and Political Problems.* New York: Charles Scribner's, 1953.

——. *Christianity and Power Politics.* New York: Charles Scribner's, 1940.

——. *An Interpretation of Christian Ethics.* New York: Harper, 1935.

——. *Moral Man and Immoral Society.* New York: Charles Scribner's, 1932.

——. "Must We Do Nothing?" *Christian Century,* March 30, 1932.

Oates, Whitney J., ed. *The Basic Writings of St. Augustine.* Vol. 2. New York: Random House, 1948.

O'Brien, William V. *The Conduct of Just and Limited War.* New York: Praeger, 1981.

————. "Just War Doctrine's Complementary Role in the International Law of War." In *Legal and Moral Constraints in Low-Intensity Conflicts.* Edited by Alberto R. Coll et al. International Law Studies 67. Newport, R.I.: Naval War College, 1995.

————. *The Nuclear Dilemma and the Just War Tradition.* Lexington: Lexington Books, 1986.

————. *Nuclear War, Deterrence, and Morality.* Westminster: Newman Press, 1967.

————. *War and/or Survival.* Garden City, N.Y.: Doubleday, 1969.

O'Brien, William V., and John Langan, eds. *The Nuclear Dilemma and the Just War Tradition.* Lexington: Lexington Books, 1986.

O'Donovan, Oliver. *The Just War Revisited.* Cambridge: Cambridge University Press, 2003.

————. "Payback: Thinking About Retribution." *Books & Culture,* July-August 2000.

Origen. *Contra Celsum.* Translated by H. Chadwick. Cambridge: Cambridge University Press, 1953.

Orsi, Michael P. "Expand 'Just War' Theory to Probable Cause." *Social Justice Review,* July-August 2003.

Pavlischek, Keith J. "Just War Theory and Terrorism: Applying the Ancient Doctrine to the Current Conundrum." *Witherspoon Fellowship Lectures* 21 (2001).

————. "The Justice in Just War." *First Things,* May 2000.

Peters, Ralph. *Beyond Terror: Strategy in a Changing World.* Mechanicsburg, Penn.: Stackpole, 2002.

————. "Rolling Back Radical Islam." *Parameters,* autumn 2002.

Phillips, R. L. *War and Justice.* Norman: University of Oklahoma Press, 1984.

Powers, G., et al., eds. *Peacemaking: Moral and Policy Challenges for a New World.* Washington, D.C.: United States Catholic Conference, 1994.

Prunckun, Henry W. *Shadow of Death: An Analytic Bibliography on Political Violence, Terrorism, and Low-Intensity Conflict.* Lanham, Md.: Scarecrow, 1995.

Pryce-Jones, David. "We Are Waging a Just War." *New Criterion,* November 2001.

Ramsey, Paul. *Again, the Justice of Deterrence.* New York: Council on Religion and International Affairs, 1965.

———. *Basic Christian Ethics.* 1950. Reprint, Louisville: Westminster John Knox, 1993.

———. "The Biblical Norm of Righteousness." *Interpretation* 24, no. 4 (1970).

———. "Christian Love in Search of a Social Policy." In *The Christian and His Decision.* Edited by Harmon L. Smith and Louis W. Hodges. Nashville: Abingdon, 1969.

———. "Christianity and Modern War." *Theology Digest* 16, no. 1 (1968).

———. *Deeds and Rules in Christian Ethics.* New York: Charles Scribner's, 1967.

———. "Dream and Reality in Deterrence and Defense." *Christianity and Crisis* 21, no. 22 (1961).

———. "The Ethics of Intervention." *Review of Politics* 25, no. 3 (1965).

———. "Farewell to Christian Realism." *America* 114, no. 18 (1966).

———. "Force and Political Responsibility." In *Ethics and World Politics.* Edited by Ernest W. Lefever. Baltimore: Johns Hopkins University Press, 1972.

———. "The Great Commandment." *Christianity and Society* 8, no. 4 (1943).

———. *The Just War: Force and Political Responsibility.* New York: Charles Scribner's, 1968.

———. "The Just War Theory on Trial." *Cross Currents* 13, no. 4 (1963).

———. *The Limits of Nuclear War.* New York: Council on Religion and International Affairs, 1963.

———. "Love and Law." In *Reinhold Niebuhr: His Religious, Social, and Political Thought.* Edited by Charles W. Kegley and Robert W. Bretall. New York: Macmillan, 1956.

———. "A Political Ethics Context for Strategic Thinking." In *Strategic Thinking and Its Moral Implications.* Edited by Morton A. Kaplan. Chicago: University of Chicago Press, 1973.

———. *Speak Up for Just War or Pacifism.* University Park: Pennsylvania State University Press, 1988.

———. "The Uses of Power." *Perkins Journal* 18, no. 1 (1964).

———. *War and the Christian Conscience: How Shall Modern War Be Conducted Justly?* Durham, N.C.: Duke University Press, 1961.

Rebard, Ted. "Justice: Moral Virtue in Society." *Ethics & Medics* 19, no. 12 (1994).

Regan, Richard J. *Just War: Principles and Cases.* Washington, D.C.: Catholic University of America Press, 1996.

Reichberg, Gregory M. "Is There a 'Presumption Against War' in Aquinas's Ethics?" *Thomist* 66 (2002).

Riley-Smith, Jonathan. "Rethinking the Crusade." *First Things,* March 2000.

Rist, John M. "Saint Augustine on the Exercise of Power." *Canadian Catholic Review* 4 (1986).

Robertson, D. B., ed. *Love and Justice: Selections from the Shorter Writings of Reinhold Niebuhr.* Philadelphia: Westminster Press, 1992.

Rommen, Heinrich A. *The Natural Law: A Study in Legal and Social History and Philosophy.* Translated by T. R. Hanley. Indianapolis: Liberty Fund, 1998.

Russell, F. H. *The Just War in the Middle Ages.* New York: Cambridge University Press, 1975.

Ruyter, Knut Willem. "Pacifism and the Military Service in the Early Church." *Cross Currents* 32 (1982).

Sabrosky, Alan N., and Robert L. Sloane, eds. *The Recourse to War: An Appraisal of the "Weinberger Doctrine."* Carlisle Barracks: U.S. Army War College, 1988.

"The Schleitheim Confession of Faith." In *Glimpses of Mennonite History and Doctrine.* Edited and translated by J. C. Wenger. Scottdale: Mennonite Publishing, 1940.

Scott, James B. *The Spanish Origin of International Law: Lectures on Francisco de Vitoria (1480-1546) and Francisco Suárez (1548-1617).* Washington, D.C.: Georgetown University Press, 1929.

Shannon, Thomas A., ed. *War or Peace: The Search for New Answers.* Maryknoll, N.Y.: Orbis, 1980.

Sheils, W. J., ed. *The Church and War.* Oxford: Basil Blackwell, 1983.

Sichol, M. *The Making of Nuclear Peace: The Task of Today's Just War Theorists.* Georgetown: Georgetown University Press, 1990.

Silverman, Adam L. "Just War, Jihad, and Terrorism: A Comparison of Western and Islamic Norms for the Use of Political Violence." *Journal of Church and State,* spring 2002.

Stayer, James M., *Anabaptists and the Sword.* Lawrence: Coronado Press, 1972.

Stern, Jessica. *Terror in the Name of God.* New York: Ecco, 2003.

———. *The Ultimate Terrorists.* Cambridge, Mass.: Harvard University Press, 1999.

Stevenson, William R., Jr. *Christian Love and Just War.* Macon, Ga.: Mercer
    University Press, 1988.

Stone, Ronald H., and Dana Wilbanks, eds. *The Peacemaking Struggle: Mil-
    itarism and Resistance.* Lanham: University Press of America, 1985.

Swift, Louis J. "Augustine on War and Killing: Another View." *Harvard Theo-
    logical Review* 66 (1973).

―――. *The Early Fathers on War and Military Service.* Wilmington, Del.:
    Michael Glazier, 1983.

―――. "St. Ambrose on Violence and War." *Transactions and Proceedings
    of the American Philological Association* 101 (1970).

Tertullian "On Idolatry." In *The Ante-Nicene Fathers* II. Edited by Alexander
    Roberts and James Donaldson. Grand Rapids: Eerdmans, 1968.

Tucker, Robert W. *The Just War: A Study in Contemporary American Doc-
    trine.* Baltimore: Johns Hopkins University Press, 1960.

―――. *Just War and Vatican II: A Critique.* New York: Council on Religion
    and International Affairs, 1966.

United Methodist Bishops. *In Defense of Creation.* Nashville: Graded Press,
    1986.

Vitoria, Francisco de. *De Indis et de Iure Belli Reflectiones.* Edited by Ernest
    Nys. Translated by J. P. Bate. New York: Oceana, 1964.

Walters, LeRoy B. *Five Classic Just War Theories.* Ph.D. diss. Yale University,
    1971.

Walzer, Michael. *Exodus and Revolution.* New York: Basic Books, 1985.

―――. *Just and Unjust Wars.* 2nd ed. New York: Basic Books, 1992.

―――. *The Revolution of the Saints.* London: Weidenfeld & Nicolson, 1966.

Weigel, George. "Just War After the Cold War." In *Idealism Without Illusions:
    U.S. Foreign Policy in the 1990s.* Washington, D.C.: Ethics and Public Pol-
    icy Center, 1994.

―――. *Tranquillitas Ordinis: The Present Failure and Future Promise of
    American Catholic Thought on War and Peace.* Oxford: Oxford Univer-
    sity Press, 1987.

Weigley, Russell F. *The American Way of War.* New York: Macmillan, 1973.

Werpehowski, William, and Stephen D. Crocco, eds. *The Essential Paul
    Ramsey: A Collection.* New Haven, Conn.: Yale University Press, 1994.

White, Jonathan R. *Terrorism: An Introduction.* 3rd ed. Belmont: Wadsworth
    Thompson, 2002.

Wilson, James Q. "What Makes a Terrorist." *City Journal,* January 13, 2004.

Wrigley, Paul R. "The Impact of Religious Belief in the Theater of Operations." *Naval War College Review* 49 (1996).

Yoder, John Howard. *Nevertheless: The Varieties and Shortcomings of Religious Pacifism.* 2nd ed. Scottdale: Herald Press, 1992.

———. *The Original Revolution: Essays on Christian Pacifism.* Scottdale: Herald Press, 1971.

———. *The Politics of Jesus.* Grand Rapids: Eerdmans, 1994.

———. *What Would You Do?* Scottdale: Herald Press, 1983.

———. *When War Is Unjust: Being Honest in Just-War Thinking.* 2nd ed. Maryknoll, N.Y.: Orbis, 1996.

Young, Frances. "The Early Church: Military Service, War and Peace." *Theology* 92 (1989): 491-503.

Zampaglione, Geraldo. *The Idea of Peace in Antiquity.* Notre Dame, Ind.: University of Notre Dame Press, 1973.

Subject Index

DATE DUE

JUL 0 5 2007			
11-16-07			
7-2-8			
DEC 0 3 2008			
FEB 15 2009			
MAR 0 5 2009			
MAY 17 2009			